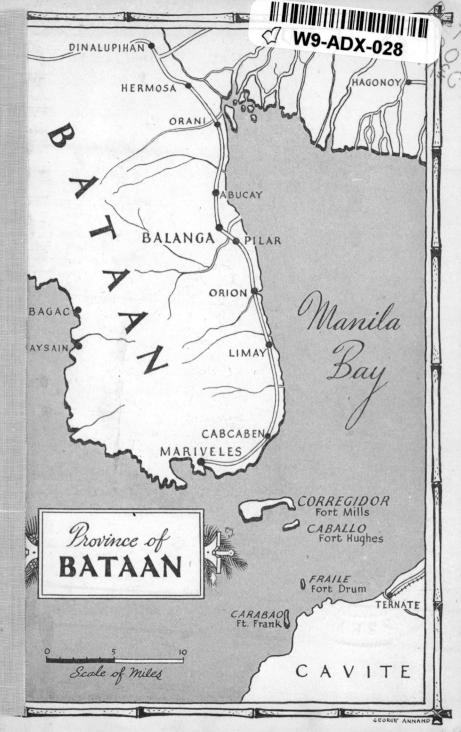

DINALUPIHAN

HERMOSA

HAGONOY

ORANI

B A T A A N

ABUCAY

BALANGA

PILAR

ORION

BAGAC

Manila Bay

AYSAIN

LIMAY

CABCABEN

MARIVELES

CORREGIDOR
Fort Mills

CABALLO
Fort Hughes

Province of
BATAAN

FRAILE
Fort Drum

TERNATE

CARABAO
Ft. Frank

0   5   10

Scale of Miles

C A V I T E

GEORGE ANNAND

The Good Fight

President Manuel Luis Quezon

This portrait of President Quezon was painted in the Waldorf-Astoria Hotel, New York City, on the occasion of President Quezon's visit to America in 1937. At the time of the Japanese invasion of Manila, the painting was hanging in the Reception Hall of Malacañan Palace, residence of the President. The painting is by Leon Gordon.

The Good Fight

[*The true story of the man who started as a young revolutionary to fight against the American people and their flag; who fought bravely, who surrendered and gave his parole in Bataan, who took to his heart the great democratic principles of America, who inculcated them in his own people, and who forty years later threw himself and his brave countrymen back into the hell of Bataan and Corregidor when the American flag was attacked by a treacherous enemy. This story is told in President Quezon's own words.*]

by Manuel Luis Quezon

LATE PRESIDENT OF THE COMMONWEALTH OF THE PHILIPPINES

INTRODUCTION BY
General Douglas MacArthur

D. APPLETON-CENTURY COMPANY
INCORPORATED

NEW YORK   LONDON

PRINTED IN THE UNITED STATES OF AMERICA

TO MY WIFE AND CHILDREN
whose courage in the presence of the greatest
dangers and whose devotion to me and to
the cause for which we were fighting, was
my inspiration during those dreadful days on
Corregidor, and on our long journey since then.

INTRODUCTION

(Note: The following Introduction was prepared by General Douglas MacArthur in 1942 and sent to President Quezon in Washington. President Quezon died August 1, 1944.)

I AM honored to comply with the request of the author of this book to write the introductory note. My only regret is that I must do so at a time when the pressure of military campaign is such that I cannot give it the leisure it deserves. For President Quezon's book, about to be published at this time, is an invaluable contribution to the war effort of his country as well as to that of the United States. It carries with it the message of a liberty-loving people hurled against those who would trample under foot man's most precious heritage, freedom.

Manuel L. Quezon is the President of the Commonwealth of the Philippines. He has been twice exalted to that eminent position by the peaceful suffrage of the Filipino people. When he speaks, however, he does not do so merely as the official representative of his country. He speaks as the acknowledged leader of a race that has raised him to dominance for the last two decades. When he writes, therefore, of the stirring days of American occupation of the Philippines, of the fruitful results of America's unique colonial policy, and stresses the gratitude of his people for what America has done in the Philippines, he is in effect firing the deadliest of weapons against the enemy—he is telling the story of a nation that was given by the United States a new birth of freedom achieved in a manner unparalleled in the history of colonization.

From the shadows of Corregidor in a proclamation to the Filipino people he said: "The determination of the Filipino people to continue fighting side by side with the United States until victory is won has in no way been weakened by the temporary reverses suffered by our arms. We are convinced that our sacrifices will be crowned with victory in the end and in that conviction we shall continue to resist the enemy with all our might." From the beginning he has pledged complete loyalty to America. As far as he is concerned, there shall be no half-way measures, no cowardly compromise with the national destiny.

He has been called by more than one American writer one of the greatest of living statesmen. With uncanny premonition, he created on the first day of his administration as President, the Philippine national defense program. The army that was the result of this foresight proved in battle the wisdom that created it, and has passed into immortality. His decision to continue the struggle is of a piece with that first premonition. It springs from the same well of tested wisdom, and the issue will be the same. His career spans the most glorious half century of Philippine history. His biography is the history not only of that epoch but of the Philippines as a modern nation. He has fought innumerable battles and won them all. And well may he now say, after the character in Browning's poem:

> "I was ever a fighter, so—one fight more,
> The best and the last!"

To-day he is fighting, at the head of his people and side by side with America, the greatest battle of all—a battle that shall determine, perhaps for centuries to come, the fate of his people. God cannot fail to bless him in so sacred a cause.

Douglas MacArthur

June 18, 1942
Melbourne, Australia

AUTHOR'S PREFACE

I<small>N THE</small> last months of the year 1899, the division under the command of General Arthur MacArthur, the father of General Douglas MacArthur, made an attack against the bulk of the Filipino Army and practically destroyed it. This compelled the President of the short-lived Philippine Republic, General Emilio Aguinaldo, to seek refuge in the mountains of northern Luzon and drove my chief, General Tomas Mascardo, up into the hills of western Pampanga. From there General Mascardo transferred his headquarters to the forests of Bataan, on the China Sea coast between Bagac and Morong. A council of war, held by the Filipino generals under the presidency of Aguinaldo, himself, had decided that, at the proper time, guerrilla warfare would be resorted to by the Filipino forces. When it became evident that organized resistance to the American Army was no longer possible, it fell to my lot to command the guerrillas that operated on the tip of the Bataan Peninsula. This spot, forty years later, was destined to be the last stronghold of the combined American-Filipino forces against Japanese invasion under the gallant and superb leadership of General Douglas MacArthur.

In the spring of 1901, General Mascardo ordered me to surrender to Lieutenant Miller, the officer in command of the American garrison in Mariveles, among other reasons for the purpose of ascertaining if it was true that General Aguinaldo had already been captured by General Frederick Funston in Palanan.

On January 18, 1936, two months after my inauguration as the first President of the Philippine Commonwealth, I visited the fortress of Corregidor, which lies just off the tip of Bataan, upon the invitation of the then Commanding General of the Philippine Department, Major General Kilbourne, who accompanied me on the trip.

While the presidential yacht, S.S. *Arayat*, which took us to Corregidor, was struggling against strong winds and big waves to dock at the pier, I heard the firing of the salute due my rank. The scene before my eyes suddenly took me back to by-gone years. The contrast between the memories of the past and the realities of that day filled my heart with an overpowering emotion. Thirty-five years before, I had walked down the slopes of Mariveles Mountain, a defeated soldier, emaciated from hunger and lingering illness, to place myself at the mercy of the American Army. Thirty-five years later, there stood at the pier of Corregidor, facing that majestic mountain, the

American General in command of the fortress, with a full American regiment at attention, waiting to render me honors second only to those paid the President of the United States. What a contrast! What an indescribable history of generous conduct on the part of the victor towards the vanquished! In the short span of a generation, America, the conqueror, through a policy unprecedented in colonialism, had permitted that I, one of the conquered, be raised from the lowest rung of the ladder to the highest seat of authority in the gift of my people!

What had happened to me vividly illustrates the great human experiment which the United States had successfully carried out in dealing with the Filipino people.

Is it any wonder that, when the American flag was attacked by Japan, the people of the Philippines stood by the United States to the bitter end?

The following pages—showing my life as a rebel against, and as a supporter of, the United States—are more than mere accounts of my personal experiences. They, in effect, portray the struggle of the Filipino people in their quest for freedom, first against and then in support of the great republic of North America.

My aims in writing this book are: first, to keep alive in the memory of the American people the service rendered by the Philippine Army in the heroic defense of Bataan and Corregidor; second, to throw into bold relief the fruit of America's policy in the Philippines, namely, the voluntary sacrifice made by the Filipino people of their lives and their fortunes, fighting side by side with the United States against a common foe; and third, to offer, inferentially, a pattern which may be followed if the redemption of the teeming millions of subjugated peoples is ever to be attempted.

M. L. Q.

PUBLISHER'S NOTE

In the *past twenty-eight years,* it has been my privilege to publish a number of books —some of serious import and permanent value, and others intended only to divert and amuse the reader. Both such types have their place and function.

Well as I have known many authors, this is the first occasion on which I have felt impelled to have a personal part, however insignificant, in the actual presentation to the reading public, of a book bearing my Company's imprint.

But the circumstances are unusual.

The author of this book is to me more than an author; for thirty-seven years he had been my close personal friend. I first knew him when I was a member of the Philippine Commission and Secretary of Public Instruction in 1907. He had been elected a member of the First Philippine Assembly, and I always had to speak to him in Spanish for he knew hardly any English at that time. Many have been closer to him in the recent years of his high public responsibility, but no one, I venture to hope, has fol-

lowed his signally successful and enlightened public career, and his splendidly sincere and human private life, without realizing that he is one of those few who, from every race, in every epoch, and under whatever seeming handicaps, raise a flaming torch of progressive leadership by which their fellowmen may steer.

For nine years, I had besought my friend, Manuel Quezon, to write a book of his experiences. While he never refused, there was always some claim with a priority on his time and energy.

It took the Japanese attack on his country and its consequent bringing him in exile to this, his second fatherland, to drive him to sacrifice his well-earned rest, and give of his harassed mind and body, in producing this, to me, fascinating story of a genius unconsciously earning its just reward.

In the sub-title, it is stated that this story is in President Quezon's own words. That is literally true. Every page of it, except three short chapters indicated later, which were given by him in recorded conversations, was dictated by him in English to his own Filipino secretary, Señor Serapio D. Canceran, and written out in English.

Then it reached my desk, day after day, and I changed a word here, a tense there—all too trifling to be mentioned.

Then it went into type.

President Quezon necessarily wrote almost entirely from memory, since his diaries and personal docu-

ments either were left in Malacañan Palace, the Phil-
ippine "White House," before he joined General
MacArthur on Corregidor, or fell into the hands of
the Japanese who captured the launch, Princess of
Negros, *off the town of San Carlos in the Island*
of Negros on March 16, 1942.

To those privileged to hear Manuel Quezon speak
to his countrymen in his native Tagalog, as I have,
even without understanding him, and to those who
have heard his impassioned addresses in perfect Cas-
tilian—as I often have—it is a rare treat to see the man
reveal himself, with the candor of a child, in a difficult
foreign language of which he knew not a word until
long after becoming of age.

I am rash enough to say that the brave Filipino peo-
ple would have had no finer paladin.

W. Morgan Shuster

New York City,
  August 18, 1944

CONTENTS

[xix]

CONTENTS

ILLUSTRATIONS

[xxi]

ILLUSTRATIONS

ILLUSTRATIONS

ILLUSTRATIONS

The Good Fight

"The people of the United States will never forget what the people of the Philippine Islands are doing these days, and will do in the days to come. As President, I wish to express my feeling of sincere admiration for the fight they are now making. I give the people of the Philippines my solemn pledge that their freedom will be redeemed and their independence established and protected. *The entire resources in men and materials of the United States stand behind that pledge.*"

—From PRESIDENT ROOSEVELT'S *message to the Filipino people on December 28, 1941.*

CHAPTER I

Birth and Childhood

FROM the lips of my mother I learned that I was born in Baler, on August 19, 1878, at seven o'clock in the morning. Since no Filipino resident of Baler at that time had a watch—for they were all too poor to own even the cheapest kind—I asked her how she knew that it was seven o'clock in the morning. "They were ringing the church bells for the first time," she answered. I understood. The 19th of August was the "town fiesta" of Baler—the feast-day of the patron saint—and it was both a civic and a religious holiday. Under the old Spanish régime, on such occasions, there was a high mass at eight o'clock in the morning and before the mass started they rang the church bells three times—the first at seven, the second at seven-thirty, and the third at eight, just at the moment when the priest started from the sacristy to the altar.

My mother, who was a very devout Catholic, added: "My boy, nothing happens in this world by accident. Everything answers a divine purpose. I believe that the fact that you were born on the day of our patron saint is indicative of God's will that you follow the vocation of priesthood."

On the other hand, my father, who had been a sergeant in one of the regiments of the Spanish Army, insisted that I should be a soldier. As a boy he dressed me in the uniform of a "Cabo de la Guardia Civil" or Corporal of the Civil Guard.

Now let me say something about the town fiesta in the Philippines or the feast of the patron saint.

Up to December, 1941, it was the greatest day of the year for every town in the Islands. The streets were adorned with beautifully woven arches of split bamboo, decked with palm leaves. The brass band which is the pride of every town in the Philippines played without rest throughout the day and on into the night. Fireworks lighted up the evening sky. It originated this way. As is well known, the conquest of the Philippines by Spain was undertaken both for the glory and aggrandizement of the Spanish monarch and the conversion of the inhabitants to the Catholic faith. With Legaspi, the conqueror, went the Augustinian friar, Father Urdaneta, the missionary. As the conquest proceeded and a town was taken by the Spaniards, the friars consecrated it to a patron saint. The patron of Baler is Saint Luis, Bishop of Toulouse. Hence my middle name, Luis, given to me by my mother.

The custom in the Philippines was that the day before the celebration of the fiesta everybody came to town, even the poorest and those who lived in the farthest barrio. Since there were no hotels, those who came to celebrate found shelter in the house of a relative, of a friend, or of the family who owned the land they were cultivating. Every house was full of people who were tucked away as best they could be. The well-to-do kept their houses open to guests all day long, and every table groaned beneath the weight of food. No visitor might leave his host's house until, whether hungry or not, he had eaten and drunk at the hospitable board.

The most important part of the fiesta, however, was the high mass celebrated in honor of the patron saint and attended by all who came from far and wide. All wore their best clothes, and many poor people spent their savings and even ran into debt to show themselves and their children to advantage.

For the expenses of the public entertainment during the fiesta, which usually lasted three days, contributions were collected. Of course, there was a cockfight—the national "sporting gamble"—during the fiesta. The cockfights always started after the mass and continued until late afternoon. Then the public entertainments began, sometimes with the *Carrera de anillo* or tilting at "rings" made of gay ribbons. Each ring was given by a fair maiden of the village, and each young gallant tried to carry off his lady love's ring, so that he might wear her colors for the day.

At night they had a *moro-moro* and, at times, Spanish comedies, depending upon the financial capacity of the townpeople to use only local talent or to import actors from Manila. The *moro-moro* is a play in the native tongue and the protagonists are on one side a Christian prince with his court and army and on the other, a Mohammedan potentate also with his court and his army. The plot was taken from Spanish literature in vogue before Cervantes wrote his *Don Quixote*—which effectively killed the earlier sort of novel. All the characters were dressed in costumes of the ancient times, with plenty of gold tinsel and plumage. In the spirited fight with swords and spears which ensued upon their meeting, the Christian prince was, of course, the victor; sometimes single-handed he killed the infidel hordes.

This particular year of Our Lord 1878, my father celebrated the double event of the birth of his first son and the town fiesta of Baler, not wisely, but too well. So often, indeed, did he look upon the fiery drink which Americans in the Philippines called *Bino* that before evening came he had lost all further interest in the proceedings. This unfortunate slip from the straight and narrow path made my mother very unhappy, for in those days, to be under the influence of liquor was considered in my country almost a disgrace. Hence, my disagreeable reaction to the sight of people who are drunk, although I enjoy a cocktail or two before meals and a bottle of good wine or beer with my food.

When I first saw the light of day, Baler was but a tiny and almost inaccessible village. It lies at the mouth of the Aguang River on Baler Bay, a few miles north of Cape Encanto, which sticks out into the vast Pacific Ocean. A ship's small-boat could not cross the river bar except at high tide. Forty-five miles to the north there lay the little town of Casiguran, accessible only by sea. To the south of us the nearest town was Infanta, a village which likewise could be reached only by sea and was seldom accessible during the typhoon season. Directly back of the coastline lay a range of trackless mountains rising from three to six thousand feet in height and sparsely inhabited by wandering bands of Ilongot head-hunters, the fiercest of the pagan tribes. Inland from Baler, up the river and on the long journey toward Manila, there was in those days only the most primitive and hazardous of trails to the nearest human habitation through some thirty miles of jungle and up and down steep declivities; this path frequently forded the crystal river in which the best fresh-water fish in the world were found. Finally, by this forest track one reached the frontier village of Pantabangan. The journey was, in those days, made either afoot or on the back of a spirited little stallion.

Baler was then an enchanting paradise on earth; the hardy inhabitants lived on their tiny rice fields; an abundance of fish was to be found in the sea and the rivers; and deer were hunted with bow and arrow in the mountains.

Baler became famous in the last days of Spanish rule because of the heroic siege of the town in which a small Spanish garrison held out until long after peace had been declared between America and Spain.

My father was a Tagalog, born in the suburb of Paco in Manila. In his youth he was drafted into the infantry unit that Spain maintained in the Philippines, composed entirely of Filipino soldiers, officered with few exceptions by Spaniards. He retired at the end of his regular term as sergeant. His love of adventure took him to faraway Baler. There he met my mother, a Spanish *mestiza*, the belle of the town, who was the school-teacher for the girls. (Co-education was then prohibited.) Since my father was soon appointed the school-teacher for boys, they formed a friendship which carried them to the altar and held them together for life. Each of them as teacher received a salary of twelve pesos ($6.00) a month, a sum which in Baler was quite an income for those days. They also had a rice paddy of some two acres which gave them enough for the yearly sustenance of the household, and what they did not consume they exchanged for fish, venison, or pork, which with our own poultry fed us well.

In a community as poor and as primitive as Baler, we were considered the number one family. We were the only family who could speak Spanish and could

The village of Baler, President Quezon's birthplace—a view taken from an airplane coming in from the Pacific Ocean

The Beach at Baler

The house in Baler where President Quezon was born

converse in their own tongue with the three Spanish officials stationed in the town—the military governor of the district who was a captain in the Army, the parish priest, a Franciscan friar, and the Corporal of the Civil Guard whose whole force consisted of at most six men. The reason for keeping this detachment in my town—not every town had it—was to protect it against the Ilongotes who were then head-hunters and occasionally from ambush attacked travelers between Baler and Pantabangan, cut off their heads, and took them home as trophies. The worth of an Ilongot amongst his tribesmen was measured by the number of skulls he collected, including those of other Ilongotes from different localities, for they cut off heads without discrimination. Whenever the Ilongotes attacked Christian Filipinos, the Guardia Civil, accompanied by townsfolk armed with spears and arrows, would go to the mountains and inflict a severe punishment upon these savages.

There was also a great deal of brigandage during the Spanish régime, and the duty of the Guardia Civil was to go after these bandits. However, while the towns of Pantabangan and Bongabong to the west of Baler and Infanta to the south, were pillaged now and then by bandits, these never dared to attack Baler because it was known that it had been the custom in our community from time immemorial, when the Moros were pillaging the coastal towns, for every man to rush to the public plaza with his bolo and spear or bow and arrow, and with these primitive weapons to resist the pirates. They also helped one another when there was fire or some other public disaster like a flood or typhoon. The sense of community interest was so high that every Sunday the men gathered after mass in the municipal building to discuss matters of common importance, and the decisions arrived at by a majority vote of all those present were obligatory for all, including the mayor and the other municipal officials. The mayor of the town presided over these meetings and the other public officials attended them.

My mother taught me to read and write Spanish, the four fundamental rules of arithmetic, and my catechism.

When I was about five years old, I got angry with a boy my age and size and slapped him in the face. My father saw me and beckoned me to approach him. "Don't slap anybody in the face," he said. "When you must hit some one do it with your fist. A slap in the face is more than a punishment, it is an insult."

The following year I did something my father did not approve of. Instead of calling me to account immediately, he let it go until the following day; so I did not know he had caught me. "Did you do anything yesterday morning that I have told you not to do?" he asked. I answered, "No, sir." He slapped me in the face. "Do you remember what I told you about slapping a man in the face?" "Yes, sir," I said. "A liar deserves no respect and may well be insulted," was his stern admonition. "Always tell the truth regardless of the consequences," he added.

From that time on, I have never concealed my feelings or my thoughts from either friend or foe. I have heard or read that in politics one cannot be too frank without being sooner or later politically ruined. My personal experience does not sustain this theory. I have never been defeated in any of the innumerable political battles I have gone through. People, I think, are more indulgent with the weaknesses and mistakes of public men if they avow them candidly. It may sound presumptuous, but it is a fact, nevertheless, that few men in public life have held the confidence of their constituents as continuously and as long as I have. Since 1905 I have been holding elective public office, without interruption and always in the ascendant, although my opponents have accused me of every crime of commission and omission.

When I was seven, my parents sent me to live with the Spanish Franciscan friar, the parish priest of Baler, who had agreed to teach me religion, geography, history, and Latin. Father Teodoro Fernandez was a saintly but severe man. I still remember how he pulled my ears when I did not study my lessons or got into some mischief.

After I had been living under the roof of Father Fernandez for over one year, Father Angulo, the parish priest of Palanan, where Aguinaldo in 1901 was captured by Captain Funston, came to spend a few weeks with his brother Franciscan in Baler. One morning after saying his mass Father Angulo invited me to go with him to the beach and take a bath. It was the month of January when the northeast monsoon blows hard on the east coast of Luzon. The waves rolling straight from the vast Pacific were big, as they always are during the monsoon season; sometimes they are almost mountainous; and the undertow is very strong. Two young men, both good swimmers, came to bathe with us. One was my first cousin, and the other also a relative. A tremendous wave knocked down the priest and me and the undertow carried us out to sea. Our companions came first to my rescue as I was the more helpless, and with great difficulty they succeeded in saving me. They went back for the priest afterwards, but they could not find him. Help came from the town but to no avail. At five in the afternoon the corpse was carried to the beach by the current. It was my first near-meeting with death, a meeting which in after life has been repeated more than once.

Two years later, when Father Fernandez was transferred to the main house of the Franciscans in Manila, my parents asked him to take me with him to be his mess boy in order that I might pursue my studies in San Juan de Letran College. I stayed in the Franciscan convent for one year until Father Fernandez was again sent to the provinces. Then my father took me to the house in Manila of a cousin of his, married to an officer of the Spanish Army, where my room and board cost twelve pesos a month. I was not happy in this house. In the first place, it was more than half an hour's walk to my school in Intramuros—the historic Walled City —and I had to go to and fro four times every day. In the second place, my uncle treated me, as well as his own children, rather roughly. So I requested my father, when I started my second year in school, to take me away. My dear parents, after discussing the matter between themselves, called me and said, "We have decided to enter you as boarder in San Juan de Letran. The cost of your stay there including your matriculation fee and incidental expenses will amount to more than both of us are making every year from our salaries, but we have saved some money and our savings plus what we can sell from the products of our farm will be enough to put you through college until you take your A.B. degree. After that, if you desire to take a course in law or medicine or prepare for the priesthood [the only professions besides pharmacy then being taught in the Philippines] you must find some way of supporting yourself and paying for your studies."

I became a boarder in the College of San Juan de Letran. It was not long before I was having fist fights and taking active part in every conspiracy to break the rules of the house. Since the rod was then still considered the only means of keeping order and discipline, I was receiving almost daily doses of this medicine. However, my teachers were relatively lenient with me because I always admitted my guilt.

It took me five years to graduate as a Bachelor of Arts, Summa Cum Laude. On such occasions, the Governor-General used to attend and preside over the exercises, and I had the great privilege of being called to shake hands with him. I was dazzled by the unexpected honor.

Although the trip from Manila to Baler was a hard one, I always longed to visit my home during vacation time. The journey took a week and was made partly in a *carromata*, a sort of buggy, the rest of the way either on horseback or afoot. The trip, besides being tiresome, was dangerous, for along the trail through the mountains the traveler was likely to be ambushed by the Ilongot head-hunters unless there was a large party composed of men armed with spears, arrows, and bolos, or perhaps some one carrying a shotgun. In that case, regardless of the number constituting the party, the Ilongotes never dared attack, for they had a wholesome fear of this "diabolical" device, as they called it. Since my father was the only man in Baler who owned a shotgun, he always went to Manila to take me home when vacation came. My visits to my home town were a source of great happiness to me. I enjoyed immensely the company of the illiterate boys of my age, just as much as I did before I went to Manila. We played our native games like *sipa* and *palabasan*. Baseball was unknown to us then.

Two years before my graduation, my father did not let me come home because he could not go to Manila to fetch me. He was too busy trying to earn more money, for his savings were running low and my expenses were increasing. I spent my vacation with classmates of mine who took me to their homes. After my graduation, father sent the father of my future wife, Uncle Pedro, for me, and upon arriving home I found my mother hopelessly ill with tuberculosis. The sight of her broke my heart.

Later in the day, my father called me aside and told me that they had spent everything they had for my education and had even incurred debts. He repeated his earlier warning: "If you want to go to the university, you will have to find means of supporting yourself."

The following day my father took me to be introduced to the parish priest. I did not know the man. We found him seated in one of those comfortable chairs that the friars invented, with his right leg up resting over one of the long arms of the chair. When we entered the spacious parlor hall the priest did not change his position. Although I had seen the same thing many times before when I was a youngster, on this occasion I felt inside me a sense of revulsion. It was then customary for the Filipinos to kiss the hand of a priest as a mark of respect. My father kissed the hand which the friar held out to him. When my turn came, I merely took the hand and shook it.

The friar did not hesitate to show his displeasure by completely ignoring me. We stayed not more than five minutes. My father made no comment about the incident. Later I learned the priest said that my studies in Manila had spoiled me and that if he were my father he would keep me in Baler and after giving me a good whipping would make me work on the farm.

After visiting the parish priest, my father accompanied me to pay my respects to the Comandante Político Militar—the military governor of the district —and then to the corporal in command of the Civil Guard. I confess that the reception these Spanish officials gave us, like that of the priest, was no different from the manner in which the representatives of Spanish sovereignty in Baler used to receive my father when I was a boy. But this time I saw things in a different light. I realized that we Filipinos were treated as inferiors and my racial pride was deeply hurt. In college there were some Spanish students who were not only indolent but plain stupid, and many Filipinos were superior to them both in character and in intellect. In my innermost self, I resolved to change that humiliating state of affairs.

In the ensuing weeks, I spent a great deal of time taking care of my mother, until one day, late in the afternoon, she asked me to fetch the priest because she was dying. I rushed to the parish house, conveyed to the priest the wishes of my mother, and ran back to her side. The priest followed me, administered her the last sacraments, and a moment later she died in my arms. Meantime, I had sent for my father who, with my two brothers, was on the farm. When they arrived, all was over. My father broke down completely and after the burial he became seriously ill. For several months he was almost out of his mind. This prevented me from returning to Manila to start my law course.

While in Baler, I learned more and more about the abuses that the three Spanish officials including the priest, then also a sort of public official, were guilty of in their dealings with the people. The Corporal of the Guardia Civil was the worst of the lot. He was nothing but a beast, a monster of lasciviousness and cruelty. He would go after young girls and compel their relatives, through threats, to deliver the innocent creatures to him. Whenever he failed, as he always did except once, he would make good his threat by arresting the person who refused to help him and having him flogged almost to death. I realized then how despicable some of the Spaniards in the Philippines were, and I began to fully understand the *why* of the "Katipunan."

To my surprise, this Corporal of the Civil Guard, Pio Enriquez by name, went out of his way to win my friendship. He would pay me a visit and invite me to his quarters which were also the barracks of the small detachment. One night he insisted that I stay for dinner and while we took our coffee he told me, in the most confidential manner, that he had fallen in love with one of my cousins. Then he insinuated that I should use my good offices to convince my cousin to yield to his advances. Knowing the man, I understood what he meant. My first impulse was to pull out the dagger which I carried on my right hip hidden under my coat and kill him. This deadly weapon I had started carrying with me when I learned what a brute this man was. However, realizing that to kill him then was tantamount to committing suicide, I repressed my anger and merely said: "You understand, Sr. Enriquez, that I cannot do what you are asking me to do." He immediately showed himself in his true color. He called one of his soldiers and said: "*Trae el látigo!*" (Bring the lash!) The soldier obeyed and came back with the horrid instrument in his hand. I lowered my arm under the table, gripped the hilt of my dagger, gritted my teeth, and strained every sinew —determined to plunge my poniard through his heart at his slightest move.

He hesitated a while, ordered the soldier to leave and, addressing me, said: "Did you see that lash? Unless you do what I want you to do I shall lash you till you are dead and then bury you in this yard and nobody will ever know what has happened to you."

The party was, of course, now at an end. As I reached the last rung of the ladder of his house, I vowed to myself that I would get him at the first opportunity.

All night long I tossed in my bed. I saw no escape from the trap I was in. I either had to commit murder or allow myself to be murdered. There was only one choice, and that same night I planned the commission of the crime. I would wait till the first dark evening came. There were no lights in the streets. I would invite him for a walk and upon reaching a deserted place with no houses around, I would attack him without warning. The thought that my dagger would leave his blood on my hands made me shiver with horror. So I decided to hit him in the head with a club and leave him dead on the road. For days, I could neither eat nor sleep. I was terrified at the prospect of being a murderer. I prayed God for light. I dared not go to my father and seek his advice for I was afraid that he, himself, would kill the man. I avoided meeting Sr. Enriquez, hoping that he might change his mind. But one evening he came to our house and asked for me. In vain I tried to hide although my father got me out of the room. He invited me to go for a walk, but I excused myself on the ground that I had not had my dinner. He insisted, and I promised to meet him later in the town plaza. He left. I took no dinner; instead, I went back to my room and sought the intervention of my mother whose soul I knew was in Heaven, that the Lord might save me from the imminent danger that was awaiting me. I knelt on my knees and prayed with all my soul.

Then I kissed my father good-night, not knowing

whether I ever would see him again, and went out with the club which I had prepared for the occasion. I met Sr. Enriquez at the appointed place and he asked me to go to his house. As usual he was carrying a hardwood cane. I suggested that we stroll for a while and he agreed. It was a very dark night and there were no people in the street. I wanted to attack him when he was not on his guard, but the treacherous act was so repulsive to me that it paralyzed my arm. Finally he asked what I had done to comply with his wishes. I stopped. The blood rushed up to my head and I forgot everything. *"Canalla!"* (Dirty dog!) I shouted, and hit him with the club. He fell, six feet long, on the ground. I thought he was dead and ran away from him in the direction of the hills.

I walked the whole night without knowing where I was going, for I was unfamiliar with the thick forest around my town. Every shadow I saw I thought was a civil guard hunting me, and I would stop and wait until satisfied of my mistake. I was torn by the fear of being caught and shot, on the one hand, and by the voice of my conscience crying in my ears the word "murderer," on the other. With all the vicissitudes that I have gone through during my long and eventful life, that was the worst night I ever had. I was in complete despair and did not even dare to call on God for help for I thought I had been doomed to eternal damnation. Morning found me far, but not too far from the town. I was on the little farm of one of my relatives.

When the woman who owned the farm arrived in the afternoon, on seeing me she asked: "Where have you been? Your father has been looking for you all morning, telling the people that you did not go back home last night."

Ignoring her remarks, I inquired: "Did anything unusual happen last night?"

She answered, "Yes, the Cabo de la Guardia Civil was heard crying for help in the thick of the night while running in the street; and when the *cuadrilleros* [policemen] rushed to his aid, he told them that he had seen an evil spirit which disappeared instantly." (The belief in apparitions was still common among the Filipinos.) I breathed a deep sigh of relief. Neither hell nor a firing squad was waiting for me. I had not committed murder and my victim was ashamed to admit that a young man half his size had given him a beating.

Now I was more afraid of my father than of the Cabo de la Guardia Civil. I decided to face the music and confess the whole business. I went home and told my father everything from beginning to end. Instead of reproaching me as I thought he would, he merely counseled me to come to him whenever I was in trouble. Then with wrath in his eyes, he added: "That cabo will never see you again except in my presence, and if he ever attempts to do you any harm I will shoot him."

Three days later, the Military Governor sent for my father and me. He was solemn and severe. He told my father that I was a member of the Katipunan, that he had conclusive evidence in his possession proving this fact.

Then addressing me, he asked: "Where were you at ten o'clock, two nights ago?"

I paused a moment to remember if this was the night when I assaulted Cabo Enriquez. No, I was certain I was home, for the assault had taken place the night before.

"I was at home, sir," I answered.

"And these eyes that have seen you and these ears that have heard you haranguing the people and inducing them to join the Katipunan—are my eyes and ears telling a lie?"

"Señor," I retorted, respectfully but firmly, "those eyes could have seen me and those ears could have heard me only in my own house."

"Enough!" he shouted. "You will be confined in the school-house [it was vacation time] until I send you to Manila to be tried by a Military Court and shot."

"At your order, sir," I replied. We were dismissed and my father who was still the school-teacher, took me to the school-house and became my warden.

For fifteen days I was locked in the school-house and no one but my father was allowed to see me or bring my food. He was forbidden to talk to me, and he complied strictly with the order. We only looked at one another whenever he came with my meals, neither of us showing what our hearts felt, both certain that I was a victim of grave injustice.

At the end of the second week of my imprisonment, my father, with evident sign of joy in his face, came to tell me that I was free; that he had convinced the Military Governor of my innocence; and that the governor had consented to my going to Manila to pursue my studies on the assurance given by my father, upon his word of honor, that I would not join the Katipunan or be a revolutionary. My father had discovered that the Cabo de la Guardia Civil and, in a way, the priest, were responsible for my detention. Later the whole town learned the truth that I had clubbed the Cabo de la Guardia Civil, and since the Spaniards were looked upon by the natives not only with respect but almost with awe, my daring was considered as a heroic act, and the good submissive people of Baler hailed me as their hero. My only brother still living has kept the club with which I attacked Cabo Enriquez.

The following day my father and I left for Manila. He still had no money with which to support me and was deeply in debt. During his illness he had received no salary as teacher and our farm had been practically abandoned. I told him not to worry, that I would work my way through the university.

Upon our arrival in Manila, I went straight to the University of Santo Tomas (Saint Thomas) and presented myself to the Director of the Interns, Father Tamayo, who had been my professor in the College of San Juan de Letran, and told him my story. Father Tamayo immediately said: "I will give you free tuition and free room and board. Your work will be to help those students who need coaching in mathematics. You will also do such other work as may be given to you." I agreed.

I told my father that I was assured of my room and board and that for my clothing and other necessary expenses as a student, I would do some other work in my spare time. My father was the happiest man on earth. "My son," he said, "I shall be going back home in two hours. I won't bother you with any advice. Just be good and be just to your fellowmen. No matter how high your station in life may be, never forget that you came from poor parents and that you belong to the poor. Don't forsake them, whatever happens."

"God bless you," he said when we parted. I never saw him again.

Mrs. Quezon before her marriage

A corner of the old Spanish Walled City in Manila

Parian Gate in the old Spanish walls, opposite which was the dungeon where President Quezon was confined

CHAPTER II

Youthful Romance and Law Studies

L EST the reader may think that my days in Baler had been constantly spent in a gloomy atmosphere of pain for the death of my mother, indignation over the abuses of the Spanish officials, or the anguish resulting from the almost tragic incident with the Cabo de la Guardia Civil and my confinement in the school-house, I desire to tell a little episode of my youth which took place in the midst of these more serious events.

The town of Baler was always famous for having an abundance of beautiful girls. At the time of which I now write, although only seventeen years old, I was no longer indifferent to the attraction of beautiful eyes and well-shaped figures. There was one girl in particular whose eyes were irresistible to me, and I quickly fell in love with her. Courting in the Philippines during the Spanish days was indeed a most trying enterprise. Girls were always chaperoned whenever they attended a dance, nor were they allowed out of the house alone. Letters through the mail, addressed to a girl, were sure to fall into her parents' hands and never reached the addressee. When a girl was visited in her home, she was not permitted to sit near her suitor, and some one was always present so that the conversation could never refer to anything so personal as the object of the call. In my own town the young man would be asked to sit on a bench— and the prevailing rules of etiquette required that one must not walk straight to the bench, but had to do it step by step, stopping after each step, until the invitation to sit was repeated three times. Then at last the tortured victim would have the right to sit down. The girl would sit at the farthest point away, the mother or the chaperon sitting with solemn face between them.

This procedure was too elaborate, too formal, and too burdensome for my impatient temperament. So I never subjected myself to the ancient ritual. There was another permissible manner of courting a girl more agreeable to my inclinations, and that was by serenading. This consisted of standing in front of the girl's house after the family had retired for the evening, and from the street playing melancholy tunes and singing love ditties. Some austere mothers would let the serenaders remain long in the street before inviting them to come up, doubtless in the hope that the intruders would get tired and leave. Usually, however, after the third musical selection, the lamps were lighted and the cavaliers invited to come up. Then would follow an impromptu dance which would last, depending upon the boldness of the suitor, until two or three o'clock in the morning. The music on such occasion consisted usually of only a flute or a violin and a guitar. I chose the serenade as the means of promoting my pretensions, and with two old friends who played the guitar and the flute, I courted the girl of my dreams. She was an orphan, living with her aunt, the most stern and implacable old lady of the town. As soon as the latter noticed that I was paying attention to her niece, her attitude toward me changed radically. She assumed that I would never marry her girl and therefore condemned me *a priori* as a villain. I went about my business unperturbed. She would keep me waiting in front of her house with my musicians as long as courtesy under the code would permit, and then in a rather hard voice and not concealing her displeasure, would ask us to come up, "*if we wanted.*" Of course, we did every time and then I would dance with the girl and although one had to hold his partner at least one foot away, I still managed to whisper a v. ord or two indicative of my deep personal feeling. After noticing that the girl was not indifferent to my advances, I used to carry with me whenever I serenaded her, a sheet of paper containing the most romantic letter I have ever produced. She never answered my letters, much less ever said that she reciprocated my love, for that was bad form in those days. Finally, on one occasion, I succeeded in finding her alone and kissed her on the cheek.

There was no protest, but it was the end, for fate took me away shortly after this incident.

The law course in the University of Santo Tomas at that time took seven years—one of preparatory and six of law proper—and no one was permitted to matriculate who did not have the degree of Bachelor of Arts. Santo Tomas being the only university in the Philippines then—it is older by twenty-five years than Harvard—all the A.B. graduates from the different colleges who wanted to take a university course met in its classrooms. There I made the acquaintance of Sergio Osmeña who came from the college of the religious order of Saint Paul established in Cebu, Vicente Singson Encarnacion, and many others who graduated from the Ateneo of Manila. This preparatory course in law was also attended by Vicente Madrigal, Juan Sumulung, Emilio Jacinto, Flaviano Yenko, and many more who graduated with me as Bachelors of Art from San Juan de Letran. Sergio Osmeña and Vicente Madrigal, besides being my classmates, were also boarders in Santo Tomas, and we formed a friendship that has lasted throughout these many years of our lives.

Emilio Jacinto became the secretary of the Katipunan and was the brains in the camp of Andres Bonifacio, the untutored leader during the early days of the revolution against Spain. Jacinto sealed with his life his love of freedom for his people. Flaviano Yenko became a general in Aguinaldo's army in Cavite and died gloriously in the defense of Sapote Bridge a few months after the revolution of 1896 broke out.

Sumulung and Singson Encarnacion became the leaders of the party which in popular parlance was called "Americanista." Sumulung became very influential during the first years of the American régime and was appointed by the President of the United States a member of the Philippine Commission, the body which after the establishment of the Civil Government exercised exclusively both the executive and legislative powers of the Philippine Government, and was composed of a majority of Americans and a Filipino minority who took part only in the legislative functions.

Madrigal never entered politics; but although he was so poor as a student that he was able to follow an academic career only by the charity of the Dominican Order, he was so brilliant, so hard-working and so keen a businessman that before he reached the age of fifty he became one of the few multimillionaires in the Philippines. And I may add in passing that every cent he made, he made honestly and by the sweat of his brow.

Osmeña and I joined our political forces in the leadership of the Nacionalista Party—the party which from the start advocated immediate independence for the Philippines. For many years Osmeña was the leader of the Party—from 1907 to 1922; at that time I succeeded him as the head of the organization.

In my preparatory course, there were two notable professors—Father Farpon, the professor of physics and chemistry, who was a real scientist (which for a friar was exceptional, for generally their interest lay in the study of scholastic philosophy, theology, and classics); and Father Valentin Marin, the professor of Spanish literature. Father Marin was not only a Spanish scholar, a playwright, and a poet, but also one of the most liberal-minded priests I have ever known in my life. I think only the Dominican Order, of all the religious orders, would have tolerated such an outspoken man. He went beyond the bounds of prudence at times in criticizing the Spanish Government and his own brothers of the Order. He was so popular among the students that I had a slight suspicion that Emilio Jacinto and Flaviano Yenko had hinted to him their connection with the Katipunan.

Years had not improved my conduct. I was the same gay and unruly student, more inclined to make than to avoid trouble. However, the need of earning a little money for my expenses, other than my tuition and room and board which were free, forced me to devote a great deal of time not only to coaching those students whom the Director of Santo Tomas, Father Tamayo, put under my charge, but also other students who came to me for help.

After finishing my preparatory course, I matriculated in the first year of law. An old Dominican priest who was teaching canonic law in Santo Tomas and who had become very much interested in me, advised me to take at the same time a course in dogmatic theology. "In case," as he said, "you may discover later that you have a vocation for the priesthood." Remembering what my dear mother had told me as a probable reason for my birthday falling on the feast of the patron saint of Baler, I readily followed the advice of the old priest. The professor of dogmatic theology that year was Father Vaquero who had been teaching in the College of San Juan de Letran during all the years that I was a boarder in that college. He of course knew me very well, and seeing me enter the classroom, he bluntly and in the presence of the other students, asked me this question: "What are you doing here?" Humbly and in a low voice, assuming that that was the proper attitude of a would-be priest, I answered: "I think I am going to study for the priesthood." He burst into laughter and said: "Who has deceived you into believing that you should ever be a priest? Don't waste your time. Get out of here and proceed with your law course." Thus the career for which my mother so devoutly prayed was nipped in the bud.

Discontent in the Philippines against the Spanish rule had then become rampant. The Katipunan was rapidly being extended everywhere. Although I knew from my own personal experience in my home town how well-founded was the discontent, I would not join the secret society because of the pledged word of my father to the Military Governor in Baler.

When I was spending my Christmas vacation in the town of Aliaga, province of Nueva Ecija, Jose Rizal, the national hero of the Filipino people, was executed, after a cooked-up military trial, in Bagumbayan, afterwards the beautiful Luneta drive and park. The death of Rizal, which the Spanish Government thought would end the subversive agitation and the incipient rebellion in the Philippines, accomplished just the opposite. More than any other Filipino before him or during his time, Jose Rizal had succeeded through his writings in arousing the dormant if not extinct national consciousness among his countrymen. He opened their eyes to the intolerable abuses that were being committed by their oppressors. His martyrdom, in a public plaza, before the startled and weeping eyes of his people, with deafening cries of *"Viva España"* from the Spaniards who witnessed the execution, was the spark that set off the Revolution. Shortly afterwards there was a general uprising.

The insurrection was started by Andres Bonifacio with his *grito de Balintawak*—the Cry of Balintawak— and Aguinaldo immediately seconded the movement with the uprising of Cavite. Here the insurrectos, armed only with a few shotguns and bolos, won easy victories and captured the Spanish garrison in the province. The success of the insurrection in Cavite astonished the Spaniards and the Filipinos alike, including Aguinaldo and his followers themselves. In my own home town of Baler, at the instigation of one Luis Novicio Luna (an Ilocano born in Baler and up to that time the only one who was a member of the Katipunan), a group of about fifty men armed with bolos and clubs attacked by surprise the barracks of the Guardia Civil and another detachment of infantry under the command of a sergeant; the revolutionaries took a number of Spanish prisoners and their rifles along with them. Among these prisoners was my old "friend," Cabo Enriquez who, despite his cruelty and despicable treatment of the people of Baler, was nevertheless spared from death. The larger part of the infantry garrison which was quartered in the ground floor of the Military Governor's house under the command of a lieutenant, escaped this attack for the guards were alert. My brother Teodorico, who did not know of my father's promise, led the attack against the Guardia Civil and captured Cabo Enriquez. That same night the inhabitants of the town of Baler, including my father, took to the near-by hills with the exception of those who were caught by the remaining Spanish soldiers. Among them was the family of my future wife, whose father was sent to jail in Manila and was kept there as long as the first uprising lasted. The rest of the people of the town remained in the hills until the Pact of Biaknabato, by virtue of which the first uprising against Spain was ended. I kept aloof studiously from anything that in any way might involve me in the revolution. I meant to honor my father's word. I continued my studies and never went back again to Baler for my summer vacations.

The rules of the house in Santo Tomas University permitted the boarders who were full-fledged university students to go out by themselves twice a week from five to seven o'clock, at which time the doors were closed and supper was served. In my second year of law, I discovered that the cook went home every night after supper through a side door which was opened for his exit. This discovery suggested to me the idea that whenever I pleased I could stay out until nine o'clock and use the cook's door to reënter the building. It did not take long for Father Tamayo, the director of the house, to discover my scheme, and one night as I entered the door I found him waiting for me. Without further parley, he sent me away for good. Fortunately, the punishment did not include my expulsion from the classes. Thereafter I boarded in a students' boarding-house in Intramuros, the Walled City, where the declaration of war between Spain and the United States found me residing.

When war was declared, the Spanish authorities and newspapers started a campaign of vilification against the Americans. They called them infidels, for in those days a non-Catholic was an infidel in the eyes of the Spanish friars in the Philippines. We were told, even from the pulpits, that the Americans, unlike the Spaniards' who Christianized the Indians in Mexico, killed the Indians living in the United States and took their lands. They assured us that victory for the invincible Spanish arms was a foregone conclusion. It was widely advertised that the entrance to Manila Bay on either side of Corregidor was so well mined that no fleet would dare enter unless it sought its own destruction.

While this anti-American publicity was going on in the Philippines, the American Consul-General in Singapore, Mr. Pratt, was negotiating with Aguinaldo for the help of the Filipinos in the war against Spain. It will be remembered that after the Pact of Biaknabato in 1896, Aguinaldo agreed to be exiled in Hongkong, and the beginning of hostilities in the Spanish-American War found him there. To this day Aguinaldo maintains that Consul-General Pratt and Admiral Dewey had both promised him that if the Filipinos took the side of the Americans in that war, upon the defeat of Spain and the signing of the peace treaty, the independence of the Philippines would be recognized by the United States. Aguinaldo says that in his conferences with these American officials, it was pointed out to him that the war was declared by the United States against Spain for the purpose of liberating Cuba and that, therefore, he easily believed that the country that fought for the liberation of

Cuba would not deny the Filipinos their freedom. Commodore Dewey—later Admiral—denied most emphatically that he had ever made such commitment to Aguinaldo, although it is officially recorded that he did inform the Government of the United States, after the termination of the war, that the Filipinos were more capable of governing themselves than the Cubans.

Early on the morning of the first of May, 1898, I heard the boom of heavy cannon from Manila Bay. I jumped up and told my fellow student-boarders who were in the same room with me that the American Fleet was attacking the Spanish Fleet lying over at the naval arsenal of Cavite, a few miles to the west. Nobody, including myself, believed what I said, but just the same we all went down and ran for the beach which was only about a thousand yards from the house. Americans who came to Manila a few years after the event I am narrating could not possibly understand what I mean when I say that the distance between Magallanes Street where I was staying and the beach was only about one thousand yards. The explanation is that during the American régime this water area was filled in, from the Malecon Drive which bordered the beach, for several miles. This is now called the Port Area, at the end of which were built the piers of Manila.

From the beach I witnessed the Battle of Manila Bay which, as far as I can remember, did not last long.

By eight o'clock Dewey's fleet steamed away, and the Spaniards who were on the beach shouted, *"Viva España!"* doubtless believing that Dewey was on the run. Their cheers, however, were of short duration, for very soon we saw Admiral's Montojo's ships all afire.

After having destroyed the Spanish Fleet and captured the naval arsenal of Cavite, Dewey sent one of his ships to get Aguinaldo and his associates in Hongkong and bring them to the Philippines in accordance with their concerted plan. Dewey did not have with him any land forces, and until he could get them from the United States, he had to depend upon Aguinaldo and his insurgents.

On the other hand, the Spanish Government in Manila, from the time that it became apparent that a war between the United States and Spain was imminent, called for Filipino volunteers to join the Spanish forces. Several battalions were organized. One contingent was composed of Macabebes from Pampanga under the command of the leading citizen of the town of Macabebe, Mr. Blanco, who was given the rank of major and later was promoted to a full colonelcy; another was under the command of Mr. Felipe Buencamino, a prominent lawyer of Manila, who was likewise given the rank of major. There were other battalions recruited from different provinces, and last but not least, there was the Manila Battalion and the Guerrilla de San Miguel, all commanded by a majority of ranking Spanish civilian officials.

As soon as Aguinaldo landed in Cavite, he issued a manifesto addressed to the Filipino people telling them that Divine Providence had at last heard their prayers and that their freedom and independence were at hand; that America, the mother of republics, had through Admiral Dewey assured him that if the Filipino people sided with the United States in the war against Spain, they would be granted independence upon the termination of the war. The arrival of Aguinaldo in Cavite was the signal for a new uprising all over the Philippines, and the Spanish Governor-General then offered the Filipinos, in the name of the government in Madrid, complete autonomy under the Spanish Crown if they would remain loyal to Spain. Some of the leading Filipinos were inclined to accept this offer, but they soon found out that the masses of the people were flocking to the banner of Aguinaldo and that even entire battalions of volunteers in the provinces had forsaken the cause of Spain and had gone over to Aguinaldo. So no one dared to come out and advocate the acceptance of the offer.

Before the American landing forces arrived in the Philippines, Aguinaldo, with the rifles that Dewey gave him from the Cavite arsenal, started a siege of Manila but was forbidden by the American high command to attack the city. After the required number of American troops had landed, an ultimatum was sent by General Anderson and Admiral Dewey to the Spanish Governor-General for the surrender of Manila. The answer was negative, but after a sham battle wherein only a few shots were fired, the white flag was raised and the Spanish conquest of the Philippines came to an inglorious end. I was then in the city and saw the American flag taking the place of the flag of Spain.

I confess to a feeling of deep sadness when I saw the old flag come down forever. After all, I inherited from my mother some Spanish blood, I spoke from childhood the language of Castile, and although the last Spanish friar, parish priest of my town, was far from what his vocation required him to be, one of his predecessors had been my teacher. Again I felt very grateful to the Dominican friars who had given me free tuition and free room and board for three years and who, despite my derelictions as a student, always treated me kindly. I felt, as I still do, grateful to them.

When Manila was occupied by the American forces, neither Aguinaldo nor his army was permitted by General Elwell S. Otis to enter the Walled City or any of its suburbs. In passing, I may add that the ultimatum, the sham battle, and the occupation of Manila took place on the 13th of August, 1898, after the armistice had already been signed by duly authorized representatives of Spain and the United States.

The denial of the fruits of victory to those who took a very important part in their achievement marked the beginning of the suspicion, jealousies, and misunderstandings between the two former allies which culminated in the outbreak of hostilities on the 4th of February, 1899.

After the occupation of Manila by the United States Army, law classes having been closed since the beginning of the war and I having nothing to do, I decided to visit Baler. I had not been in communication with my father or any one from Baler since the siege of Manila and was naturally very anxious about the fate of my family. When I arrived in Baler, I learned that my father, with my young brother who had gone to the provinces before the siege of Manila, had been murdered by bandits on their way home. It appears that my father had succeeded in collecting his back salary and had gone to Nueva Ecija not only to fetch my brother but to buy some merchandise with the idea of entering into the retail business. The bandits not only took everything they had, but murdered them besides. Years afterwards when I had become a prosecuting attorney, I succeeded in capturing every one of these bandits myself in company with my other brother, and I then prosecuted them for murder and robbery, and succeeded in securing life imprisonment for them.

I stayed in my home town, living with the family of my future wife, whose mother was a sister of my mother. At that time my little cousin was only about ten years old and I used to play with her.

The old town was deserted by its inhabitants, all the houses having been burned. Only the church and the adjoining parish house were standing and had been converted into a fortress by the Spanish garrison which was beleaguered for many months and had refused to surrender. No more glorious page in Spanish military history, I think, has been written than that which this small garrison wrote in the siege of Baler. Hunger and sickness had reduced the garrison from a hundred and fifty men to about fifty and only one of the officers commanding the company remained alive—Lieutenant Martin. Emissaries from Manila were sent by the Spanish General ordering them to give up the fight on the ground that the Philippines were no longer Spanish territory, since the treaty of peace had already been signed between Spain and the United States. The commander of the garrison did not listen to the emissary, but instead threatened to shoot him unless he went away. Finally Aguinaldo agreed to let these Spaniards come out from the church-fortress and go to Manila without surrendering and to carry with them all their rifles.

I was in Baler when the hostilities began between America and the Filipino forces. It was already known all over the world that in the treaty of peace America had insisted on the transfer by Spain of her sovereignty over the Philippines to the United States.

President McKinley had issued his proclamation formally declaring that the people and territory of the Philippines be placed under the sovereignty of the United States, and General Otis was commanded to take the steps that would bring about acceptance on the part of the Filipinos of the new situation. Although the language of the proclamation was couched in the most diplomatic terms, Aguinaldo and his advisers were in no way misled. They realized its full import and meaning, and as answer thereto, Aguinaldo convened at Malolos the First Filipino Congress, which was inaugurated with all the ceremonies and the solemnity demanded by the occasion. The Philippine Republic was formally proclaimed. The joy and exultation of hundreds of thousands of Filipinos that gathered in Malolos from all parts of the Islands knew no bounds. Aguinaldo, however, deliberately avoided a serious clash with the Army of Occupation.

Meanwhile, President McKinley created the First Philippine Commission headed by Jacob Gould Schurman, the President of Cornell University, with instructions to go to the Philippines and explain to the Filipinos America's purpose in taking the Philippines from Spain: namely, not to subjugate the people of the Islands, but to educate and train them in the art of self-government. In his message to Congress of that year, President McKinley with uncanny premonition stated: "I believe and confidently expect that the day will come when the Filipino people will bless the day when Divine Providence placed their country under the protecting hand of the United States." Unfortunately, when the Commission arrived in Manila, the peaceful, if strained, relations between the American and Filipino forces had terminated and war was actually in progress.

The news of the hostilities which began on February 4, 1899, reached Baler almost overnight. I decided at once that my duty lay in fighting for the freedom of my country. Neither my father, while he was alive, nor I had any commitment with the United States Army. On the contrary, it was that army, as I thought, which had broken faith with my people.

CHAPTER III

I Join the Revolution

In PANTABANGAN, I presented myself to Colonel Villacorta, a good and valiant soldier but almost an illiterate man. He had fought from the beginning of the first insurrection and never laid down arms even after the Pact of Biaknabato. He was only too glad to take me. He had known me in Baler, for he had been in command of the forces that had besieged the Spanish garrison there.

Villacorta made me a second lieutenant and a sort of aide-de-camp. When we arrived in Cabanatuan, General Llanera, having heard of a hideous crime committed by a band of *ladrones* (highwaymen) in the town of Aliaga, ordered Villacorta to send some of his men to go and capture the band. Villacorta gave me the mission, and in Aliaga I was informed that this band had attacked the house of one of the richest people in the town, taken everything they had and murdered everybody in the family, not excluding the children. After two days' hunting, I caught the whole gang. They were court-martialed and executed in short order. I was promoted to first lieutenant in recognition of this service.

For several months I was stationed in Cabanatuan. When later Aguinaldo, pressed by the American advance, transferred the seat of his government from Malolos to Cabanatuan, I was detailed to form a part of his staff. The General in command of all the forces operating in Luzon was Antonio Luna, a highly educated man who had spent many years as a student in Spain and in France. No braver soldier was ever born in any clime or any land. Whenever a key position was at stake, he always took personal command of the Filipino forces and was the last to retreat. At Calumpit, one of the most bloody battles fought during the war of resistance against the United States, he was wounded, but did not enter a hospital.

Soon after Aguinaldo had gone to Cabanatuan, the Filipino Congress held a session there. It was generally believed that at this session the Congress had decided to appoint a committee that would go to Manila and negotiate peace terms with the Philippine Commission sent by President McKinley on the basis of Philippine autonomy under an American protectorate. But General Luna, having heard of the action taken by the Congress, came rushing to Cabanatuan and arrested the members of the Congress whom he found there, including those who had been appointed members of the committee. That was the end of the Malolos Congress as well as of any attempt to negotiate peace with the American Government. It was also rumored that General Luna, after insulting some of the members of Aguinaldo's cabinet who had approved of the action of the Congress, demanded from Aguinaldo their dismissal. Whether the rumor was true or not, the fact remains that after Luna's trip to Cabanatuan, to which place the Congress had returned, the members of the cabinet presented their resignations and they were accepted. On the other hand, Aguinaldo prevailed upon Luna to release the members of the Congress whom he had arrested.

General Benito Natividad, who was seriously wounded in the battle of Calumpit, was brought to Cabanatuan in a hammock carried by his men. General Natividad was one of the right-hand men of General Luna, and by orders previously given by this general he was to be taken to Luna's headquarters in Bayambang. Colonel Sitiar of Aguinaldo's staff instructed me to escort General Natividad to Bayambang. After safely placing my patient in the hands of his friend and chief, I departed the following day for Cabanatuan. Upon reporting that my mission had been performed, I found that I had been promoted to the rank of captain.

Not long afterward Aguinaldo once again transferred the seat of his government from Cabanatuan to Angeles. We made the trip on horseback from Cabanatuan to San Isidro, where we found a force composed of at least three thousand men under the command of General Gregorio del Pilar. General Aguinaldo, after reviewing his guard of honor, ordered all the officers who were then in San Isidro to come up to his residence, and there, without any explanation for this unexpected as well as unusual procedure, he made us swear that we would fight by his side against all comers. Very early the next morning, we proceeded in the direction of Bayambang where we arrived late at night. On this trip for the first time I saw General Aguinaldo dressed in his military uniform with his insignia as full general. I asked him if he was celebrating some happy event, and he just smiled and said nothing.

Before midnight it was rumored in Bayambang that Luna had been murdered in Cabanatuan by the personal guards of Aguinaldo who were left in that town to protect his mother and wife. While this terrible news was being whispered all around, we received orders to board the train which was to take Aguinaldo with the forces of General Gregorio del Pilar to Angeles. Angeles was the headquarters of General Concepcion, another of General Luna's trusted men, who was in command of the forces which were facing the Americans in San Fernando. General Concepcion was evidently unaware of our arrival, for he showed his surprise when he was faced by the Commander-in-Chief of the Filipino forces. The following day official announcement was made of the killing of General Luna and that of his senior aide-de-camp, Colonel Paco Roman. His two junior aides were put in prison.

The brigade defending the line facing San Fernando was the crack brigade of the old Philippine Army. It had been organized by General Luna himself and was composed of veteran soldiers of the defunct Spanish Army and commanded by officers who had also served and fought many battles under the Spanish flag. Quietly but hurriedly, General Aguinaldo recalled these officers, sent them to other brigades, and replaced them with his old trusted officers of the Revolution.

We did not remain long in Angeles. From there we went farther north to the town of Tarlac where Aguinaldo, in personal command of the Philippine Army since Luna's death, remained for several months. While in this town, I lived in the house of Colonel Alejandro Albert of the Medical Service, whose kind wife was one of the most widely read Filipinas of her day. She treated me like a son, and I can never forget her generous hospitality. It was in her home, too, in Manila, that I found haven whenever I needed lodging in after years. When I became influential in the government of the Philippines, although Colonel Albert belonged to the opposition party, my first recommendation to Governor-General Harrison was the appointment of Dr. Albert as Under-Secretary of Public Instruction, a position he held until he was no longer physically able to perform the duties of the office.

While in Tarlac, I received orders from General

Aguinaldo to go to Baguio and replace the officer in command of the garrison there until another officer could be sent to take my post. It was my first visit to the place which has been, since Governor-General Taft's day, the summer capital of the Philippines. It was a long trip from Tarlac on horseback to the high altitude of the Baguio mountains.

Baguio was nothing but a forest of pine trees with Igorrot huts. There were, however, three houses made of timber; one occupied by a German, Dr. Sheer, married to an Igorrota by whom he had a pretty daughter and a fine boy; another occupied by a Dutchman, and the third by a full-blooded Igorrote—Carino—who was appointed by Aguinaldo governor of the province. These two distinguished representatives of occidental civilization, instead of imposing their own civilization upon the Igorrots, evidently preferred to adopt that of their hosts, for I saw them in G-strings exactly like those of the Igorrots.

The Christian settlement at that time was Trinidad, about three miles from the city hall of Baguio and a couple of thousand feet lower than Baguio proper. The Spanish Military Governor of the Mountain Province resided at Trinidad, and there the garrison remained until they were captured by the Filipino forces during the Second Rebellion. Americans who have fine homes in Baguio and have enjoyed its delightful climate, perhaps one of the best in the world, and its beautiful scenery, will be surprised to hear that at that time not gold but coffee made the province of Benguet—which includes Trinidad and Baguio—famous. When I returned to Tarlac, I carried with me two sacks of coffee which I presented to my hostess, Mrs. Albert, and one small tube of particles of gold taken from the river, which I presented to General Aguinaldo's mother.

As a member of Aguinaldo's staff in Tarlac, I only did office work and it became tiresome to me. I felt ashamed of the fact that although there was actual war going on I had been promoted from first lieutenant to captain without having heard, even at a distance, the whistle of a bullet. So one day I asked permission to see General Aguinaldo and told him what I felt. I requested him to send me to the front, so he sent me to General Mascardo with a letter of introduction in his own handwriting. General Mascardo had his headquarters then in the town of Porac, Pampanga. I arrived at his place at dusk and remained with him for the evening.

The following day he sent me to the front as member of the staff of Colonel Leysan, who was in command of the Filipino forces on the line between San Fernando and Porac.

Our advance post was in Bacolor. Colonel Leysan was quartered in a nipa house about one mile back of the lines and with him were staying Major Galura, the Chief of Staff, and another officer whose name I do not now remember. That night we played *tres siete*, a game of cards somewhat like bridge. At five o'clock in the morning the roar of small pieces of artillery made us jump out of bed. We hurriedly put on our uniforms and rushed to the line. As we were getting nearer the trenches, I heard for the first time in my life the whistle of a bullet. I ducked. Then the number of the flying bullets became too numerous to duck and I felt inside myself an irresistible impulse to run away. Before this, I had a very high opinion of my own valor. Indeed one of the reasons why I asked General Aguinaldo to send me to the front was because I felt pretty certain that I could be one of the national military heroes of Philippine history. But when the test came, I discovered that the fear of death was instinctively quite strong with me. My whole body was shaking and my knees became so weak that I felt they could only carry me if I turned around and ran in the opposite direction; not another step could they take in the direction from which the bullets were coming. What made my fear so overwhelming was the fact that I had not been to confession for a long, long time and I thought that the loss of life in this world to me meant hell fire. I was too panicky to be able to concentrate and make an act of contrition. Indeed, I could not even finish the Lord's Prayer which I started to say as soon as the first bullet had whistled over my head. I was about to run away as fast as I could when I heard a voice behind me saying, "*Joven, cuidado que los soldados le estan observando.*" (Young man, you'd better be careful because the soldiers are watching you.) A sense of shame and humiliation, stronger even than the fear of death, brought me instantly back to myself. From that time on, I stood erect and noticed no longer the noise of bullets. My attention was now directed to the movements of the enemy and to encouraging my own soldiers. By ten o'clock in the morning, Colonel Leysan ordered me to go and tell Major Liraz whose battalion was on the other side of the road between Bacolor and Porac, to move his forces and cover our right flank, for the Americans had started to envelop us in that sector. I found Major Liraz standing, seemingly unconcerned, in the middle of the road at the head of his battalion. I had not finished transmitting the order when a burst of shrapnel cut short Major Liraz's life. I lifted his head to see whether he was still alive, but he was truly dead. Four soldiers carried him away and the following day he was buried with the military honors due a real hero. He left a widow and seven children.

Colonel Leysan put me in command of Major Liraz's battalion until the battle was over at six o'clock that evening. The Americans had taken Bacolor. We had withdrawn to Porac, and General Mascardo's headquarters had been transferred to the village of Dolores in the hills. The advance continued the following day and Porac fell into the hands of the Americans sooner than Bacolor did because our soldiers had not had anything to eat during the battle the day before, nor had they had enough rest during the night. It was a hot day when the Americans entered Porac. Although our forces had not only withdrawn but had practically run, I decided to hide in the bushes and trees that were thick back of the river, to find out what the Americans did when they entered a town. I had about ten soldiers with me, armed with rifles. At about eleven o'clock in the morning, I saw a number of Americans, some on horseback and others afoot, going down the river. I wondered if they were coming to hunt for me, but my doubts were soon dispelled for although they were armed they dropped their rifles, left their horses, and began to undress. Evidently they had come for a swim. In nature's bathing-suits they plunged into the water. Before I could stop it, one of my soldiers fired a shot and the swimmers ran for their guns, although not for their clothes. They immediately returned that fire in our direction and we left.

At one of the formal dinners that, as President of the Commonwealth, I gave to new Commanding Generals of the Philippine Department, having learned that my guest of honor on this particular occasion had been under General J. Franklin Bell, I asked him if by any chance he was in the attack of Porac and he said yes. Then I told him my little experience with the swimmers and he admitted that he was one of them.

In the toast that I offered to the health and success of my guest of honor—there were no ladies present—I made reference to the difference between the uniform which he wore when I first saw him in the river and the one he was wearing that evening.

After Porac, General Mascardo appointed Leysan his Chief of Staff and ordered him to his headquarters in Dolores. Leysan took me with him as his assistant. It appears that General Aguinaldo had appointed General Mascardo as Commanding General of all the Filipino forces operating in Central Luzon, which at that time was the only real field of action. General Mascardo, who was a hero in the First Revolution against Spain when he had been wounded four times in four different pitched battles, was an expert in guerrilla warfare, but knew nothing about military strategy and tactics, as did his predecessor, General Luna. As Colonel Leysan had served with ability and distinction as officer of the Spanish Army, Mascardo rightly considered him well prepared to be our Chief of Staff.

The first few weeks of our stay in Dolores were marked by lull and quiet in the lines. This was not unusual for since the campaign started the Americans would give us respite from time to time. During these quiet days our needs for relaxation took the form of certain emotional outbursts. We had dances and courted the fair girls of Pampanga, either in the unoccupied towns or out in the villages where some of them went to hide. A brother of General Mascardo who had lost his left arm in a hand-to-hand fight in the First Revolution, was making love to a girl in Guagua. Although the town was no longer defended by Filipino troops, the Americans on their part had not occupied it, so Major Mascardo was able to visit his girl. He always went with about fifteen men, all of them including the major on horseback—I will not call them cavalrymen because they really were not. We never had a force of cavalry except what General Luna organized, composed of fifty men as his personal guard who accompanied him everywhere.

One day Major Mascardo invited me and Lieutenant Betus to go with him for they had planned to have a little dance in his girl's house. We arrived there about two o'clock in the afternoon so as to have time to take a bath and change our clothes for the dance which was to begin at five o'clock. By four, we were notified that a troop of American cavalry was in the outskirts of the town. Instead of escaping as we should have done (and we had ample time to do it), Major Mascardo decided that he would show his girl the brave man that he was. So he invited us to come to the street with our rifles ready to fire as soon as the American cavalry came.

In the first exchange of shots Mascardo fell dead with a bullet through his head. The rest of us ran for our lives. We were not pursued by the enemy, and by nightfall I sent a courier to find out if the Americans had left and what had happened to the major's corpse. The courier came back with the information that the cavalry had returned to Bacolor, had taken his watch and everything else of value that Major Mascardo had with him, carried the dead officer to the Presidencia or town hall, laid him on the municipal council table, and left a letter for General Mascardo in the hands of the mayor of the town. I went back and found the body of Major Mascardo no longer in the Presidencia but lying in the parlor of his girl's house placed on a bed with four lighted candles around him. The whole town was there mourning the death of a patriot.

The letter addressed to General Mascardo was handed to me. It was written in English on a sheet of paper with no envelope. I did not attempt to read it for neither I nor any one else in the house understood its language. Taking the letter, the watch, and the money removed by the Americans from Mascardo's pockets, which were handed to me by the mayor, we went back to headquarters with the corpse carried in a hammock. General Mascardo raised hell with us and gave definite orders that thereafter no one should go to the unoccupied towns except with his permission.

At headquarters there was an officer, Major Kunanan, who was educated in Europe and knew English well. The letter as translated by him to us read more or less as follows: "To Major General Mascardo,

Commanding General of Central Luzon: I regret to have killed your valiant brother. As evidence of my admiration for him and my high regard for you, I had his body carried to the town hall, placed it on a table, and entrusted everything he had with him, including his revolver and his rifle, to the mayor of the town for delivery to you. I beg to express my sympathy in your bereavement."

The letter made a profound impression on all those who knew of its contents. What a different picture it gave us of the kind of men the Americans were from that depicted by the Spaniards in the early days after the declaration of war by the United States against Spain.

Sometime later we were surprised by the arrival of two Japanese officers—Captain Hara and Lieutenant Nakamori. They came with a letter from General Aguinaldo informing General Mascardo that they were military observers sent by the Japanese government. Both spoke English, but Captain Hara was the only one who ever joined in our conversation. Nakamori went to the front and Hara remained at headquarters with us.

At last General Mascardo instructed Colonel Leysan to formulate a plan for an attack against Angeles—the town farthest north along the railway line occupied by the Americans. My general thought that there was something wrong with the American Army when they remained for so long a time without attempting to make further advance. Captain Hara was consulted. The plan contemplated an attack against Angeles from three sides—north, east, and west. On the south, there would be a force prepared to intercept reinforcement that might come from San Fernando, the next town to the south. We started to advance at four o'clock in the morning. It was a fiasco. One company commanded by a very excited captain began firing before their bullets could reach the positions occupied by the Americans. At this time our ammunition consisted of cartridges reloaded in the most primitive way, and our weapons were old Spanish Mausers and Remingtons which we had taken from the Spaniards. Their effective range was not more than three or four hundred yards. The Maxims, which the Americans had, started on their deadly work and we had to withdraw before we could even get within range for our guns.

General Bell, then a major or lieutenant colonel of the volunteers of theAmerican Army, soon returned the compliment to us. We found one morning while we were having breakfast at headquarters that he was at the head of his cavalry and attacking our small garrison there. By following a trail, he had succeeded in going through out lines unobserved. Fortunately, we were all dressed and our horses were ready, for General Mascardo was about to go out on an inspection trip. So we jumped on our horses and let loose our bridles. By a mere matter of five minutes the whole staff of General Mascardo, including himself, escaped from falling into the hands of Major Bell.

This unexpected and unwelcome visit of the enemy forced Mascardo to transfer his headquarters to a safer place at the farthest end of a small valley. To reach it one had to go between two hills which exposed the would-be intruder to cross-fire. I was left in command of two companies guarding the entrance to the valley. Not having learned my lesson properly from the previous surprise attack of Major Bell, and confident that before the Americans could reach our place some resistance would be offered by our forces in the front line, I preferred to stay in a rather nice farmhouse, somewhat distant from the hills where the forces under my command were located. The Japanese Captain Hara stayed with me. We had hardly been one week in this new position when one morning we were notified of the approach of Major Bell by bullets going through the house. Captain Hara actually flew, for in one second he had jumped on one of the two horses we had at our disposal tied near the house and was galloping without saddle at full speed. I jumped on the other horse to take command of the companies that were posted to defend the approach to General Mascardo's headquarters. I had just taken my position at a point on the hill to the left side of the entrance to the valley when I saw the American cavalry approaching cautiously. I got my field-glass and recognized the man whom I thought was commanding the troops. From the descriptions given us, I felt certain he was the same man who had killed Major Mascardo—the man who almost took us prisoners in Dolores. I decided to kill him with my own hands, so I took a Mauser from one of the soldiers near me and watched him approach. I gave orders not to fire until I did. I waited until my chosen victim was near enough even for our almost useless cartridges. I put my finger on the trigger and just as I pulled it he dismounted and the bullet struck his saddle. The horse ran away to the hills and later in the day we got it and its saddle with the bullet embedded in it. I aimed again and again until I fired ten shots, always missing my target. I gave it up and returned the rifle to the soldier.

By this time Major Bell had mounted another horse and after a while withdrew with his force. Evidently, they were merely reconnoitering.

I went to General Mascardo's headquarters; it was deserted. I looked for him and his staff and found them on the other side of the hills, on the bank of a river. By noon Captain Hara appeared still mounted on his unsaddled horse.

"Where have you been?" I asked him in Spanish. The Japanese, theretofore always solemn in words as well as in action, his face as blank and unmoved as that of a marble statue, was now glowing with joy and happiness and literally shouted: *"Nacimiento! nacimiento!"*

Captain Hara only spoke to us in English through

our interpreter, Major Kunanan, but this time he managed to express his feelings in one Spanish word, *nacimiento*, which means birth. He doubtless meant to convey the thought that he had gotten a new lease on life. Thus, my first experience with a Japanese army officer did not conform with the utter disregard for life which they showed many years later in the conquest of the Philippines.

After the occupation of Angeles, all the forces in Central Luzon were dispersed and took to the hills, since it had become impossible to maintain our lines. Aguinaldo had fled from Tarlac and was sharply pursued by the American forces. He was almost captured before he reached the Caraballo Mountains. Only the determined resistance put up by General Gregorio del Pilar at Tila Pass—where this young general lost his life to save that of his chief—gave Aguinaldo a chance to get to Palanan on the east coast of Isabela, the remotest and most isolated town in Luzon. Here Aguinaldo remained for many months in hiding, his own generals not knowing where he was, although he continued to communicate with them. General Mascardo himself, pressed day and night by Major Bell, had withdrawn his own brigade to the mountains separating Bataan from Pampanga. But Bell made it so difficult for us to get food supplies from the Filipinos in the plains of Pampanga that General Mascardo decided to send me to Bataan which, according to our information, had not as yet been occupied by the Americans. I was to look for the best place to which he could go with his remaining forces.*

With twenty-five soldiers I proceeded immediately to comply with this order. I took as guides two Negritos, the nomad aborigines of the Philippines—tiny little fellows, black with kinky hair. The trip was one of the hardest I ever made in my life. We walked barefooted up and down the mountains and swam rivers infested with crocodiles. Our food consisted of a little rice and salt, and when we slept at night we lay on the ground covered only by the sky above. On the third day, we came down to the plains of the province of Bataan, and from Dinalupihan I made the rest of the trip on horseback.

On reaching Orani, I was met by Major Vister who, only two months before, had captured a small launch carrying a few American soldiers and made prisoners of them. The launch had gone to Orani and had run aground in shallow water—an accident which sealed the fate of its passengers. Later, the prisoners

---

*As far as I can remember, upon the dispersion of the Filipino forces in the Island of Luzon, they were scattered in the provinces of northern and central Luzon as follows:

General Tinio remained in command of Northern Luzon; Generals Makabulos and Llanera in Tarlac and Nueva Ecija, respectively; Generals Aquino and Hizon in Pampanga east and west of the railroad line from Manila to Dagupan; General Pekson with Colonel S. Miguel, in Bulacan; General Geronimo whose forces killed General Lawton, in Rizal, with General Del Pilar; General Malvar, the last Filipino general to surrender, in Batangas and Tayabas; General Trias, in Cavite; and General Mascardo in Bataan and Zambales.

were released by order of General Mascardo. In Balanga, the capital of the province, I discovered that the Military Governor, Lieutenant Colonel Bautista, together with his forces had abandoned his post and with the scanty funds of the government had run back to his old home town in Cavite. Two former bandits during the Spanish régime who had styled themselves generals when the first revolution broke out but who never received recognition from General Aguinaldo for their "patriotic services," had gathered their old gang and on their own authority replaced the deserting revolutionary chief. Although I did not intend to recognize their assumed military rank and power, I nevertheless sought their advice as to the place best suited for General Mascardo's headquarters. They received me with undisguised displeasure for which I later found the explanation. This, however, did not stop them from giving me the information I wanted as they told me that the forest between Bagac and Morong on the China Sea coast would be the best hiding place for my chief, General Mascardo.

I went to Bagac and satisfied myself that the old bandits were right. So I sent the information to General Mascardo who, within fifteen days, followed me with all his forces—about three hundred men armed with rifles and five rounds of ammunition apiece. Before Mascardo's arrival, and while I was in Pilar, I had received information that a house in a barrio of Balanga had been pillaged by a band of men armed with rifles. I went to the place with my twenty-five soldiers and in the house which had been robbed, I met the two self-styled generals with about forty men, some armed with rifles and others with bolos. From the look on their faces, it appeared clear to me that they were ready for trouble if I attempted to investigate them. So pretending that because they had taken charge of the case, I felt that I had nothing more to do with it, I left the house with a courteous bow.

As soon as I was out of their sight, I concealed myself with my men in the bushes from which I could see them going back to the town. Half an hour afterward, they were gone. I returned to the house and asked its owner for particulars about the robbery. While making this investigation, a man came looking for his hat which he had left the night before. I asked him why he had been there and he plainly told me that he had been a guide for the bandits. I inquired whether he knew the chief of the gang or any of its members, and without hesitation he answered affirmatively and gave me the name of the chief of the band. With him I went back to Pilar which, to avoid a clash with the old bandits who were in Balanga, I chose for my quarters while waiting for General Mascardo.

That same night I succeeded in getting hold of the man who was responsible for the robbery. I told him to make his confession or I would order his execution the following day. I sent for the parish priest who gladly performed his religious duty. At midnight, one of the old chieftains came to see me and interceded in behalf of my prisoner. He pleaded forgiveness upon the ground that the prisoner as well as himself and his companions had rendered patriotic service during the First Revolution. After exacting from them the promise that the crime would not be repeated, I dismissed the case and freed the prisoner. From that time on I never had trouble with these "patriots" and my authority was never challenged by them.

When General Mascardo came, it was no longer safe to travel through the towns bordering Manila Bay, so he made the trip all the way to Bagac through the woods. On his arrival at this last named town, he was given a rousing welcome. Then we went to the place I had selected, where he remained until he surrendered months later to the American forces in Zambales. It should be stated here that the Filipino troops in this last named province were also under the command of General Mascardo. They consisted of about two hundred men, commanded by a colonel whose name I have forgotten, and Lieutenant Colonel Gabriel Alba, a former companion of mine in the college of San Juan de Letran. Our troops in Zambales were already carrying on guerrilla warfare and they had succeeded in capturing a few rifles from the Americans.

Once he was located in his new and last encampment in the forest between Bagac and Morong,

Mascardo divided his forces in Bataan into three commands: one under Colonel Vister operated from Abucay to Dinalupihan, including the territory between Bataan and Pampanga; the second under me operated from Balanga to Mariveles; and the third from Bagac to Morong was commanded by Colonel Leysan who continued to be the Chief of Staff and stayed in Mascardo's headquarters. It fell to my lot to be placed in command of the guerrilla band that would operate between Balanga and Mariveles—the tip of the peninsula which forty-two years later was destined to be the last stronghold of General MacArthur's army. The two Japanese officers, Hara and Nakamori, as soon thereafter as they had the chance, went to Manila and thence to Japan.

Following Mascardo's transfer to Bataan, the American forces took possession without opposition on our part of the towns of the province. In Balanga where the military commander of the province was, the larger part of the forces was stationed, and there was one company each in the towns of Dinalupihan, Orani, and Orion. The other towns, including Mariveles, had only small garrisons. Upon the occupation of the province of Bataan, following the same practice that they had adopted in all the occupied provinces, the Army of Occupation appointed the local officials of the town and started to open up schools with some of the non-commissioned officers as teachers. Every man appointed to these municipal posts, whether he happened to be the same Filipino official appointed by Aguinaldo's government or a new one, when the former was suspected of being disloyal, accepted their new appointment only with the consent of General Mascardo and upon the understanding that the appointee would continue to serve the revolution either by helping us to secure food supplies or by giving us information as to the movements of the American troops whenever they planned to attack our encampments, or in any other way that might be necessary.

Not long after the American occupation of Bataan, Mascardo decided to attack the small garrison in Hermosa. He gathered almost all the forces he then had in the province and we made the attack at night. Before we could do much harm to the garrison, help came from the near-by towns and we retreated, losing one major killed and several soldiers wounded. Knauber, a Scandinavian, whom I met later after the establishment of the Civil Government as officer of the Constabulary, gave a good account of himself on that occasion. With such disastrous results, we gave up the idea of ever attacking again the American garrisons and decided that the safest and most effective tactic was to ambush them whenever they went out to the hills in search of our guerrillas.

The 24th of December, 1899, arrived. To be eating only boiled rice up in the hills did not appear to me a very appropriate way of celebrating the birth of Our

Lord Jesus Christ. Hence, I sent word to the American-appointed mayor of the town of Orion that I would come down with my one hundred soldiers and spend Christmas Eve and Christmas Day in his town. The mayor was agreeable and assured me that if his instructions were literally followed, he would smuggle into town every man with his rifle, distribute us in different houses, and the Americans would not be any wiser. More still, he promised me *lechon* (roast young pig) and abundant fresh sea-food for our hungry band. We entered Orion from different places after nightfall without being noticed. The man in command of the American force was Captain Goldman whom later I met when he was Governor of Bataan after the establishment of the Civil Government. I was taken to the house of the mayor, one of the finest in the locality, made of hard wood with fine furniture and two comfortable bedrooms. Captain Goldman lived in the parish house, as usual the largest and best. The next day after the mass, as was the custom of the municipal officials during the Spanish régime, the Presidente or mayor with his subordinates, called on Captain Goldman to wish him Merry Christmas. No doubt with more sincere feelings they called on me, too. My soldiers filled up with good food, and some of them even went to the cockpit on Christmas Day. That night there was gambling in the house of one of the prominent citizens of the town—the well-known game of chance called monte. American soldiers who had already learned the game attended and bet their dollars. My whole fortune consisted of P5.00 ($2.50 in American money) and I decided to back my luck against my enemies. The old adage "lucky in love, unlucky in cards" evidently also means "unlucky in war, lucky in cards," for with my five pesos I won one hundred dollars which, under the circumstances, looked to me to be quite a fortune. So I decided to spend this money in Manila. It was Christmas and even then I already had a very pronounced inclination for the frailties of the so-called civilized, modern man. Indeed, my prolonged nomad life as an insurrecto was beginning to weigh heavily upon my nerves. So, with my liking for quick decisions, I instructed Lieutenant Baluyot, my second in command of the guerrillas, to take the men back to the hills and keep on with the job in my absence. I gave him a letter for General Mascardo begging pardon for my temporary relinquishment of the command.

Disguised as a fisherman, I sailed for Navotas in a fishing boat from one of the coastal towns of Bataan. Cabesang Doro, from Pilar—his full name was Isidoro Paguio—accompanied me in this sea trip. This generous man treated me like a son and later on saved my life.

We stayed in Malabon in the house of Cabesang Doro's friend long enough for me to secure clothes that would give the appearance of a university student. I entered Manila without the slightest difficulty and spent my holidays in the house of Colonel Albert, the same man who, for several months, had me as boarder in Tarlac. The house was located in what was then named calle Ronquillo (Ronquillo street), just in front of the quarters of the military police in the suburb of Santa Cruz. I thought the safest place was where no one would suspect that an insurrecto would dare be. By this time, the American soldiers had learned a few Spanish words, such as *"buenos dias"* (good morning), *"mucho bueno"* (very good); the correct Spanish expression, however, is *"muy bueno."* *Buenos dias* and *mucho bueno* were frequently exchanged between my adversaries and myself.

In this house, I learned that Aguinaldo's family had presented themselves to the Americans and had been set free, although they were closely watched. They were guests of Señor Leyva, one of the rich widowers of Manila, whose son, a real athlete, had been the aide of Aguinaldo and had been murdered by robbers in Pangasinan.

From my gambling winnings, I bought one chicken and a basket of fruit, and with the double purpose of leveling suspicion and paying my respects to my Commander-in-Chief's family, I called on them. Not much was said between us. We were afraid that even the walls had ears.

New Year's Eve was celebrated in Manila by the

men not on duty in the Army of Occupation, in the old American style.

Lastly on the morning of New Year's Day, which is also my Saint's Day, I went to the University of Santo Tomas to hear mass. My old professors were glad to see me. They invited me to breakfast assuming that I had returned to the ways of peace. They were amazed, and I guess scared, when they discovered that I was still an insurrecto. They tried to dissuade me from going back to the hills. "Further resistance is of no use," they asserted, "and then the Americans are fair. They treat the Filipinos well, they have allowed the reopening of the schools, and President McKinley has promised to grant us self-government in due time." The Spanish friars who previously had reviled the Americans had evidently become their friends. I was unmoved. "Dewey," I said, "fooled Aguinaldo once. McKinley would fool us again."

Shortly afterwards I reported to General Mascardo's headquarters. At that time only General Mascardo and the men staying with him had even a limited ration. The rest of us ate if and when there was food to be had. Almost everybody, including General Mascardo himself, became affected with malaria and a few of our soldiers died from this illness. I myself woke up one morning with very high fever and sent for my very dear friend who had remained in the town of Pilar. He appeared with a man whom he called a doctor. This fellow had been a sort of nurse in San Juan de Dios Hospital during the Spanish régime, had settled in Pilar, and became the town physician. He brought with him some pills which he gave me to take, all at once. It was not long before I felt that I was dying. They sent for the parish priest who administered to me the last sacraments and gave me also a five-dollar gold coin. It was the first American gold coin I had ever seen. I have an idea that the famous "doctor" had given me an overdose of aspirin, but I survived, and when I was strong enough to be moved away, Cabesang Doro brought some men and a hammock to carry me through the town of Pilar to the beach where a fishing boat was ready to take me to Navotas. The people of Pilar, as I learned later on, watched the movements of the Americans to make certain that they did not catch me while I was being transported through the town.

I spent a month in the house of Cabesang Doro's friend in Navotas. This old man had amassed so much money from the fishing business that he had been able to send a son to be educated in Europe. While convalescing at his house, I read books which left in my mind some doubt as to the certainty of the existence of hell as taught me by my friar teachers—doubts which in after years contributed to my leaving for a long time the Catholic faith and joining the Masonic Order. I returned to the old church after my children had grown up. My orderly, a young man from Bohol, had accompanied me on this trip and most generously devoted himself to helping me regain my health. This boy is the only man to whom I had owed so much but whose services I was unable to repay at a later date. By the time I was in a position to do something for him, he had joined his Maker.

Once I had fully recovered, I decided to return and rejoin my comrades in arms. This time, instead of using my usual means of transportation, I preferred to go on one of the Yangco launches then making daily trips between Manila and Bataan. Through a messenger, I notified the Presidente of Pilar—a man whom the American garrison considered a loyal Americanista—of the day and time of my arrival on the Yangco launch. This I had to do so that I would not have to go in the regular rowboat that met the passengers on the bay to bring them ashore. As I boarded my little *banca* (canoe) the man paddling it delivered to me a letter from the mayor in which I was told not to come to the outskirts of Pilar at the mouth of the river during the daytime, but to remain instead in the bushes near the beach. He knew that a scouting platoon was going to the village some time that day.

When night came and the platoon did not come, I went to the outskirts feeling certain that the danger had passed as it was not customary for the American forces to venture outside the town at night in small numbers. I intended to proceed to the hills after dinner that night, but before I had finished my meal the people of the village came rushing through the street to their houses, and I was notified that American soldiers were approaching. I went down and hid under the house which was fenced with bamboo. After a while, I realized that every building was being searched and, indeed, two soldiers came to the house under which I was hiding. They found my little valise containing my picture and that of a young lady I was courting while I was in the province of Pampanga. This discovery apparently convinced the platoon that I was in the village and they did everything to force the villagers to confess where I was. Whether it was because no one really knew my whereabouts at this moment or that the people simply wanted to protect me, the fact remains that, evidently exasperated by their failure, the American troops burned the houses in the village. These all being made of nipa and bamboo, the fire spread everywhere, including to my hideout, in five minutes. In the face of what I thought was certain death, I had to decide whether I preferred to be burned or shot, and as far as I was concerned there was only one choice—the less painful of the two. I looked out to the only street of the village. It was full of soldiers. I signaled to my orderly who was hiding with me to get ready to run. We jumped out, running toward the river which was less than twenty-five yards from our hiding-place.

Several shots were fired in our direction. I reached the river and dove all the way to the other side. When I reached the opposite bank I flew rather than ran, for in my athletic days in the college of San Juan de Letran, I was one of the faster runners. They did not pursue and after midnight I cautiously approached the village to find out what had happened. Not a house was left standing. The Americans had left for dead my orderly who had been shot through the body three times. As best we could, we attended his wounds and that same night I had him taken to Navotas on a fishing boat, there to be treated. He was saved although he remained lame the rest of his life.

I went back to the hills, this time with murder in my heart. I was determined to take revenge. Practically every man in the little village followed me, armed only with their bolos. They were just as resolved as I to get even with our foe. For several days we waited until at last the news came that a force from Balanga was getting ready to cross the mountain and go to Bagac. Walking all night long, I led fifty men armed with old Spanish Mausers and only two rounds of ammunition. These were Sanda Tahanes * from the burned barrio of the town of Pilar.

I took my men and ambushed them on either side

* Sanda Tahanes was the name given to the insurrectos armed only with bolos who constituted practically the only force with which the revolution against Spain was started, for shotguns were very scarce.

of the trail at the back of the mountain that divided the two coastlines of the province of Bataan. By noon of a very hot day, a force of about thirty Americans headed by an officer on horseback came up, men and animal with their tongues hanging out from heat and fatigue.

At the first discharge of our rifles the horse ran away with his rider and instinctively the tired soldiers followed their leader. We killed two whose corpses I had buried. It was my last engagement with the American troops, for from that time on my malaria came back and I was never well enough to indulge in any guerrilla warfare. I picked out a hut in the mountains of Bataan, which the American troops never reached at that time, but which became familiar to them during the recent Bataan campaign.

The American forces had occupied the whole province of Bataan, but the Filipinos including those living in the towns were still loyal to the Revolution. They told us the movements of the American troops and occasionally, whenever they could, sent us some food.

About the end of February, we received reports to the effect that General Aguinaldo had been captured in Palanan. We did not believe it. We thought that it was part of a plan to dishearten and induce us to quit, for, by that time, there had already been organized in Manila a political party which was co-operating with the United States to bring about the restoration of peace at an early date. However, the news about the capture of Aguinaldo became so persistent that, at the end of March, General Mascardo summoned me to his headquarters and gave me orders to surrender to the American forces. I was to try to find out if the capture of Aguinaldo was a fact. The General said: "You have served your country well as a soldier. But you are sick and have been suffering from malaria so long that you simply cannot stand this hard life much longer. It is better for you to surrender. The Americans will let you free as they have done in the case of most of those who have already surrendered. Go back to your university, continue with your studies and finish your career. Our country needs men with education. You will be of service to our people in other fields. Besides, I have a special mission for you. I want you to find out definitely if General Aguinaldo has been captured. If he has, try to get in touch with him and tell him of the situation of our forces here in Bataan and over there in Zambales. Ask him to instruct me whether I should surrender or continue on fighting till my last man."

With a heavy heart, I took leave of my General and started for Mariveles without saying good-by either to my comrades at headquarters or to the men under my command. General Mascardo did not want anybody to learn of the mission he had given me.

One early morning in the month of April, 1901,

clad in a worn-out uniform of a major of General Aguinaldo's army, emaciated from hunger and lingering illness, I walked down the slopes of Mariveles Mountain, accompanied by two soldiers, to surrender to the American post stationed in the little town of Mariveles. The mayor of the town, a Filipino, had previously negotiated my surrender with Lieutenant Miller, the commandant of the post. I was met at the outskirts of the town by Lieutenant Miller, the first American with whom I had ever come into personal contact. After an exchange of greetings, Lieutenant Miller told me through an interpreter that I could consider myself free and should keep my revolver and my dagger, but that he would take the rifles carried by my soldiers and would give them in exchange thirty pesos each. I handed Lieutenant Miller my dagger as a present. (This same dagger he sent back to me soon after I was elected President of the Commonwealth, thirty-five years later.) Lieutenant Miller invited me to come and stay in his headquarters until the next day when a launch would take me to Manila. During the day I turned over in my mind whether I should tell Lieutenant Miller of the special mission which General Mascardo had confided to me, and having come to the conclusion that by so doing I would sooner find out whether General Aguinaldo had been captured or not, I decided to do so. Lieutenant Miller said: "Of course, it is true that General Aguinaldo has been captured; he was captured by

General Funston in Palanan. He is now a prisoner of war, but he is living in Malacañan Palace where the Military Governor, General Arthur MacArthur, lives, and where he is treated with the utmost courtesy and consideration. I will inform Manila of your mission at once; perhaps they will let you see Aguinaldo with your own eyes."

That night before I fell asleep I heard shooting in the streets of Mariveles. Later I learned that the detachment operating between Orion and Mariveles had attempted to attack the garrison, but withdrew after an exchange of a few shots. I assumed that my old comrades, believing that I had deserted them, intended to punish me. On the other hand, Lieutenant Miller now suspected that my surrender was a stratagem. My calmness when he entered my bedroom with a revolver in his hand convinced him of my innocence and without further ado he left the room.

On the afternoon of the following day, a small launch carried me from Mariveles to Manila and I was conducted directly to Malacañan Palace—the holy place from which Spanish Governors-General had ruled the Philippines, and which I had never seen before. I was ushered into the office of General Arthur MacArthur, the father of the hero of the Battle of the Philippines. Fred Fisher who, in after years, became a member of the Supreme Court of the Philippines, acted as interpreter. He told General MacArthur in English what I had said in Spanish;

namely, that I was instructed by General Mascardo to find out if General Aguinaldo had been captured. The American General, who stood erect and towered over my head, raised his hand without saying a word and pointing to the room across the hall, made a motion for me to go in there. Trembling with emotion, I slowly walked through the hall toward the room, hoping against hope that I would find no one inside. At the door two American soldiers in uniform, with gloves and bayonets, stood on guard. As I entered the room, I saw General Aguinaldo—the man whom I had considered as the personification of my own beloved country, the man whom I had seen at the height of his glory surrounded by generals and soldiers, statesmen and politicians, the rich and the poor, respected and honored by all. I now saw that same man alone in a room, a prisoner of war! It is impossible for me to describe what I felt, but as I write these lines, forty-two years later, my heart throbs as fast as it did then. I felt that the whole world had crumbled; that all my hopes and all my dreams for my country were gone forever! It took me some time before I could collect myself, but finally I was able to say in Tagalog, almost in a whisper, to my General: "Good evening, Mr. President."

"Good evening," he answered rather coldly.

I continued: "I have been sent by General Mascardo to find out whether it is true that you have been captured and if so to receive your instructions as to whether he should continue fighting or surrender."

General Aguinaldo did not answer. It was clear from the expression of his face (and very seldom did General Aguinaldo betray his thoughts) that he suspected me of being a spy. So I turned my head and showed him a scar on my neck caused by a treatment used by Filipino herb doctors in the villages to cure a fever. As soon as he saw the scar his face brightened somewhat, and he said: "I am glad to see you. How many more men has General Mascardo?"

I answered: "About three hundred in Bataan, one hundred and fifty or two hundred in Zambales, with two or three rounds of ammunition."

"How are you getting along with your food?" he asked.

"Sometimes we eat nothing for twenty-four hours; most of the time we have rice twice a day, and very seldom we get fish or meat," was my reply.

The General then proceeded: "As you see, I am now a prisoner. I have taken the oath of allegiance to the United States and I have no right directly or indirectly to advise you to go on fighting. On the other hand, if I were to send word to General Mascardo to surrender, he might think that I am acting under duress and he would have the right to disobey me. General Mascardo has to assume the responsibility and decide for himself, whether he wants to surrender or not. If you see him, give him my best regards and tell him what you have seen, that is, that I am in Malacañan, very well treated by the Americans, but a prisoner just the same."

With tears in my eyes I prayed, "God keep you, Mr. President," and left. I went to the house of Dr. Alejandro Albert, a former colonel of the Philippine Army, and spent the night there. I did not sleep. I thought of General Aguinaldo, my country and the future—a very dark future as it seemed to me then!

CHAPTER IV

In Manila Again

AFTER completing my mission, I stayed in the house of Dr. Albert with the idea of remaining there until I could find work and resume my study of law. Before I could find a job, however, my siesta was interrupted one afternoon by a most unwelcome visitor. This suspicious looking fellow told me I was wanted by the Provost Marshal. On reaching the Provost's office, I was told to follow an American sergeant who knew what to do with me. The sergeant was a gentleman. He conducted me to a big house which during the Spanish régime had been occupied by the Civil Governor of the province of Manila. It was now the stopping place for the leaders, civilian and military alike, and for intransigent chiefs of the revolution. Mabini, the greatest character of his time and many times the Prime Minister of Aguinaldo, had hallowed its halls. Two Filipino generals were then unwilling guests in the house. I was left in a nice room where I lived for two months, eating good food but not knowing why I was confined there.

[81]

One day the two generals were taken out, General Diokno to his own house and General Aquino to Bilibid Prison. The latter had been court-martialed and sentenced to death for the alleged murder of an American prisoner. However his sentence was commuted by the President of the United States to life imprisonment, and he was later set free when the general armistice was proclaimed.

I, on the other hand, was taken to another prison —a room by the Postigo Gate inside the stone wall which surrounds the Old City of Manila. During the Spanish régime, this room had housed the keeper of that gate. I found in this dungeon more than thirty men, and we slept there almost on top of each other. It was a damp place with only two small windows. Our food consisted of rice and canned salmon. Here I remained for four months without having to answer any charge. At long last, one stormy night the officer in charge of my cell came to notify me that I was free. He had been doing this humanitarian service from time to time as the jailed insurrectos were successively set free. He used to read from a sheet of paper the names of the fortunate ones. On this particular evening, as soon as I heard my name I jumped from my seat and almost cracked my head against the ceiling. On noticing my excitement, the officer, doubtless with good intentions, told me that since it was raining that night, I could postpone my departure until the next day. I thanked him for his kindness and promptly left, not for the house of Colonel Albert but for my old hiding place in Navotas. There I waited until I could verify whether I had been let loose by mistake or not. It was my firm determination to go back to the hills if they tried to arrest me again. To this day I have never known why I was so badly treated. Of course, this made me more anti-American than ever before. After becoming convinced that I really was free, I returned to the house of Dr. Albert.

I was, in effect, penniless when I surrendered to Lieutenant Miller in Bataan. All I had with me then was the five-dollar gold coin given to me by the parish priest of Pilar which I had saved and had spent before I was imprisoned. The Alberts gave me room and board while I was looking for work. Before I could start working I had a nervous breakdown. Upon the request of the Dominican friars, the then acting Archbishop of Manila, Bishop Alcocer of Cebu, gave instructions that I be given a room in the Catholic hospital of San Juan de Dios. Here I was treated for many months by the best physicians in the hospital—Doctors Miciano, Valdes, and Singian. When I was convalescent, Dr. Singian whom I had met in San Juan de Letran, although four years my senior, took me to his home and kept me with him until he married the daughter of the Filipino Chief Justice of the Supreme Court—Justice Cayetano Arellano—a leading member of the bar in the later years of the Spanish Government, whom Mr. Taft praised as the equal of the best lawyers in the world.

By the time that Dr. Singian was married, I had completely recovered from my malaria and my nervous breakdown, and was again the strong, healthy young man that I was when, for the first time, I joined the revolutionary forces. I began work for twenty-five pesos a month as clerk in the Monte de Piedad—a sort of pawnshop established as a charitable institution. During the Spanish régime it had been administered by a board appointed by the Governor-General and, upon the transfer of sovereignty to America, was taken over by the Archbishop of Manila and administered by a board appointed by him. Years afterwards, the same Archbishop converted the Monte de Piedad into a trust and banking institution.

Once I had this job, I lived in the house of Mr. Antonio and stayed there until I took my bar examination in April, 1903.

By the time I resumed my study of law I did not have to attend classes at the university. The American Government had by then enacted a law reorganizing the whole educational system of the Philippines which provided, among other things, that any one who had taken a three-year course in law was entitled to practise the profession after passing the bar examination. Since I already had fulfilled this condition I proceeded to prepare for the examination, and in April, 1903, I was admitted to the bar. The day that I learned of the results of my examination, I bid good-by to Mr. Sotelo, the cashier and chief of the department where I worked. The old man advised me to stay in my post. He reminded me of the fact that many lawyers were starving in the streets. "Here," he said, "you have your future assured. In a few years more your present salary of P25.00 [$12.50] will be doubled and who knows, it may be that before you have grown too old you will be receiving as much as I am getting now." (He was perfectly satisfied with his salary of P200 [$100] a month.) After thanking him for his fatherly counsel, I left.

Two days later, I was sent for by Francisco Ortigas, at that time the head of one of the best and most successful law firms in Manila. Francisco Ortigas had been an intern in the College of San Juan de Letran where the Dominican friars for five years had given him, as they had done with many others, free room and board, free tuition, and even clothes and shoes. He had known me as a youngster in San Juan de Letran and also as a freshman, sophomore and junior in the University of Santo Tomas. He invited me to work in his office at P150.00 a month to start with, with the right to have my own clients in cases where the client came to seek my professional service. I accepted the offer and I still remember the thrill of my heart when I won the first case that Ortigas entrusted to me—the defense of five ignorant men accused of aiding the few revolutionaries still fighting in the hills. The first month that I worked in the law firm of Ortigas I made only the P150.00 that he paid me as salary. The second month, I made P50.00 besides from a case brought to me by my first client. The third month, I made from my own clients twice as much as I was receiving as salary from the law firm, so I decided to open my own law office. There were then plenty of civil as well as criminal cases while lawyers were still few in number.

I may say here that I had not as yet been reconciled to the American régime. I was proud of the fact that I knew nothing of English and was determined not to learn it. How contemptible seemed to me those Filipinos who belonged to the Federal Party—a political organization which advocated permanent annexation of the Philippines to the United States on the basis of eventual statehood. I blamed this party for the cessation of Filipino resistance to the American régime for it was the party's campaign praising America and its libertarian policy that induced the people to refuse to us, the revolutionaries, further aid and support.

In October, 1903, I had to go to the province of Tayabas to attend a case in court that affected me personally. Upon the death of my father, his lifelong rival—one Fabian Hernandez—had taken possession of our little farm in Baler pretending that my father had sold it to him. Hernandez had falsified my father's signature. It was not so much the value of

Ayuntamiento Building, Manila, which contained the offices of the early American Governors and members of the Philippine Commission

New Post Office Building, Manila

Legislative Building, Manila

my small two-acre farm that forced me to abandon temporarily my profitable practice in Manila. It was the fact that that tiny piece of land had supported my family and myself for many years and that as a young man I had sweated in clearing those fields. Then I felt that somehow, by this act of usurpation of my father's property, Fabian Hernandez had become in some way implicated in the murder of my father and young brother. So I went to Lucena, the capital of Tayabas province. Although by this time Baler had become a part of this province, I knew no one there, for during the Spanish régime, Baler, San Jose, and Casiguran constituted a district under a sort of military government. There had been no intercourse whatsoever between Baler and Lucena.

Before I embarked for Tayabas, I got a letter of introduction from another lawyer—a friend of mine—to the governor of Tayabas who was a Filipino, for since 1902 the American Government had permitted the people to elect their provincial and municipal officials. On my first day in Lucena I delivered to Governor Paras the letter of introduction. In line with the proverbial Filipino hospitality, Governor Paras invited me to stay in his house until I was ready to go to the town of Tayabas where the court was holding sessions.

With the governor I talked about the situation of our country. He was an honest and a real patriot. He told me that he did not seek the job, but accepted it because it was his sincere opinion that the only way of promoting the freedom as well as the welfare of the Filipino people was by coöperating with the American Government. He pointed out to me that the founders of the Federal Party (branded by most of the Filipinos as the Americanista Party) were already taking part in the highest council of the civil government, and that the steps taken so far by the United States all confirmed the policy enunciated by President McKinley that America had come to the Philippines not to subjugate but to train the Filipino people in the art of self-government so that in due time they might become a self-governing nation.

Although I dissented from the opinion of Governor Paras, his words made some impression on me. I wondered, in my own mind, if the freedom which we lost by fighting America could not be won by coöperating with her. The idea flashed through my head that I might renew the same fight by peaceful means, by taking active part in the political field. "Why not start with the governorship of Tayabas?" I asked myself.

Governor Paras introduced me to Colonel Bandholtz who immediately befriended me. He invited me to his house, presented me to Mrs. Bandholtz and asked me to come to lunch before I went to Tayabas. Colonel Bandholtz was a very unusual man. Although an American, he had been the first elected governor of Tayabas. He had learned the Spanish language well and knew a few words of Tagalog, the native tongue in that province. He made me feel at home in his company and asked me to come to him whenever I was in need of his services. In this way my first meeting with Colonel Bandholtz almost made me forget the ill-treatment which I had received while a prisoner in the Postigo Gate.

I easily won my case in the court of Judge Linebarger, who knew as little of the Spanish Civil Law as I did of the American Common Law. Judge Linebarger boasted of having studied law in Spain and indeed, like Colonel Bandholtz, he also spoke Spanish well. He dictated his decisions following the Spanish form, but his legal attainments did not go any further. This judge was industrious and perfectly honest. He presided over the courts of Tayabas, Mindoro, and Marinduque. Soon after my own case had been disposed of, I received other cases—the most famous one being my defense of the mayor of the town who had been persecuted by the most influential family in Tayabas who had bossed the town since Spanish days. It was generally expected that my client would lose, for the Filipinos still believed that judges favored the rich. Furthermore, the prosecuting attorney was a member of this family and although he took no part in the prosecution it had been taken for granted that he would have great influence with Judge Linebarger. To the surprise of most people, although with manifest public approval, my client was acquitted, a fact which not only inspired confidence in the American courts but at once gave me some legal reputation throughout the whole province.

Thereafter clients came in numbers to my law office in Tayabas—the rich as well as the poor. I adopted two rules, one for the rich client, whom I charged heavy fees, and one for the poor client, whom I served gratis with as much interest and zeal as I did when working for money. I decided to establish myself permanently in Tayabas; in the first place, I was making much more money than I expected to make in Manila, and in the second place, I had more opportunities to defend my old comrades in arms who would yield neither to force nor to prosecution. It is worthy of note that after the establishment of the American Civil Government (replacing the American Military Dictatorship) which was vested with both executive and legislative powers during the first years after its establishment, a law was enacted imposing up to twenty years' imprisonment of any revolutionary who had not surrendered or been captured before that time, or of any one who in any manner or form helped those who still kept up the guerrilla warfare. The law defined both the guerrillas and their helpers as *bandoleros* (bandits). In the latter part of 1903, and even during the first half of 1904, every provincial jail in the Philippines was filled with the so-called bandits. Innocent Filipinos living in faraway villages who were put in jail on mere suspicion or on woefully deficient evidence, were innumerable. I volunteered to defend all those who had no lawyers to represent them in court, and I hope I may be forgiven if I proudly state that I won the liberty of every man whom I defended. As usual, I divided my time in reasonable proportions between making money—and plenty of it—and serving the poor without charge.

The neighboring towns of Tayabas—Lucena, Sariaya, and Lucban—which from time immemorial had been the richest and gayest places in the province, were in turn the scenes of my social diversions. Judge Linebarger became fond of me and placed much reliance upon my knowledge of Spanish substantive law and procedure. Colonel Bandholtz, whose house was in the near-by town of Lucena, continued to ask me to visit him and our friendship developed from day to day.

By the end of 1903 Judge Linebarger called me to his office after the court session one day and inquired whether I would like to be the prosecuting attorney of the province of Mindoro, a position then vacant. He said that the salary of the office was about three thousand pesos ($1,500) a year. I told him I would give him my answer, one way or another, in twenty-four hours.

I pondered over this matter. Neither from the point of view of experience and knowledge that I would gain as a lawyer, nor from the viewpoint of pecuniary return could the offer be seriously considered. A prosecuting attorney only dealt with criminal cases and the annual salary of the prosecuting attorney of Mindoro was much less than what one of a number of my cases had netted me. My conversation with Governor Paras came to my mind with striking force, for the kindness of Colonel Bandholtz as well as his fairness in dealing with the Filipinos, together with the honesty, if not the learning, of Judge Linebarger, had already inclined me to try in practice the advice of my provincial governor. I said to myself: "This position which is being unexpectedly offered to me may be the starting point set by fate for a greater service that I may render to my people in their work of self-redemption." Anyway, as a sort of mental reservation, I told myself that I could always resign the post and return to my law practice if I should be disappointed.

I saw Judge Linebarger at the appointed time and gave him an affirmative answer. Dr. Trinidad Pardo de Tavera was then visiting Tayabas on an official inspection trip. He with two other Filipinos were members of the Philippine Commission, a body originally constituted entirely of Americans appointed by President McKinley and invested with all governmental powers to administer the affairs of the Philippines, though subject to the supervision and control of the Secretary of War. Dr. Tavera, a distinguished Filipino scholar in the last decade of the Spanish régime, had been the founder of the Federal Party which advocated full and unreserved coöperation with the United States. In his hands Judge Linebarger left the matter of my appointment as prosecuting attorney of Mindoro. Upon Dr. Tavera's return to Manila, Civil Governor Taft signed my commission and I went to the dreaded Island of Mindoro.

This province was said to be infested with malaria, although in the towns the disease was not so prevalent as in the hills. My office was located in Calapan, capital of the province, and there I met the governor, Captain Offley of the American Army. At that time the province of Mindoro had not been listed as one of those entitled to choose their own governor. My duty, of course, was to prosecute criminal offenders. After going over the papers left by my predecessor, I came to the conclusion that two-thirds of the men in prison on the serious charge of banditry had been put there without sufficient evidence. At that time, recourse to the writ of habeas corpus could not always be had in the provinces where judges with jurisdiction to grant the writ were only available during the regular or extraordinary sessions of the court. So I had to wait until the arrival of Judge Linebarger and then move for the dismissal of all cases unsupported by proper evidence.

After serving six months as prosecuting attorney here I was promoted to Tayabas. On my return I still found my old friends, among them Governor Paras and Colonel Bandholtz.

Colonel Bandholtz then insisted that I should learn English and offered to be my teacher. He set the day for my first lesson after presenting me with an English grammar. We did not get very far. The lessons could not be given regularly either because he was on an inspection trip of the Constabulary forces under his command, or because I was too busy with my cases, but a beginning had been made. I no longer boasted, but rather was sorry that I spoke no word of English.

The case which definitely established my popularity in Tayabas and which, in my opinion, later contributed to my election as provincial governor, I shall call the "Mason Case," because that was not the name. Mason was an attorney and, accompanied by his secretary who acted also as his interpreter, he came to my office one day with twenty-five different deeds of sale of agricultural properties which he wanted me to register in his name. (The prosecuting attorney was then at the same time the register of deeds.) I took the papers from him and said that I would attend to it as soon as possible, and he left.

I placed the papers in one of my drawers and was so busy that I forgot all about them. A week later Mason's secretary came to see me in behalf of his principal to inquire whether I had registered the deeds and I told him no, explaining my reasons, promising, however, to do it immediately. One hour later, Mr. Mason himself, accompanied by the same secretary, came to my office with his hat on and without even greeting me, shouted: "What did you do with the papers I gave you?" I repeated the answer I had given an hour before to his secretary. He then threatened that he would complain to my superiors in Manila unless I registered the deeds immediately. My temper, which I had been trying to control since he entered my office, gave way and getting hold of my inkstand, I ordered him out of my office, saying that otherwise I would break his head. He left, but not without repeating his threat.

No man is really brave who does not feel completely blameless, and since I knew that I had not been too busy to have registered the deeds, as soon as Mr. Mason left I took the papers from the drawer and proceeded to examine them. I found that the documents covered sales of lands planted with coconut trees, including the working animals, and that all in all, the twenty-five deeds of sale represented several thousand acres with about 50,000 coconut trees and two or three hundred working animals. The total value of the properties exceeded P60,000.00 ($30,-000). The owners of these properties were all in the provincial jail of Tayabas. They had signed the deeds while in jail, with Mr. Mason's secretary and one of the jail guards acting as witnesses. The Justice of the Peace of the town in those times performed the duties of notary public. The consideration for the transfer of the properties to Mr. Mason was his services as a lawyer to be rendered in defense of these men, all of whom were charged with banditry (violation of the act to which I have before referred).

I was most suspicious of the whole transaction, so I went immediately to the provincial jail of Tayabas. I asked the first prisoner if he knew Mr. Mason and he said yes, as he was his lawyer. I asked him if he had given Mason his farm and working animals in consideration of Mason's services as his lawyer, and he answered most emphatically, "No." Then the man told me this story: "Mr. Mason came to me and offered to defend me. I said I had no cash but that I owned some land planted with coconut trees and a few working animals. He then promised to take my case if I would pay him P300.00 ($150.00), the amount to be delivered to him after I was out of jail, but he demanded as guarantee my land with the coconut trees, plus my working animals. I agreed."

"Is this your signature?" I asked, pointing to his name written in the deed for sale. He answered affirmatively.

"How do you know the paper you have signed contained what you have just told me?"

"That was the information given me by Mr. Mason."

All the other prisoners told me the same story. I sent for the justice of the peace who confirmed the declarations of the men. I asked the justice of the peace, who knew Spanish, the language in which the deeds were written, if he had read the documents, and he answered in the negative, adding that after hearing what Mr. Mason told the prisoners in his presence, he felt that it was unnecessary to read the documents for that would be a proof of lack of confidence in Mr. Mason who, being a lawyer, must be an honorable man.

I got everybody to sign the necessary affidavits in accordance with their testimony and went back to my office to prepare immediately the presentation of twenty-five cases for *estafa* (swindling) against Mr. Mason. After giving his bail, Mr. Mason left for Manila. He immediately accused me to the Attorney General of the Philippines, of concocting those cases to cover my negligence in failing to register the deeds. An American newspaper in Manila was quick to attack me, but Colonel Bandholtz who was still the Chief of the Constabulary in Tayabas, and whose duty, among other things, was to go after violators of the law, gave me his support after making his own investigation of the case. The office of the Attorney General sent to Tayabas to help me try these cases, a Mr. Basset, a bright young lawyer who had just arrived from the United States. Mr. Basset later became one of the most successful lawyers and respected businessmen in all China and is now in America. It should be stated before going any farther that in the Philippines there was not then, nor is there now, any trial by jury, so that Mr. Mason was tried only by an American judge. When the day of his trial arrived, four of the best lawyers of Manila came to defend him. They were Judge Kinkaid, Mr. Fred Fisher, Judge Bishop, and Mr. Green, who practised law mostly in Tayabas. Mr. Basset and I entered into an agreement with the defense that we would try one case first, and if the defendant was acquitted either by the court of first instance or, on appeal, by the Supreme Court, we would ask for the dismissal of all the other cases.

Mason's case caused a commotion in the province of Tayabas, if not in the Philippines. It was the first time since the beginning of American occupation that an American—and an American lawyer at that —had been prosecuted in the courts of the Islands, and what amazed the Filipinos most was the fact that the prosecutor was a Filipino. Those were still the so-called "Days of the Empire," when the majority of the Americans in the Philippines were decidedly anti-Filipino and looked upon us with contempt. Men like Bandholtz and few others were rare exceptions. Governor Taft himself was not only disliked but actually hated by the majority of his compatriots because he delivered a speech entitled "The Philippines for the Filipinos." It was in those days that the expression originated: "He [the Filipino] may be a brother of William H. Taft, but he ain't no brother of mine."

Needless to say, Mason was convicted. He appealed the case to the Supreme Court. While the case was on appeal, he went to Hongkong and on learning that the decision of the lower court had been confirmed, he forfeited his bail and never returned to the Philippines. A few years later, I saw him in a hotel in Shanghai.

CHAPTER V

Law Practice and Public Office

THE Mason case of course increased my popularity amoung my countrymen, but although Colonel Bandholtz and my immediate superior in the office of the Attorney General, Judge James Ross, became even stronger friends of mine thereafter, some unknown enemies started persecuting me. Behind my back I was investigated for several charges and when finally I learned what was going on, contrary to the advice of my friend Judge Ross, I insisted upon resigning as prosecuting attorney. I resumed immediately the practice of my profession in the province of Tayabas.

I must pause here to relate an event which later developed into one of the most important steps in my life. To it I owe having been the happiest of husbands and the proudest of fathers.

Once I was installed in Tayabas as prosecuting attorney, I wrote a letter to my Aunt Zeneida who was already a widow, inviting her to come and stay with me, with her two unmarried daughters, Amparo and Aurora. This aunt and my mother had loved each other dearly and had been the closest of friends even after their marriages. The youngest daughter of my aunt, Aurora, had been raised by my mother from childhood in my home and the little girl had been my father's pet. (Earlier in this book I mentioned that during my visit to Baler after the American occupation of Manila, I stayed in the house of my Aunt Zeneida.) The family accepted my invitation and came to live with me. My cousin Aurora looked very pretty. I sent her to Manila to study in the Normal School. The government had a boarding-house for girls under the care of Miss Colman, and there Aurora stayed except during vacation time when she came and joined her mother and sister in my house.

On resuming my practice, I made more money than before albeit I continued to give free service to the poor. Within six months, I had clients from the remotest towns of the province.

When the election of 1905 for provincial governor was approaching, I was already a convert to the policy of coöperation with the Government of the United States. Every pronouncement made by the highest spokesman of the American people was to the effect that America was in the Philippines as the liberator, not as the oppressor of the Filipino people.

General Bandholtz by this time had been transferred to Manila and I had met his successor, Colonel J. G. Harbord, now the chairman of the Board of

Directors of the Radio Corporation of America. Colonel Harbord was a different type of man from General Bandholtz. I make no comparison of the two men who became very dear friends of mine, especially since one has died, while the other, thanks be to God, is still alive. But I must say that no American in those early days had as much influence in forming my high conception of public duty or gave me a better idea of American manhood than the then Colonel Harbord. General Harbord is, in my opinion, one of the greatest men I have ever met. After a conference with him I decided to run for governor and easily defeated my two other rivals for the office.

My first visit to my home town after my election as governor of Tayabas I made with Colonel Harbord. He wrote of that visit as follows:

> As Constabulary District Commander I had a Coast Guard cutter under my orders, and asked the young Governor to let me take him back to his native Baler for his first visit since he had left it as a young insurrecto eight years before. He came on board the cutter at Atimonan on a June evening 1906 and the next morning found us opposite Baler. Once the fishermen along shore sighted us, the news quickly spread to the village. When we landed through the surf, the narrow sandy beach was filled by a great crowd of Filipinos of both sexes. The whole population of Baler was there on the

The Escolta, principal business street of Manila

Acme

President Quezon standing at attention to receive the nineteen-gun salute after taking the oath of office as first President of the Philippine Commonwealth, on November 15, 1935

International News Photos

General view of inaugural ceremonies of President Quezon in Manila, in front of the Legislative Building

rumor that the Governor had come back to his native village.

The procession formed in a long column headed by the young Governor. His parents were no longer living but dozens of relatives and older people who had known them and him in his youth crowded into the column. The village band played gay and patriotic airs all the way from the beach to the town. The officials, the teachers of the schools, the local business men, and most important, the Spanish parish priest who had known the Governor in his boyhood, and still remained in the town, marched at the head of the procession. Few Spanish priests still lived and headed their old parishes after the Insurrection had ended. Old women who had known the boy from babyhood crowded to march in turn with arms around the young Governor, with many cries of "Manuelito," and there was much joyous laughter and some weeping over the home town boy now grown into a great man.

At the village we found the plaza crowded with more people who were anxious to do honor to the distinguished visitor. The whole day was given over to rejoicing. Speeches were made in Tagalog, Spanish, and English. Native games were played all afternoon. Fencing contests showed the method of instructing young boys in the handling of native weapons. Dances were danced never before seen by Americans and the whole day was a gala day. That evening there was a great banquet * with more speeches, much music and more dancing. The full moon of tropic night lighted us down to the beach when the feasting and dancing were over, and we went down accompanied by the whole village.

In twelve years in the Philippines I saw many moving spectacles of joy and sorrow but that day at Baler remains in my memory as the most dramatic and touching day passed in those twelve crowded years. I never have seen my friend Governor Quezon again without a different feeling toward him than I have toward any other Filipino, and I have know the best and brightest of his contemporaries. Nearly forty years have passed and I am proud to say that our friendship is still the same. What I saw that day is the explanation to me of the wonderful hold he has over the hearts of his people, which has enabled him to lead them as a unit against the invader who followed Pearl Harbor.

As governor of Tayabas my main concern was to prove that the Filipinos were capable of governing themselves. I gave complete freedom to the town mayors and municipal councils to manage the affairs of their respective localities and insisted that I be

* If the name of banquet could be given to typical Filipino food served in the most ordinary plates, but with plenty of fish, crab, chicken, and vinegar.

[104]

given by the authorities in Manila a free hand in governing my province. The Executive Secretary of the Governor-General then was Frank W. Carpenter. It was he who did the actual supervision of the provincial and municipal governments and he did not interfere with my work. He was a very capable executive and a hard-working man.

By an Act of the United States Congress, it had been provided that two years after the taking of the census, if peace and public order prevailed in the Philippines, an election for members of a lower house of the legislature would be called by the Governor-General. Thus for the first time in their history the Filipino people would be allowed through their elected representatives to take part in the legislative department of their government. As pointed out heretofore, America had governed the Philippines, during the occupation and pacification of the Islands, through a military government, and after the organized resistance of the Filipinos had been overcome, a civil government was inaugurated, the powers of which, both executive and judicial, were concentrated in the hands of the Philippine Commission headed by Mr. Taft who also was the Chief Executive. This body, in the early days of the Civil Government, was composed exclusively of Americans, but very soon three Filipinos—Legarda, Tavera, and Luzurriaga—were added as members of the Commission although possessing legislative powers only, and forming but a minority even in the legislative functions of that body.

The Judicial Department was constituted by Courts of Justices of the Peace, Courts of First Instance, and the Supreme Court. The Governor-General appointed the Justices of the Peace and Judges of the Court of First Instance, all removable at his discretion. The President of the United States appointed the members of the Supreme Court, likewise to hold office during the President's pleasure. The majority of the members of this court were Americans, although from the beginning the Chief Justice has always been a Filipino.

When the election to the National Assembly was called in 1907, I announced my willingness to occupy a seat in the new elective body if my district wanted to elect me. By this mere announcement, I was elected to the Assembly by practically unanimous vote of my district.

In the first election of the Philippine Assembly, as was the case with every succeeding election, the Nationalist Party to which I belong—and which carried the banner of immediate, absolute, and complete independence—won by an overwhelming majority. The Governor-General was then the Honorable James L. Smith of California, while Mr. Taft had been promoted to the position of Secretary of War. Representing President Theodore Roosevelt, Secretary Taft went to Manila and inaugurated the National Assembly.

In his address at the inaugural ceremonies, Secretary

Taft reiterated the American policy of granting the Filipino people an ever-increasing measure of self-government as they proved themselves to be capable of assuming and exercising greater responsibilities.

The law that created the National Assembly also provided for the election by the Philippine Commission, acting as the upper house, and by the Philippine Assembly, acting as the lower house of the legislature, of two Resident Commissioners who would represent the Philippines before the Government of the United States, with a seat but no vote in Congress. Messrs. Legarda and Ocampo were elected the first two Commissioners.

At the first session of the Philippine Assembly, Sergio Osmeña, upon my motion, was chosen by unanimous vote Speaker of the House. This, despite the fact that sixteen members from the opposition had been elected as members of the body. I became the floor leader and was appointed by the Speaker Chairman of the Committee on Appropriations, which also had jurisdiction over revenue bills.

My first clash with the American Government while serving in the National Assembly was about a bill pending in the United States Congress to provide for the trade relations between the United States and the Philippines. The bill contemplated the establishment of free trade relations between the said two countries. Certain private interests in the United States were opposed to the bill for selfish reasons and Secretary of War Taft, under whose department the Philippines then were, instructed the Philippine Commission to indorse the proposed bill and to secure the concurrence of the Philippine Assembly to its action. I fought the measure upon the ground that free trade relations between our countries would result in making the Philippines absolutely dependent upon the markets of the United States. This, I contended, would create a most serious situation in Philippine economic life, especially when the time came for the granting of our independence. The Assembly, by overwhelming vote, supported me, only the opponents of immediate independence taking the other side. My contention was proved sound when finally the question of Philippine independence was taken up by the Congress of the United States.

After the first session of the National Assembly, Secretary of War Taft reported to President Theodore Roosevelt that the Filipinos had lived up to the expectations of their friends and proved a disappointment to their enemies.

In the closing days of the second session of the Philippine Assembly, the State Department in Washington transmitted to the Governor-General of the Philippines an invitation from the government of the Czar of Russia to an International Congress of Navigation which was to be held in Saint Petersburg. Governor-General Smith informed Speaker Osmeña of this invitation. I told the Speaker that I should like to go although I was as competent to take part in that Congress as a shoe-peddler would be. My purpose in mind was to have my first glimpse of the outside world which, as I thought, would prepare me for the next post to which I was then aspiring—that of Resident Commissioner to the United States. My wishes were fulfilled, but needless to say, I was attacked right and left by the press and properly so, although I might say that the trip eventually proved to be not a bad investment for Filipino taxpayers.

I took with me two secretaries—one to act as my interpreter, an American who knew Spanish well, and a Filipino newspaper man who, years afterwards, occupied positions in the executive and legislative departments of the Philippine Government. We took a Japanese steamer, for our itinerary contemplated going from Manila to Japan and thence to Russia by way of the Siberian railroad. Our ship called at the ports of Nagasaki and Shimunaseki; then we crossed the mainland of Japan by train and took a boat on the opposite coast, to Vladivostok.

Of my first impression of Japan, I wrote to a friend in the Philippines the following: "The Japanese people are less capable of self-government than we are."

In Russia I met, among other persons, Alexander Kerensky, who later played for a short time an important part during the days of the Russian Revolution. I was too late to participate in the Navigation Congress, but I had occasion to observe the extreme poverty and ignorance of the masses of the Russian people while their grand dukes were swimming in luxury.

From Russia I went to Berlin, thence to Paris, London, and finally to the United States. I arrived in New York in summer and President Theodore Roosevelt invited me to lunch with him at Oyster Bay. In my first meeting with President Theodore Roosevelt, what made the most striking impression on me was the simplicity and democratic manners of an American President. I had read of European monarchs and their courts and never suspected that America had truly discarded their ways and ceremonial practices! I had seen, if only from a distance, Spanish Governors-General riding in a carriage drawn by six white horses, preceded and followed by cavalry escorts!

President Theodore Roosevelt greeted me warmly and took me to his table without ceremony. The other two guests were Secretary Cortelyou of the Treasury, and my interpreter, Mr. Escamilla. After the luncheon, President Roosevelt had a short conference with me. He said he was pleased with the conduct of the Philippine Assembly and assured me that the policy of the United States was to grant the Philippines their independence in due time. Being only a very provincial Filipino, knowing nothing about protocol, nor of the injunction against quoting heads of state, I repeated to newspapermen what President Roosevelt had told me. I was promptly listed by presidential decree as a member of the "Ananias Club"!

On my return to Manila, I was given a hearty welcome by the Nacionalista Party. Not unnaturally my partisans preferred to give credit to what I said rather than to the subsequent denial by the President of the United States.

At the second and last session of the first Philippine Assembly, I was elected Resident Commissioner to the United States to succeed Pablo Ocampo. I arrived in Washington on the afternoon of December 24, 1909, about the same hour that, years later, I arrived on Corregidor with my family, and in the company of High Commissioner Sayre, on December 24, 1941. Only there was a slight difference between the circumstances under which the two trips were made.

CHAPTER VI

In Washington

IT WAS an extremely cold night in Washington and I feared that I might catch pneumonia, against which I had been warned before leaving Manila by my friend, Mr. W. Cameron Forbes, then Secretary of Commerce and Communications. Secretary Forbes is known as the road-builder of the Philippines. So I spent my first Christmas Eve in Washington duly shut up in my rooms at the Champlain Apartment House. The following day, however, although the streets were covered with snow, I ventured to go out, protected with fur-lined gloves and fur overcoat. After walking for a little while I rushed back to my apartment fearing that I would lose my ears.

On New Year's Day, 1910, the senior Resident Commissioner, Mr. Legarda, took me to wish Happy New Year to President Taft, Vice-President James S. Sherman, and Speaker Joseph G. Cannon.

Mr. Taft, while at the head of the Philippine Government, was called "the friend of the Filipinos." In later years the feeling of my countrymen towards him changed somewhat because of his insistence that it would take no less than two generations before the Filipinos could be capable of self-government; but, although I never had the opportunity of being close to President Taft, either while he was Civil Governor of the Philippines, Secretary of War, or President of the United States, and regardless of whether his conception of our capacity for self-government was right or wrong, in the perspective of history I am bound to affirm that President Taft had deservedly won that title. It is hard to believe now how much opposition and abuse the first Civil Governor (afterwards the title was changed to Governor-General) received from the early American residents in the Philippines. Many of them doubtless remembered how the Southerners were dealt with after the Civil War and, therefore, felt that no better treatment should be given to the "brown brothers." Still others were told by English and Dutch subjects how foolish it was—and how *dangerous*—to attempt the experiment of "shooting" democracy into the fabric of "Oriental" minds. These critics overlooked the fact that more than three hundred years before the Spaniards *did* shoot—and successfully—the Christian religion into the souls of the Filipinos, and that Christianity had prepared us for democracy since Christ's teachings were indeed the essence of democratic ideals and principles.

Anyway, the fact remains that Mr. Taft, in a moment of unsuppressed anger, called his newspaper critics "the lions of the Press" and pointed out the way of escape to those who did not approve of the American policy—"the Philippines for the Filipinos." The exit through Corregidor, he asserted, was wide enough for every dissenter to get out.

After the Christmas holidays, Commissioner Legarda introduced me to the House of Representatives and I was sworn in.

My service in the House of Representatives was one of the most pleasant and fruitful periods of my life. No one can possibly imagine how much of human value there is to be found under the two wings of the Capitol. This imposing building is at once the best university and the nicest playhouse in the world. To the outsider, the Senators and Representatives may be mere *politicians* with only one purpose in mind— to satisfy the whims or promote the interests of their constituents. To one who has heard them in debate or delivering eloquent addresses; to one who has conversed with them in their cloak rooms, their offices, or while taking their meals; to one who has been with them in formal affairs or on small private parties; to one who has even taken part in a few more lively gatherings where some of them have been present; to such a person, especially if he be a foreigner more inclined at first to discover faults than to find virtues; to that person, I say, it is a great privilege to have spent amongst these legislators six of his youthful and inquisitive years. When I left Congress for the Philippines to be the first President of the first Philippine Senate, I had already learned many lessons in leading and handling men, whether as a mass or as individuals, in any walk of life.

In the following condensed narrative of my work in Congress, I shall only mention the names of those who, by reason of their assignment to the Committees which dealt with Philippine affairs, took an active part in Philippine legislation.

The War Department, from the first day of American occupation of Philippine territory until after the enactment of the Independence Law, had charge of the Government of the Philippines. It was during the Taft administration that I had the honor of meeting the present Secretary of War, the Honorable Henry L. Stimson. He was then holding the same portfolio. From the start he gave me the impression that I had met a great man. The time that has elapsed and further official and personal association with him, has enhanced my admiration and affection for "my old man" as my wife affectionately calls Colonel Stimson.

It was also while I was a member of Congress that I had the good fortune to meet Secretary of State Cordell Hull. He was as handsome a man as could be seen in Washington. Although a new member of the House, he soon won the respect of his colleagues by his devotion to duty, his plain honesty, and his unusual ability.

I will be forgiven if I bring in the name of a man who had little to do with policy-making decisions or important administrative actions affecting the Philippines. But I mention him because I take pride in the fact that I discovered even then his extraordinary mental faculties and his inborn moral courage, although he was then only a young man recently graduated from Harvard. I am referring to Justice Felix Frankfurter whom I met in 1911 as an assistant to the Law Officer of the Bureau of Insular Affairs in the War Department.

The most serious obstacle to the performance of my duties in Washington was my very limited knowledge of the English language. I could not even carry on a simple conversation for any length of time. So I decided to hire a teacher who, after the style of General Bandholtz, started to give me lessons in grammar. After diligently taking my first fifteen lessons I came to the conclusion that through this method it would take me a long time before I could deliver my first speech on the floor of the House of Representatives. Thereupon, I gave up the teacher and started to teach myself. With the aid of a Spanish-English dictionary I read newspapers, magazines, books, and more important still, I launched into the social world without the company of any one who could act as my interpreter when I needed assistance. My early experiences in this respect were very amusing and sometimes rather embarrassing. When I failed to find the word to express an idea and could not make my-self understood with the help of gestures, it was my wont to supplement the sentence with the corresponding Spanish word.

In May, 1910, exactly five months after my arrival in Washington, I delivered my maiden speech on the floor of the House. My colleagues listened to me not only with courtesy but with generosity, for there was hearty applause at the conclusion of the speech. I spoke in recognition of the benefits which we had received from the Government of the United States. "But despite it all," I said, "we still want independence.... Ask the bird, Sir, who is enclosed in a golden cage if he would prefer his cage and the care of his owner to the freedom of the skies and the allure of the forest."

My next address to Congress took place when a congressional investigation was being urged by Congressman Martin of Colorado to determine how the Government of the Philippines was carrying out the policy laid down by Congress, that limited to 1024 acres the maximum area of government land that could be sold to corporations or individuals. This law had been enacted soon after the United States had taken the Philippines to prevent the exploitation of the Filipino people by capitalists, whether foreigners or natives. American capital interested in the sugar industry had acquired two very large tracts of land which the Philippine Government had bought from the friars with funds raised from bonds issued under the security of the Philippine Government. The avowed purpose in buying these extensive properties from the Spanish religious orders was to resell them in small lots to Filipino farmers, and thus to do away with absentee landlordism which had been the most serious cause of the Philippine rebellion against Spain. The reasons given for the sale of these lands to American capital by the American officials in charge of the execution of the congressional policy were twofold: First, that the Act of Congress referred only to lands of the public domain but not to lands acquired by the Government in some other way. And second, that the sale of these lands was made in order to establish the sugar industry in the Philippines on a truly grand scale under modern methods, as had been done in Cuba. It was further alleged that such a method would bring great prosperity to the Philippines.

I spoke in support of the proposed investigation, contending that the establishment of the sugar industry under those conditions would mean the debasement of the Filipinos into mere peons. "Moreover," I argued, "large investments of American capital in the Philippines will inevitably result in the permanent retention of the Philippines by the United States." At the climax of my speech I roared: "If the preordained fate of my country is either to be a subject people but rich, or free but poor, I am unqualifiedly for the latter."

The investigation was ordered by the House of Representatives, and although the sales already made were not annulled, no further sales were made in defiance of the Congressional Act.

In the autumn of 1911 I went on a speech-making tour through the New England states under the auspices of the Anti-Imperialist League whose headquarters was in Boston. The chairman of the League was that distinguished lawyer and noble man, Mr. Moorfield Storey. As honorary vice-presidents of the League, there were listed some of the best known Americans of those days—the then undisputed leader of the Democratic Party, William Jennings Bryan, ex-President Cleveland, Representative Champ Clark, Senator LaFollette, and many others, including the Chief of the Army during the Spanish-American War, General N. A. Miles.

The League had been organized to oppose the acquisition of the Philippines by the United States as being contrary to the principles propounded in the Declaration of Independence. The League feared that the American Republic would blunder away from its glorious history and follow the bloody and greedy policy of the imperialist powers.

My speech-making trip through New England was naturally advertised ahead in the newspapers of those states. When I stepped off the train in the first city in which I was to give an address, I was thrilled with emotion as I saw the railroad station full of people to give me, as I thought, a rousing welcome. I was glad that on the train I had changed my ordinary suit for a cut-away and had put on my top hat. To my surprise, the people in the station remained in their places with their eyes fixed on the train even after I had left the platform. Then I realized that the crowd had not come to meet me, but, perhaps, some notable personage who had traveled from Washington in the same train with me.

At last the train pulled out of the station and the look of disappointment was evident in every face. True enough, those people were there to see the visiting Filipino, but they had expected an entirely different figure—that of the chief of one of the tribes exhibited at the St. Louis Fair, adorned with plumes on his head, trinkets on his neck, arms and legs, and perhaps a silk G-string. Americans learned right there and then that a Filipino could high-hat them.

Another trip I want to mention was one I made to the city of Cleveland at the invitation of the late Justice Clarke. Newton D. Baker was then mayor of the city, and he presided over the meeting. This visit gave me the opportunity to form a friendship which later on helped the Philippine cause when Mr. Baker became Secretary of War under President Woodrow Wilson.

By the end of President Taft's administration, the fight between him and ex-President Roosevelt left no doubt in the minds of impartial observers as to the outcome of the election. President Wilson, in fact, was elected. Since in one of his previous writings President Wilson had said something not frankly in favor of our independence, I wrote him a letter as soon as he was elected, with a memorandum containing a report on conditions in the Philippines. I placed particular emphasis on the progress made by the Filipino people and the evidences they had given of their capacity for self-government. In his speech in Staunton, Virginia, the President-elect unmistakably took his stand for Philippine independence.

CHAPTER VII

Philippine Legislation

IN THE second half of President Taft's administration, the Democratic Party secured control of the House of Representatives and Mr. William Atkinson Jones of Virginia was made chairman of the House Committee on Insular Affairs. In view of the policy which the Democratic Party had adopted upon the acquisition of the Philippines by the United States—namely, in favor of the granting of Philippine independence—I had made it my business to become acquainted with Mr. Jones from the first days of my service in Washington. He was then the senior minority member of the Committee on Insular Affairs and, according to the prevailing practice in the House of Representatives, would be the chairman of the committee if and when the Democrats secured a majority in the House. The more I knew Mr. Jones the more I felt attached to him. He treated me with extreme kindness which, due to the difference in our ages, developed into a sort of fatherly love. He believed strongly that continued possession of the Philippines by the United States would inject the virus of imperialism into the American body politic, as did almost all the Democrats both in the Senate and House; so, also, did the progressive Republicans, whose influence in Congress was then beginning to be felt. As a matter of fact, few Republicans of any kind supported the Republican administration policy except upon the theory that the Philippine venture was of a temporary character as publicly announced by Presidents McKinley, Roosevelt, and Taft. All these Presidents asserted in more or less the same words that the Filipino people would be given the right to decide whether they would prefer Philippine autonomy under the American flag or complete independence; such question to be submitted to them for decision when they should have learned enough to make a wise one. Senator Beveridge of·Indiana was perhaps one of the very few who bluntly advocated American imperialism as the road to glory, power, and wealth.

When the Democrats captured the House in 1911 after long successive years of defeat, I induced Mr. Jones to introduce in the House a bill which had formerly been presented by Mr. John Sharp Williams of Mississippi when he had been the senior minority member of the Committee on Insular Affairs. This bill was approved in the last session of the Sixty-Second Congress, but silently buried in the Senate, which was Republican.

After President Wilson's inauguration, when both

Houses of Congress had become Democratic, I renewed my efforts to induce Mr. Jones, who remained as the chairman of the Committee on Insular Affairs, to reintroduce his bill which had been unceremoniously killed in the preceding session by the Senate. But this time Mr. Jones would not move without first securing the approval of President Wilson. I began to see the difference in political procedures when one party was in full control of both the executive and legislative branches of the government, and when it only had a majority in one of the two Houses. Not that the Democratic platform on which President Wilson was elected was no longer committed to Philippine independence. Indeed it was and, as a matter of fact, I had something to do with the writing of the plank of the platform regarding Philippine independence, since I personally appeared in Baltimore before the Platform Committee presided over by Mr. Bryan. But the vocal opinion in the United States at that time was decidedly against Philippine independence. The three former Presidents—McKinley, Roosevelt, and Taft—had created the belief that the Filipinos would not be ready for a long time to be entrusted with the government of their own country, and with the exception of some of the newspapers in the southern states, the immense majority of publications here, whether dailies or magazines, ridiculed the idea of allowing the Filipinos to govern themselves. President Wilson himself was reluctant to recommend Congressional legislation, despite his speech at Staunton and the efforts of Mr. Bryan, then Secretary of State. It was President Wilson's plan to send a man in his confidence to the Philippines with instructions to replace, as rapidly as possible, the Americans in the service there with Filipinos and thus to determine, by trial and error, the Filipinos' capacity to administer the affairs of their country.

This plan of President Wilson placed me in a somewhat embarrassing position. The Governor-General of the Philippines at the time was the Honorable W. Cameron Forbes, from Boston, who had given me clear evidences of friendship while I was Provincial Governor and member of the Philippine Assembly. Governor Forbes happened to be in the United States at the time that President Wilson was elected, and although he was a Republican, he returned to his post before the President-elect had assumed office. President Wilson one day summoned me to the White House and asked my opinion as to whether a new Governor-General should be appointed or whether Governor-General Forbes should be left in his post. To a Filipino, with Oriental ancestry, a little Spanish blood and mostly Spanish education—which was practically all that I then had—the question was very trying indeed. Friendship to me has a real meaning and personal favors are never forgotten. On the other hand, I had come to Washington to perform a sacred duty. I measured my words and gave President Wilson the following answer: "Mr. President, if it is your intention to disregard the Democratic platform and merely carry on the policies of the Republican Administration, then you can find no better man for the job than Governor-General Forbes. If, on the contrary, you intend to take immediate steps, as in my opinion you should take, to make good the now historic commitment of your party to grant independence to the Philippines as soon as possible, then Governor Forbes can neither be the spokesman for nor the executor of your policies in the Philippines."

The President made a move to indicate that the conference was over. President Wilson did not have that forceful handshake of President Roosevelt or that spontaneous and contagious laugh of President Taft. Whether Mr. Wilson had ever laughed when conversing with other people, I do not know, but this time I saw on his face the suggestion of a smile. We never talked except on official matters. But I shall always remember with gratitude that, despite my youth, he always gave to my opinions the most serious consideration. Let me say, too, that I am a great admirer of President Wilson. I sincerely believe that had he been able to prevent the conclusion of an unjust treaty of peace at Versailles and had he secured the approval by the Senate of the United States of the League of Nations, there would not have arisen this Second World War.

President Wilson appointed as Governor-General of the Philippines the Honorable Francis Burton Harrison, then the ranking member of the Ways and Means Committee of the House of Representatives. In this appointment I had something to say. President Wilson gave Governor Harrison a message addressed to the Filipino people in which the President outlined his Philippine policy looking definitely toward independence. As the first step in the execution of this policy, the Filipinos were given a majority in the appointed Upper Chamber, thus turning over to them practical control of the legislative department of their government. Governor-General Harrison took to heart the trust placed in his hands by his chief, and from the time of his arrival in Manila, he proceeded to rapidly "Filipinize" the government.

Needless to say, the so-called American "old timers" raised shouts to heaven and systematically opposed every move of the new administration. Harrison was not spared. Attacks of all kinds were made against him. It took a man with the strong will and determination of Governor-General Harrison to carry out the policy which it was his duty to do and of which he personally approved. The antagonism of his own countrymen in the Philippines found support in the newspapers in the United States. Of course, the Filipinos stood by Governor Harrison.

I believe that when cooler heads are called upon to pass impartial judgment on the history of Harrison's administration, some American historian will give him credit for the important contribution he made to the policy which won for the United States the loyalty of the Filipino people.

My work in Congress to secure legislation that would either grant the Philippines independence, or at least formally commit the United States to the policy of granting to the Philippines self-government, continued unabated. Three men in the House of Representatives were my formidable allies—Speaker Champ Clark, Mr. Jones, the chairman of the Committee on Insular Affairs, and Mr. Garrett, the senior member of that committee. There were also many others ready to help at any time. In the Senate, there were Vice-President Marshall, the President pro tem, Senator James P. Clarke of Arkansas, Senator LaFollette of Wisconsin, Senator John Sharp Williams of Mississippi, Senator Ashurst of Arizona, and, most active of all, Senator John Shafroth of Colorado, who took care of our Philippine Bill in the Senate Committee of which he was a member. Senator Hitchcock of Nebraska, the chairman of the committee, although not actively interested in Philippine independence, was nevertheless sympathetic to the cause.

At long last Mr. Jones presented a bill, but not the same one that he had introduced in the previous Congress, which had become known among the Filipinos as Jones Bill No. 1. The Democratic leadership (I think, with the previous approval of President Wilson) only agreed to a bill which in the preamble would state that it was the purpose of the United States to grant Philippine independence as soon as a stable government could be established in the islands. The body of the bill, or rather its legislative provisions, would create at once an elective Philippine Senate which, with the right to confirm all appointments made by the Governor-General, implied, as a matter of course, the exclusion of Americans from holding offices as Secretaries of Departments. There was one exception to this, however: the Secretary of Public Instruction would continue to be the Vice-Governor and an appointee of the President of the United States.

This bill, conservative as it was, passed only the House of Representatives in the first wholly Democratic Congress under the first Wilson administration. Long hearings in the Senate prevented its passage before the end of that Congress.

When the next Congress convened, Senator Hitchcock got busy and reported to the Senate early in the session the same bill which the House had passed in the preceding one. During the discussion of this bill, however, Senator Clarke of Arkansas introduced an amendment which gave an entirely different aspect to the bill. The amendment provided that independence would be granted to the Philippines not earlier than one year nor later than two years after the enactment of the law. On the personal intervention of President Wilson, Senator Clarke agreed to rewrite his amendment so as to provide that within not less than two years nor more than four after the enactment of the law, the Philippine Republic would be proclaimed and recognized by the Government of the United States. It was also contemplated that the Philippine Islands should be recognized as neutral territory, but the neutralization of the Philippines was not made a condition *sine qua non* for the establishment of the Philippine Republic. Senator Clarke's amendment passed the Senate by the deciding vote of Vice-President Marshall, many Democratic Senators joining with the Republicans in voting against it.

When the bill as thus amended was reported to the House of Representatives by Mr. Jones, a large group of Democratic members, headed by Congressman Fitzgerald of New York, voted with the solid Republican membership against the Clarke Amendment, which was thereby defeated. After this amendment had been stricken out of the bill, this measure was passed without a record vote either in the Senate or in the House. With the signature of President Wilson, it became a law and was popularly known in the Philippines as the Jones Act.

I felt then that my public career had ended. There was no longer any doubt in my mind as to the future fate of the Philippines. The Congress of the United States had at last supplemented and strengthened the previous executive pronouncements—which in the language employed by Presidents McKinley, Theodore Roosevelt, and Taft, were rather ambiguous—by an unequivocal declaration that "it was, as it has always been, the intention of the people of the United States to grant the Philippines their independence as soon as a stable government could be established therein."

So I resigned my post as Resident Commissioner after duly notifying the leader of my party, Speaker Osmeña of the Philippine National Assembly, of my proposed action. I further advised Speaker Osmeña to become a candidate for the Philippine Senate, as the presidency of this body, which would have more powers than the Lower House, would be the proper place from which to exercise the continued leadership of our party. Contrary to my advice, Speaker Osmeña decided to keep the speakership of the House and in that position also to remain as head of the party. In his cablegram, Osmeña notified me that, willy-nilly, my candidacy to the Senate would be presented by the party with a view to having me elected as the President of this newly created body.

On the eve of my departure from Washington, my friends in the House of Representatives, at a farewell banquet held at the New Willard Hotel, presented me with a gold watch with this inscription: "To Manuel L. Quezon, in recognition of his patriotic services in the House of Representatives, from his friends and admirers."

I am proud to remember the tremendous greeting which was given me on my arrival in Manila. Not even on the day of my inauguration as the first President of the Commonwealth were the people in the streets so wild in their demonstration. A typhoon was blowing in the bay, my ship was detained and in a pouring rain the old and the young alike, including children, stood for hours, waiting to cheer me when I landed. It was nightfall before I could reach the Quezon Gate—a gate which, by order of the City Board of Manila, was opened in the wall facing the college of San Juan de Letran, my alma mater. The Filipino poet laureate, Fernando Maria Guerrero, wrote a sonnet which was inscribed on a silver hatchet symbolic of the hammers which destroyed the wall to open the gate. After the public meeting, held despite the raging storm, I was escorted to Malacañan Palace where, for a few days, I was the guest of Governor-General Harrison. Other public meetings and several banquets were held in my honor and, without making a campaign, I was elected Senator by unanimous vote from my district. Upon the inauguration of the new legislature composed of two elective houses, again by unanimous vote I was elected the first President of the Senate. President Wilson sent an appropriate message which was read at the ceremonies of the inauguration by Governor-General Harrison.

By this time even the most intransigent Filipinos,

with the exception of General Ricarte, who had exiled himself from the country, had become sincere friends and loyal supporters of the United States.

Not long thereafter, the United States entered the First World War by the side of the Allied nations. The war message to Congress of President Wilson giving the reasons and stating the aims of the United States in declaring war against the Central Powers found a responsive chord in the hearts of the Filipino people. The whole country was aroused, and from the cities and countryside messages were sent to me to be transmitted to the President of the United States expressing the desire of the people to fight with America on the battlefields of Europe for the attainment of those aims.

"Self-determination" expressed in one word the cause for which the Filipinos had given their lives and their all in two successive and unequal wars, first against Spain and later against the United States. Self-determination expressed, too, the national ideals and aspirations of every subjugated race. It was then for our own cause and for our own national aspirations that America was unsheathing the sword and for the first time in her history taking active part in the bloody quarrels of old imperialist Europe. America's policy in the Philippines—its solemn pledge to grant the Filipino people their independence contained in the preamble of the Jones Act—had borne its fruit; in the hour of national peril, contrary to what they had done when they were the subjects of the Spanish monarchy, the Filipinos asked to be allowed to shed their blood mingled with American blood.

I decided to go to Washington in person and convey to the President of the United States the universal sentiment of my people. President Wilson received my message with unconcealed enthusiasm and in his characteristic well-chosen words, expressed his deep appreciation. This act of loyalty on the part of the Filipino people would conclusively prove to the statesmen of Europe the wisdom of his announced policy. The War Department was given instructions to help in every way in the organization of a Filipino Army, and meanwhile all the American forces were withdrawn from the Islands to be used elsewhere as demanded by the requirements of the war. Thus, for the first time since American occupation, the American flag was in the keeping of none but Filipino troops—the Scouts and the Constabulary. It was reported that an American Negro in the service of an American General said to his master: "Boss, we are the only Americans now in the Philippines."

On my return to Manila, the Philippine Legislature enacted a law authorizing the creation of the National Guard, the body which was to be trained by American officers and then mustered into the Federal Army. The Philippine Legislature also authorized Governor Harrison to offer to the United States one destroyer and one submarine.

[134]

Despite the sympathetic support of the War Department, for reasons unknown to us the military authorities in the Philippines were very slow in providing the civil government with the necessary help for the training and equipment of the National Guard. The result was that the division which we organized was mustered into the service of the Federal Army only a short time before the Armistice was signed. Thus we did not have the privilege of taking part, under General Pershing, in the First World War.

However, even then some Filipino blood had been shed on the soil of France. The first Filipino who lost his life in that war was immortalized in our history by giving his name, Claudio, to the training camp of the National Guard—Camp Claudio.

Because of the defeat that we recently suffered in the defense of the Philippines against Japanese invasion, due mainly to lack of air power, it is of special interest to note now that even after the National Guard had been demobilized, Governor-General Harrison, in full agreement with the Legislature, tried hard to keep up and give more impetus to Filipino aviation; but after Governor Harrison left, our common efforts in this respect went to naught. It was only after I had become President of the Commonwealth that the Filipino aviation service was again revived— too late, as it proved to be.

After the signing of the Armistice, and while

President Wilson was hopelessly matching his talent against the European foxes, I again came to Washington at the head of a delegation, this time to plead for immediate independence for the Philippines.

On this trip came with me, not as a member of the delegation but as my life partner, the woman who, for twelve long years, had been engaged to me. The opposition to our marriage of her beloved mother and my dear aunt had been removed by the will of God. Aunt Zeneida had joined our ancestors the year before. Contrary to Filipino custom which celebrates marriages at great expense and with pompous ceremonies, my bride and I were married in Hongkong in our street clothes and with the attendance of only the members of my staff. Twenty-four years of married life with the same wife have proved that matrimonial happiness does not depend upon the noise of the wedding. Nor for that matter upon closing one's eyes to the sight of other beauties and running away from their company during the period of one's engagement.

In Washington my delegation was received by Secretary of War Baker, representing the absent President Wilson. No more eloquent impromptu address have I ever listened to than that delivered by Secretary Baker on that memorable occasion. He gave us the assurance, in behalf of President Wilson, that at the first opportunity the President of the United States would recommend to Congress the enactment of a law that would grant the Philippines immediate and complete independence. After his return to Washington, and before the expiration of his term, President Wilson submitted to Congress a message recommending the granting of Philippine independence—a perpetual testimony to his abiding faith in self-determination. A hostile Congress turned a deaf ear to, and promptly shelved, the message of that great apostle of human freedom. This recommendation of the President, together with his League of Nations, went into the archives of Washington to form a part, I hope, of historical American documents.

During the succeeding administrations of Presidents Harding and Coolidge, no progressive step was taken toward either greater self-government or independence for the Philippines. Not that the Filipino people, through their Legislature, had ceased to demand independence. On the contrary, year after year, the Legislature approved resolutions asserting that a stable government had been established in the Islands and that it was time, in accordance with the declared policy of Congress, that independence be granted to the Philippines. I had been to Washington several times during those years in an effort to secure Congressional action in accordance with the Philippine Legislature's petitions, but to no avail. Of course, I had occasion to meet both President Harding and President Coolidge and, later on, President Hoover.

I had known President Harding as chairman of the Senate Committee on the Philippines. To me he was a most lovable man; so human in his acts. One day as I was sitting in his office conversing with him, Attorney-General Daugherty entered the room and President Harding said: "I want the boss of Ohio to shake hands with the boss of the Philippines."

President Coolidge left no impression on me one way or another. He would let me talk and then he would say something in such a low voice that I never understood what he said. So when I left the White House I knew no more of the presidential mind than before I entered.

I met Mr. Hoover while he was Secretary of Commerce and after it was publicly known that he would be a candidate for the presidency. My purpose, of course, was to make the acquaintance of the man before he was too busy as President of the United States, since it looked certain that the Republican candidate would be elected. I had read of his splendid relief work in Belgium and being myself naturally sensible of the sufferings of the people, I had looked at Mr. Hoover as a man overflowing with kindness and love for his fellow-men. I was, therefore, disappointed when at our first meeting I was face to face with what seemed to me a marble statue. After talking to him, I received the impression that his mind dealt with facts and figures and that his heart took no part in his business.

To succeed Governor-General Harrison, President Harding appointed as Governor-General of the Philippines the strongest Republican candidate in the primaries—General Leonard Wood. General Wood was of the opinion that Governor-General Harrison had "Filipinized" the service too rapidly and there were evidences that he would have turned the clock back, if it had been in his power to do so. He also disapproved of the part taken by the Philippine Government in acquiring or founding public utilities during Governor Harrison's administration. Here, too, he would have undone what had been done, if he could. I opposed him at every turn although our personal relations never ceased to be pleasant.

For a time and at the beginning of his administration, General Wood had with him a very able assistant General Frank R. McCoy. Perhaps the complete rupture between General Wood and his own Filipino Cabinet, as well as with the Philippine Legislature, might have been avoided had not General McCoy left for the United States.

It was partly due to my conviction that the Nationalist Party was bound to withdraw its support from the Wood administration, and partly to other causes which it is not necessary to mention here, that I forced a break with the leader of the party, Speaker Osmeña, and after carrying the fight to the electorate I became the head of the party.

I might also add that long ere this I had been trying

to return to the practice of my profession for which I had always longed, but it was Speaker Osmeña himself who had most decidedly opposed that step.

On the death of Governor-General Wood in 1927, I made a trip to Washington to see President Coolidge and to secure, if at all possible, the appointment of a successor to Governor-General Wood who would not perpetuate the break between the Philippine Legislature and the Governor-General.

I came to the United States with Mr. Osmeña who was then the President pro tempore and majority floor leader of the Senate. I had made up my mind that the best man for the position of Governor-General was Colonel Stimson whom, as I have mentioned before, I met when he was Secretary of War. Colonel Stimson had been the guest of Governor-General Wood in Manila about the time my fight with the Governor was at its height. During the visit of Secretary Stimson, I had a conference with him and told him how our official relations with Governor Wood could be improved. Without wholly committing himself, Colonel Stimson left with me the impression that some of my suggestions might be heeded. However, after leaving Manila he wrote an article which was published in the United States in support of the administration of General Wood and in criticism of the Filipinos who were fighting the Governor. I answered the article in very measured language, and I got a letter from Colonel Stimson in appreciation of the courteous and considerate manner in which I had replied to his criticisms.

Moreover, I had not changed the high opinion that I had formed of Colonel Stimson as a truly great man when he was Secretary of War, and I had not forgotten how he used to tell me, when I called at his office, that he considered the promotion of the welfare of the Filipino people one of the grave national responsibilities of the United States. He never pretended to be in favor of Philippine independence because he was anxious about the fate of the Filipino people once they were without the protection of the United States. He believed with Presidents Theodore Roosevelt and Taft that through the natural process of evolution—intellectual, political, and material—the Filipino people would arrive at the dignified state of nationhood and self-government in the manner, for example, in which the people of the self-governing commonwealths of Great Britain have become in later years masters of their own destinies, without, however, breaking completely with the mother country.

I might digress right here and now to give my personal views upon this question. Many Americans have accused me of being insincere in my advocacy of complete independence for the Philippines because on some occasions I have expressed myself as not unwilling to consider continued political relationship between the United States and the Philippines, including of course, free trade relations.

It will be recalled that when the question of free trade relations between the United States and the Philippines was first submitted to the Philippine Assembly, I fought strongly against the proposition. But my opposition having been disregarded by the Congress of the United States and free trade relations having been established, the natural consequences of this trade relationship had become evident in the course of years: the Philippines became prosperous, but at the same time largely dependent upon the profitable market of the United States. Our standard of living was raised above that of other peoples of the Far East. If I could have both prosperity and freedom without completely breaking our political ties with America, I would have been a fool had I been opposed to them.

The word "independence" never meant much to me except as a young revolutionary fighting in the hills of Pampanga and Bataan. I had learned something since those hard days. I had learned that there were countries nominally independent but which in effect were under foreign rule; and still others which had in theory as well as in fact national independence, but whose people knew no freedom except the freedom to starve, the freedom to be silent, the freedom to be jailed, or the freedom to be shot. None of those situations was I willing to see become the fate of my people. I had devoted my whole life to securing for them not the name or the form, but the substance and the essence of liberty. And the reason why I chose to follow and adopt the policy of the Nationalist Party for immediate, absolute, and complete independence was because I had always thought—and so think to this day—that it was easier to get freedom and liberty for the Filipino people through the road to independence which the average American understands than through the policy of Presidents Roosevelt and Taft, agreed to by Colonel Stimson, which, although known and practised by the English in their relations with their white subjects, was entirely alien to the American mind.

And now back to my story. Upon reaching Washington, I called on President Coolidge in the company of Señor Osmeña and told the President how important it was, from the point of view of both the United States and the Philippines, to resume the policy of coöperation which had characterized the relationship between the United States and the Philippines and which had been temporarily suspended during the administration of Governor-General Wood. I mentioned the name of Colonel Henry L. Stimson as the right man for Governor-General. President Coolidge murmured a few words which I did not get and the visit was ended.

I asked for an appointment to see Chief Justice

Taft who graciously received Senator Osmeña and me in his library at his home. He was genuinely glad to see us. He spoke of his early days in the Philippines and inquired about certain persons, calling their names. It was evident that he had been happy during his service in the Islands. Then I told him of my errand. He said that he was no longer interested in politics and did not, as a rule, talk to the President about appointments; but in this particular case, he would be willing to see the President and recommend the appointment of his former Secretary of War, Colonel Stimson, if I could convince the Colonel that he should accept the office.

I wrote a letter to Colonel Stimson who was then in New York requesting him to set a time for a visit with him. He answered by inviting Senator Osmeña and me to an informal family dinner with only Mrs. Stimson and himself at his hotel in New York. We accepted and after dinner I put before Colonel Stimson the purpose of my trip. He would not consider it for a moment. I insisted, and after reminding him of his own words that the government of the Philippines was a grave responsibility resting on the United States, and after giving him assurances of my loyal support and coöperation, bade him good-night. He had given no answer to my presentation of the case, but I felt that I had made a dent both in his mind and in his heart; and so I went back to Mr. Justice Taft and told him that I thought Colonel Stimson would not refuse the post if it were offered to him by the President of the United States.

Fifteen days later, I read in the newspaper that the Honorable Henry L. Stimson had been appointed Governor-General of the Philippines. Unfortunately, I had to go to a sanatorium in Monrovia, California, sick with tuberculosis, and Governor-General Stimson went to the Philippines without my being there to lend him my personal and official support. But Senator Osmeña had returned to the Philippines and temporarily acted as President of the Senate and leader of the party, and he conveyed to our colleagues my wishes that the new Governor-General be given their sincere coöperation and assistance.

When I went back to Manila, after recovering from my illness, I found both the Governor-General and Mrs. Stimson extremely happy with their surroundings. Governor Stimson revived the Council of State, composed of the leaders of the Legislature and members of the Cabinet of the Governor-General, which Governor-General Wood had abolished. He initiated a policy which he expected would finally end in a political status whereby the Filipino people would be essentially free and feel satisfied to remain under the American flag. Hardly did he begin to try out this policy when the sugar interests in the United States started an agitation to secure legislation from Congress which would put a limit to the free exportation of sugar from the Philippines into the United

States. I went to see the Governor in his office and told him that this was the beginning of the end of what he was trying to do. I said most emphatically to him that if the United States retained the Philippines under the American flag and taxed our products entering the United States while keeping open the Philippine market for the free entrance of American goods, I would start a revolution against the United States.

The Governor smiled and said: "I would not blame you." Then taking a very solemn attitude, he exclaimed: "That will never be tolerated by the American people and I will fight it to the end." He did so and the Timberlake Bill went by the board.

Upon the election of President Hoover, Governor-General Stimson was appointed Secretary of State and thus ended his short-lived administration of the Islands. I regretted his departure and I have a slight suspicion that he carried with him imperishable memories of his stay in the Philippines. Of course we had our disagreements, but we discussed our differences of opinion with perfect sincerity and frankness, and after the discussions were over there was never a bad taste in our mouths. It had been my wont after the departure of Governor-General Stimson to tell every one of his American successors, whether Governor-General or United States High Commissioner (after the establishment of the Commonwealth), that no representative of the United States in the Philippines had won my respect and even my personal affection more than did Governor-General Stimson. This, I added, was due to the fact that he never left me in doubt as to what he had in mind whenever he expressed his ideas on any subject. There was never any mental reservation whenever he talked to me, and he therefore made me feel that he gave me his entire confidence exactly as he would have done it if I had been an American sitting at his council table as the senior member of his official family. He and Mrs. Stimson treated Mrs. Quezon and me as close friends, and my wife used to refer to the Governor in our intimate family chats, as "*mi viejo*." (This Spanish expression literally translated means "my old man," but is also used to designate affectionately one's father.) My purpose in refering to Governor-General Stimson in the way I did when talking to his successors was not only to state a fact, but also in the hope that his successors would adopt the same policy in dealing with me and with other Filipino officials.

After Governor-General Stimson, the next Governor-General was Dwight F. Davis. He remained but a short time in the Philippines and during most of that time I was forced to be away from the Islands because of ill health. All I can say of Governor Davis is that he was the gentleman personified and was well liked by the Filipinos.

I was in Washington when the appointment of the successor of Governor Davis was being considered by President Hoover. The Secretary of War, Mr. Patrick Hurley, arranged a meeting between General Douglas MacArthur, then United States Chief of Staff, and Colonel Theodore Roosevelt, Jr., at my house in Washington. Soon thereafter the latter was appointed Governor-General of the Philippines. No American Governor-General had used the word "*Mabuhay*"—an expression of effusive greeting—as did Governor-General Roosevelt. He, too, made friends with the Filipinos, but his term of office was cut short by a telegram which he received soon after the election of President Franklin D. Roosevelt accepting his resignation as Governor-General of the Philippines.

During the latter part of the administration of President Hoover, the movement in the United States to close the American market to Philippine products took another turn. A bill granting independence to the Philippines was introduced in Congress. It included a provision for terminating the free trade relations between the United States and the Philippines. The Philippine Legislature sent a mission to the United States with Messrs. Osmeña and Roxas at its head to appear before Congress in support of independence, but also with the idea of making the bill's provisions agreeable to the Filipino people.

The bill as it passed both Houses in its final form was vetoed by President Hoover; but Congress overrode the President's veto and the bill became known as the Hare-Hawes-Cutting Act. In order to take effect the Act had to be accepted by the Philippine Legislature.

Before the law could be submitted to the Legislature, President Franklin D. Roosevelt had been elected and assumed the presidency. One of his first acts affecting the Philippines was the appointment of the present Justice Frank Murphy of the Supreme Court of the United States as Governor-General of the Philippines.

When Governor Murphy entered Malacañan Palace, a bitter political fight was going on over the acceptance of the Hare-Hawes-Cutting Act. Messrs. Osmeña and Roxas were for the acceptance of the law while I was leading the opposition on several grounds. My main objection, however, was to the provision of the law that called for the retention of military and naval establishments by the United States after the Philippine Republic should have been proclaimed. I did not object to the provision regarding the retention of naval stations so long as this was made dependent upon the consent of the Philippine Republic; but I did strenuously and definitely oppose the retention of military establishments otherwise, for it destroyed the very essence of independent existence for the Philippines.

Governor Murphy won the respect of the Filipino people by keeping aloof from this fight and maintaining the strictest neutrality. He went about his business as Governor-General as though there was no political storm raging around him. His main concern while he remained as Governor-General was social service, and he tried to save as much from the public funds as he thought could be done without stopping the wheels of government. Considering the short time that Governor Murphy stayed as Governor-General of the Philippines, it will be correct to say that during his administration he held more social parties of an informal character, where Filipinos were made to feel at home in Malacañan Palace, than any of his predecessors. When my political fight with Osmeña and Roxas over the Hare-Hawes-Cutting Act was over, Mrs. Quezon and I were frequent guests of Governor Murphy and his sister.

When the Hare-Hawes-Cutting Act was submitted to the Philippine Legislature, it was rejected by an overwhelming majority. Whereupon, the Philippine Legislature sent me to the United States to explain to the President and the Congress our reasons for rejecting the law and to work for a new one more acceptable, or at least less objectionable, to us.

In Washington, President Roosevelt received me with his well-known cordiality. He was kind enough to refer to the fact that he had met me when he was Assistant Secretary of the Navy in the Wilson administration. This thoughtful gesture on the part of the President gave me every encouragement to lay before him frankly and in detail the purpose of my errand. After paying close attention to my statement, he suggested that I present a memorandum in writing to him. I did so, but with a heavy heart. I thought that the President had imposed upon me the burden of writing the memorandum to be read by some one else and then would give me a perfunctory answer. After waiting for over fifteen days, I received word from the White House that the President would see me at a certain hour. I was ushered into his office where I found him as before, with his winning smile and gracious manner. To my agreeable surprise, my memorandum was on his desk and he proceeded to discuss every angle of the question submitted in the memorandum with such comprehension and understanding of the problems that it really astonished me. He was a new President and yet none of his predecessors knew more about the Far East and the Philippine situation than he did—at least as far as his predecessors had ever discussed those questions with me.

President Roosevelt readily agreed that the maintenance of military reservations in the Philippines after the proclamation of the Philippine Republic would, in itself, make the granting of independence a farce. "After all," President Roosevelt added, "the American military force in the Islands is too small to protect the Philippines against foreign invasion, and after we have been in the Islands all these many years, it will be impossible to induce Congress to appropriate the necessary funds for the military defense of the Islands and the maintenance of an army of sufficient size to keep any enemy at bay." He also agreed that as far as naval stations were concerned, the Philippine Republic should have something to say. As to the trade relations between the United States and the Philippines during the ten-year period that the American flag would still remain in the Islands (to which I had also objected), the President promised to have further investigation made of the matter and recommend to Congress the correction of such inequalities and injustices as might be found in the law. In accordance with my understanding with the President, a new Independence Bill was introduced in Congress by Senator Tydings in the Senate and Congressman McDuffie in the House of Representatives. After I became certain that the new bill would become a law, I sought a conference with General Douglas MacArthur, still Chief of Staff of the United States Army.

General MacArthur had been in the Philippines as a young officer and in later years had commanded successively a division and the Philippine Department. I had known General MacArthur for many years and a close friendship had grown up between us. He called me by my first name. I was fully informed of his comprehensive knowledge of the Philippines and knew of his close association with the Filipinos and his absolute faith in their capacity for self-government. He had told me also that the Filipino soldier was the match of any other soldier in the world. His world-wide reputation as a brave and brilliant general had been duly recognized by his own Government in placing him at the head of the United States Army at an early age and for a longer time than any other previous Chief of Staff. I needed the advice of a competent man on whose judgment I could depend as to the feasibility of adequately preparing the Philippines for national defense against the day when they should become independent. No man knew the answer to this question as well as General MacArthur, if he only would give it to me.

At the appointed time, I saw General MacArthur in his office in the War Department. I said: "General, I have come to see you on a matter which concerns the very life of my country. If you can give a frank and complete answer to the question I shall propound, please give it. On the other hand I want no answer from you if you would have to give it with mental reservations, because it affects military matters."

"What is the question?" he said.

"Do you think that the Philippines can be defended after they shall have become independent ten years hence?"

He answered: "I don't think so. I know that the Islands can be protected, provided, of course, that you have the money which will be required."

I asked again: "How much would be needed?"

And he answered: "With what you now spend for the maintenance of the Philippine Constabulary, which I understand is about six million pesos a year [$3,000,000], it will be necessary to spend ten million pesos more [$5,000,000] for the next ten years. Moreover," he added, "the defense of the Philippines cannot rest upon the creation of a big regular army, for that would be too expensive for you. You would have to create a citizen army on the basis of universal compulsory service. If you have a small regular force as a nucleus to be expanded by employing the citizen army in time of peril, no nation will care to attack you, for the cost of the conquest will be more than the expected profits."

I said, "General, one more question: Would you be willing to come to the Philippines and be the man to put into execution the ideas you have just expressed?"

"Manuel," he said, "I have done all that I can as a soldier in the service of my country. Unless there is another war, I do not see any prospect of further constructive work that I can do for the Government and people of the United States. The Philippines is my second country and there is nothing I would like more than to undertake the task that you are proposing. America has a great responsibility for the future safety of the Filipino people. We cannot just turn around and leave you alone. All these many years we have helped you in education, sanitation, road building, and even in the practice of self-government. But we have done nothing in the way of preparing you to defend yourselves against a foreign foe. We have trained a few officers and a few thousand soldiers in the Philippine Scouts and you have created your own Constabulary, but this force is more of a national police than an army. This is the time—if it is not too late—to help you organize your own defense. If you can secure the consent of the Secretary of War and the President of the United States to my assignment as Military Adviser of the Philippine Commonwealth, I shall consider the assignment as a fitting end to my military career."

I replied: "General, I shall proceed at once to secure the consent of the Secretary of War and the President of the United States, with the understanding of course that this plan will be carried out if I am elected President of the Philippine Commonwealth."

The office of the Chief of Staff is connected with the office of the Secretary of War by a side door. General MacArthur peeped into the office of Secretary Dern and upon finding the Secretary alone, he motioned to me to go in. I told the Secretary what I had in mind and he told me to see the President about it. President Roosevelt approved of the plan, using his influence to have an amendment made to a then existing law which permitted the Government of the United States to send military commissions to the South American republics upon their request. The amendment included the Philippines within the scope of the law.

Presently, the new Independence Act was approved by Congress and after its approval I went back to the Philippines to secure its acceptance by the Philippine Legislature. This was done by the unanimous vote of both Houses; whereupon the Independence Act became a solemn pact entered into between the Government and people of the United States on the one hand and the Government and people of the Philippines on the other, whereby it was agreed that on the 4th of July, 1946, the Philippines should become an independent republic. In the meantime, there was to be established the Government of the Commonwealth, with a constitution of its own, framed and adopted by a constitutional convention elected by the voters of the Philippines. The Constitution, once approved by the President of the United States, was to be submitted to a plebiscite of the people for their approval or rejection.

In accordance with the Independence Act, popularly known in the Philippines as the Tydings-McDuffie Law, a constitutional convention was elected which sat in the city of Manila and did, in my opinion, most creditable work. Although in its main features, the Philippine Constitution was practically a copy of the Constitution of the United States, it contained new provisions to meet the social problems of our day which did not exist when the fathers of the

American Republic drew up their own constitution. It also contained the clause in the famous Kellogg Pact that the Philippines renounced war.

Upon the approval of the Philippine Constitution by the constitutional convention, Governor-General Murphy, with a strong favorable recommendation, sent it to Washington for submission to the President of the United States as directed by the Independence Act. President Roosevelt gave his assent to the Constitution and thereafter it was submitted to a plebiscite of the Filipino people who, by practically unanimous vote, made the Constitution the fundamental law of the land.

CHAPTER VIII

My Election as President

AFTER THE general elections for the Legislature which preceded the election of the members of the constitutional convention, the breach in the rank and file of the Nationalist Party caused by the political feud between Osmeña and Roxas and their followers on one side, and my followers and me on the other, was entirely healed. In the general elections, my side won an overwhelming majority, and after our victory we invited our former comrades to join hands with us again so as jointly to give the best there was in the Filipino nation for the writing of their Constitution, and thereafter for the discharge of the grave responsibilities that the Government of the Commonwealth was to impose upon us. Thus when the elections for the officials of the Commonwealth were held, the Nationalist Party again reunited had as its standard bearers myself for President and Sergio Osmeña for Vice-President. Out in the field to oppose me were my former chief, General Emilio Aguinaldo, and also Bishop Gregorio Aglipay of the Philippine Independent Church.

After a campaign during which I made only a couple of speeches over the radio, the Quezon-Osmeña ticket came out victorious with overwhelming majorities.

As soon as the results of the elections were officially known, I cabled General MacArthur, who was still the Chief of Staff of the United States Army, to come to the Philippines as soon as possible in accordance with our understanding. General MacArthur came accompanied by a staff selected by him, arriving at Manila some time before the inauguration of the Commonwealth. He at once reported to me and submitted his whole plan for the national defense of the Philippines. He had already prepared a draft of the message that I was to submit to the new one-chamber Philippine Legislature as provided in the Constitution—the National Assembly—as well as the draft of a bill which would translate into legislative provisions his plan for our national defense. I asked him to leave his papers in my possession so that I might carefully study them. This I proceeded to do immediately, and after making certain amendments to the suggested message as well as to the proposed bill, I returned the papers to General MacArthur so that they might be written out in final form.

I invited the members-elect of the National Assembly to come to Manila some time before the day of the inauguration of the new government. I held several conferences with them during which I explained General MacArthur's plan, and after prolonged discussions, we finally agreed to approve the National Defense Act as the No. 1 Law of the Philippine Commonwealth.

President Roosevelt sent his Secretary of War, the Honorable George H. Dern, to represent him at the inauguration of the Government of the Commonwealth. A distinguished delegation of both the Senate and the House of Representatives, each headed by their respective presiding officers, Vice-President Garner and Speaker Byrns—also came to the Philippines to add solemnity to the greatest historic event in the life of the Filipino people from time immemorial.

On a beautiful morning, November 15, 1934, I left my house in Pasay by the shores of the Bay of Manila and rode with military escorts through streets decorated with American and Filipino flags, under artistic and symbolic arches, to the legislative building where the inaugural ceremonies were to take place. Hundreds of thousands of people had come to Manila from far and wide to witness the elevation to the highest office in the land of the first Filipino who would occupy the seat of power, for centuries past occupied by Spaniards and by Americans. On a grandstand built for the occasion were the highest officials of the Government of the United States, save only the President himself, and all the high dignitaries of the Government of the Philippines including the Chief Justice and members of the Supreme Court, the Secretaries of Departments, and the newly elected members of the National Assembly. There were also present my Military Adviser, General MacArthur, the Commanding General of the Philippine Department with his staff, and the Commandant of the Cavite Naval Station accompanied by other ranking officials of the United States Navy. The last to enter the grandstand were Secretary Dern as representative of the President of the United States, Governor-General Murphy, and I. Secretary Dern read a message from President Roosevelt to the Filipino people and the presidential proclamation declaring officially the establishment of the Government of the Commonwealth. Governor-General Murphy read his farewell address as Governor-General, after which I took the oath of office before Chief Justice Ramon Avanceña of the Supreme Court of the Philippines and then delivered my inaugural address.

From the grandstand, I went through streets crowded with people acclaiming their first President, on to the Palace of Malacañan, the great mansion on the bank of the Pasig River which had been the seat of power of foreign rulers for many decades past. As I stepped out of the presidential car and walked over the marble floor of the entrance hall, and up the wide stairway, I remembered the legend of the mother of Rizal, the great Filipino martyr and hero, who went up those stairs on her knees to seek executive clemency from the cruel Spanish Governor-General Polavieja, that would save her son's life. This story had something to do with my reluctance to believe that capital punishment should ever be carried out. As a matter of fact, during my presidency, no man ever went to the electric chair. At the last moment I always stayed the hand of the executioner.

From the top of the stairs, turning to the right, one saw the very large reception hall, at the end of which on either side of the hall and fronting each other, there were two rooms which reminded me of my first visit to the palace in 1901.

In the room on the right side of the hall, there stood at that time General Arthur MacArthur, then Military Governor of the Philippines, and on the left, there was the room where Aguinaldo was kept as prisoner of war. The first thought which came to me was that I had been right in placing my faith in America, for by coöperating with her my people had won their local autonomy and were on the road to complete independence.

These thoughts were suddenly interrupted by my aide-de-camp who informed me that in the executive office there were waiting for me the general who was Chief of the Constabulary, and the provincial governors of Tayabas and Laguna, whom I had summoned to my first official conference.

The night of the inauguration there was a reception and ball in Malacañan Palace in honor of the American officials, Secretary Dern, Vice-President Garner, the Speaker of the House of Representatives, and the Senators and Congressmen who constituted the Congressional Delegation. That same night, from every home in the Philippines, whether of the poor or of the rich, a prayer went to heaven for the continued greatness of America and the future safety of the Philippines.

CHAPTER IX

Executive Problems

(Note: The following chapter has been prepared by former Governor-General Francis Burton Harrison, who was adviser to the late President Quezon. At President Quezon's request Mr. Harrison kept careful notes of the former's expressed views on the subjects involved in this chapter.)

Executive life was a great change for me after more than twenty-five years of continuous service as a legislator. For the first six months of my presidency I kept intact the Cabinet which I had inherited from Governor-General Murphy; I knew them all intimately and had for years been working with them on the Council of State.

I was determined to give the Philippines the finest government they had ever had. I had one great advantage over my American predecessors as Chief Executive: I really understood my own people. In addressing audiences in the provinces I kept telling them: "Now, I am not an American Governor-General—I'm a Filipino, so tell me the truth." I knew all about the racketeers in the service and determined to get rid of them. From the very beginning the plain people responded heartily to my appeals, for was I not their leader? I myself was one of them. I had started life as a poor village boy and had never accumulated any fortune.

On the other hand, I was somewhat oppressed at first by the new duties as an executive. For the past thirty years I had been mostly in legislative life, and I hated to be tied down to executive office hours and other restrictions. I had made a great many speeches in the Senate and now I was going in for action—not talk. From the point of view of the Executive chair I began to see more clearly the difficulties of putting into effect some of the measures I had championed so ardently in the Senate. Nevertheless, I was determined with all my heart and strength that in three years' time I should have a model government in the Philippines.

The first matter of great importance before us was, of course, the creation of the Philippine Army. How deeply I regretted that the Philippine National Guard which we had organized in 1917-1918 to help the United States during the war had been abolished. In that, we had already had the nucleus for an army, including the rudiments of an Air Corps. But now we had to start again from scratch. This was the subject of my first message to the National Assembly, and the bill was signed and became a law on December 21, 1935. Later, the first general officers appointed were Paulino Santos as Chief of Staff and Generals Reyes, Basilio Valdes, and Vicente Lim. Recruiting for the new army was soon in full swing.

In the provinces around Manila public order was, at that time, in a somewhat unsatisfactory condition. General Aguinaldo, who had been an unsuccessful candidate against me for the presidency, was now a source of some uneasiness to the American Army officers in their garrison. But I thought I knew Aguinaldo better than they did. In the course of a few months his followers had entirely quieted down.

Banditry in the mountains at the other end of Laguna de Bay was still active and the Sakdalistas in the near-by provinces were still restless. I seized both of these problems quickly and with great vigor and soon settled them to the general satisfaction and without further bloodshed. This was possible because I was a Filipino and understood the psychology of those people and how best to handle them.

The truth was that when I took over the Executive power there was still an economic depression in the provinces—as, for that matter, there had been in the United States. Wages in near-by regions had fallen to sixty centavos a day and in the Ilocos regions to the north to even forty centavos. Of course, the people were restless. Eventually, I secured from the Assembly a minimum wage law fixing the rate at

Malacañan Palace and Grounds from Malacañan Park across the Pasig River

Executive Building adjoining Malacañan Palace

not less than one peso a day in the country districts and one peso twenty-five in the municipalities. The disquiet in the provinces had been chiefly on the part of the farm laborers, and it must be remembered that the Philippines are still mainly an agrarian country. The grievances of the farm laborers were due not only to the miserable pittance they were receiving as a money wage, but also to the large landholdings created in much earlier times which were so managed that those who had cleared the land and worked their small fields could get no title to their lands. Many of the largest *haciendas* were still owned by church corporations as in the stories of Rizal. The remedy proposed and partly carried out by Mr. Taft, known as the Friar Land Purchases, had not worked out as intended. The lands thus purchased by the Philippine Government and meant to be sold to the tenants seldom got into the ownership of those who had worked them and lived on them. Besides, this was a method which proved extremely expensive to the Government. I preferred and advocated the system which had been applied to settle the land troubles in Ireland by Mr. Gladstone, known as the "three F's": fixed rental, fixity of tenure, and freedom to convey, with land commissioners to administer the law. The Philippine Government was still struggling with this question so fraught with danger for the future.

In another reform I made great progress. This was in wiping out the tribal particularism which had existed in the Philippines for so many centuries. In frequent visits to the provinces, especially those far distant from Manila, I addressed large audiences and rallied them to the knowledge that we were all, first and foremost, Filipinos, and that at last they had their own government.

In the southern provinces, the most important question of all was the future of Mindanao, our second largest island, which for ages past and until recently had been under the control of the Moros. They had never been subdued by the Spanish and were never disarmed by them. Even up to the time of my childhood, they used to raid the northern islands for slaves and plunder. But the cry, "*Hay Moros en la costa*" ("There are Moros on the coast"), has not been heard in the rest of the Philippine Islands for now at least a half century.

The American Army officers used alternately to fight the Moros and then to "baby" them. The Moros are very artful and seldom agreed to any proposition made to them on the part of the Government except with feigned reluctance, and only in a manner calculated to put the Executive under an obligation. I felt that this method on their part was mostly bluff, and I now addressed them on various occasions with straight-from-the-shoulder declarations. This new method of handling them seemed to work excellently. The Moros are good farmers and fishermen, but theirs has a been a dark and bloody chapter of history, and we were glad to see them at length gradually settling into modern ways.

Aside, however, from the matter of public order, there existed an international aspect of the Mindanao question, of profound importance to the Filipino nation. Unless we fully opened up, protected and settled, and thus made use of this great, rich, only partly developed island, some other nation might some day try to move in and make it their own. For the past twenty years, continued and successful efforts to colonize Mindanao from the north have been undertaken. The modern Filipino is not afraid of his kinsmen, the Moros. Settlers from the north in great numbers have poured into the rich valley of the Cotobato. I asked General Paulino Santos to take charge of the new colony at Coronadal near Davao, which he did with conspicuous success. Secretary Rafael Alunan in the Cabinet was given supervision over all colonization affairs. Many members of the Assembly accompanied me on the S.S. *Negros* down to Davao to see the new enterprise and became very enthusiastic over the prospects. I felt very strongly that every man who could own his own land would be contented and never became a prey to the teachings of Communism. But these colonizations were very expensive for the Government and, at best, only partly met the issue. I was convinced that transportation and access were the key to full solution of this problem, so during my administration I pushed the opening of modern roads across Mindanao, and Filipinos from the north took advantage of these opportunities. The Government supplied 60 per cent of the necessary capital for the subsidizing of new and modern steamers plying to the Visayas and Mindanao from Manila. I advocated the building of a railway, to be run by electric power from the magnificent Cristina Falls in Lanao, across the island, with feeder highways at selected points.

Another settlement for which one hundred thousand hectares of land was set aside was opened in the province of Isabela. The Ilocanos, who had requested the opening of this new settlement began to settle here in great numbers, taking advantage of these immensely rich lands in Isabela.

During the first year of my administration I was continuously busy with the reorganization of the bureaus of government, cutting down and consolidating the overlapping offices which encrusted them and which had gradually grown up and deranged the administration by their eager competition with one another.

Malacañan Palace garden along the Pasig River

Mrs. Quezon's Library in Malacañan Palace

The family dining-room

Of great importance, in my opinion, was the selection of judges to fill vacancies and to sit upon the new Court of Appeals. I was determined to make no unfit appointments and even to drop those judges who had proved themselves unworthy in the past. Favoritism was to play no part in my selections for the bench— nor did it. My test for a Justice of the Supreme Court was not only integrity but also his modernity of view: Was he a man capable of interpreting the spirit of the new Constitution as well as the letter of the law? Was he a jurist and not merely legalistic? I quizzed each one of the remaining Supreme Court Justices in turn to ascertain whether they placed other human rights on an equality with the right of property. Those who sought by themselves, or with political pull, an appointment to the Supreme Court or to the new Court of Appeals were, in my view, utterly undesirable for such a post.

As for incompetency or graft in the service, I was quite ruthless. During the first quarter of the year 1936, my administration collected two million pesos more from the existing tax laws than had my immediate predecessors. I advocated an inheritance tax law and an increase in the income tax in the higher brackets. My motto in all these matters was progressive conservatism.

In educational matters I promoted the growth and welfare of the University of the Philippines, and blocked an attempt of the Church to impose religious instruction in the public schools.

On one, perhaps minor, point, I encountered considerable criticism. This was in the many improvements and additions I made to the Executive Mansion, known as Malacañan Palace. I have always had a very strong creative urge in the matter of public buildings, but in this case I knew that the Filipinos would regard the improvement and adornment of the Executive Mansion as a matter of national prestige. Moreover, these public works were not done for my own comfort and personal enhancement and that of my family, for we spent actually far less time in Malacañan than had my predecessors as Chief Executive, since I was so constantly on the move in the provinces. I really had in mind an effort to block the original "Burnham Plan" for moving the Executive Mansion, which in itself would have been very costly, and, in my opinion, nothing could really replace this old palace with its historic associations. It may also be added that in the new city named after me, some ten kilometers to the north of Manila, I had constructed by the Government hundreds of houses for the working people. These dwellings with all the comforts of sanitation and with playgrounds near-by for children were occupied at a nominal rental by the former dwellers in the insanitary barrio of Tondo.

After six months of planning and consultation my new administration was formed and the Philippine Commonwealth was fully launched upon its career.

CHAPTER X

Another Visit to the United States

FOR THE purpose of securing action that would remedy the "injustices and inequalities" in the trade relations between the United States and the Philippines as provided in the Independence Act and also promised by President Roosevelt, I came to Washington in 1937.

It was likewise my purpose to present to the American people in its true light, the nature and objective of my policy of national defense which had been the subject of the most unfair and malicious attack from certain quarters in the United States. At the same time, I wanted to obtain more enthusiastic support from the War Department. For these reasons, I brought with me my Military Adviser, General Douglas MacArthur.

On my way to America, I passed through China and Japan and was entertained, while in those countries, by government officials as well as by private persons and civic organizations. The Mayor of Greater Shanghai, General Cheng, gave a reception in my honor and in the name of his Government delivered to me a decoration given only to heads of states, which I accepted with the understanding that the constitutional requirements under the laws of the United States and of the Philippines would later be complied with.

I had met General Cheng many years before, when he was an aide-de-camp to Dr. Sun Yat-sen, on the occasion of my visit to the Father of New China in his home in Canton. It was a visit I could never forget. That wonderful patriot had explained to me at length his vast plans of political and material development for his beloved fatherland. Old Dr. ————, ex-Minister from China to Washington, was present at the luncheon which was presided over by charming Madame Sun Yat-sen. The old diplomat assured me he would live a hundred and twenty-five years, when he objected to my offer to help him up the innumerable stairs that we had to climb to reach the living-rooms of Dr. Sun Yat-sen.

After the reception of the Mayor, General Cheng, Mrs. Quezon and I were guests at dinner given by Dr. and Madame Kung. Dr. Kung is a descendant in direct line from Confucius and was, even then, one of the most influential officials in the Chinese Government. Madame Kung, sister to Mesdames Sun Yat-sen and Chiang Kai-shek would, in my opinion, grace any throne whether European or Oriental.

In Japan, Ambassador Grew honored me with an afternoon tea and a reception. While the party was going on, I was handed an envelope from the Foreign Office containing a copy of the speech which the Japanese Minister for Foreign Affairs was to deliver at the banquet he was giving in my honor that night, to which Ambassador Grew and General MacArthur had been invited. There was also a note in the envelope wherein I was requested to send a copy of my response to the toast. Since I had intended to say nothing more than a few pleasant words on this occasion, I did not have any written speech. I was, therefore, compelled to abandon the most pleasant occupation of dancing, in which I was engaged, and dictate a formal address.

I noticed that in his toast the Foreign Minister had completely ignored the United States while he stressed the need of closer coöperation between Japan and the Philippines. I made it a point, therefore, to avow our eternal gratitude to the United States for the unselfish policy pursued in all her relations with the Philippines. I stated further that it was our desire to maintain the friendliest kind of relationship with Japan, as indeed it was; that this was also our aim in dealing with all foreign countries; but that in the case of America, we were bound to give her special considerations as we would owe to her our having become a member of the sisterhood of independent nations. Among those present at the banquet was the Prime Minister himself, Prince Konoye.

In the course of the evening, the Foreign Minister

expressed his desire to have a visit from me at his office the following day, to which, of course, I readily agreed. At our conference, he expressed the appreciation of his Government for the fair treatment I was giving to the Japanese residing in or doing business in the Islands. I assured him that it was the fixed policy of the Filipino people to deal justly with every other people in the world; that we were bent on making friends and not enemies.

"Is it definitely settled," he asked, "that the Philippines will be granted independence by the United States?"

"Of course," I replied. "On the 4th of July, 1946, the Philippine Republic will be proclaimed by the Government of the United States as a separate and independent state."

"But many Americans believe," he retorted, "that Japan will take the Philippines once you are free, and these Americans, plus many others who are imperialists at heart, object, even now, to the independence of the Philippines."

I agreed with that view, adding that among the Filipinos there were also a few who feared independence because they thought that ultimately it would only mean a change of sovereignty—to that of Japan instead of the United States.

His Excellency gave me the typical smile of a Japanese diplomat and said: "Mr. President, you may tell your people—you may even assure President

Roosevelt when you see him—that Japan will gladly be a signatory to a treaty that will recognize the Philippines as a neutral territory once it shall have become independent. . . . Japan," he continued, "has no aggressive intentions towards the Philippines. All we want is your trade—to buy your products and to sell you our goods."

I expressed to him the hope that Japan and the Philippines would always be on good terms. As to trade relations, I saw no objection to his ideas.

"But you must realize, Mr. Minister," I said, again repeating what I stated the night before, "that the Philippines owe much to the United States and we are bound to give her special considerations if she should want them, so long as her wishes do not conflict with our national interests."

"I understand, of course, your position," he remarked.

I stood up to leave.

"By the way, I take it that you are informed of the impending change in the Government. To-morrow I shall cease to be the Foreign Minister, but Japan's foreign policy remains unaltered despite changes in the personnel of the Government." These were his last words.

We shook hands and he accompanied me to the door.

On the following day, His Imperial Majesty had me as guest at luncheon in the Imperial Palace. The

President Quezon after reviewing the Philippine Military Academy Cadets in Baguio, in 1936

President Quezon congratulates General MacArthur on his appointment as Commanding General, United States Armed Forces in the Far East, July 26, 1941

other guests were Ambassador Grew, the Emperor's brother, and the Minister of the Household. After luncheon, His Majesty conversed with me through an interpreter. Whether by design or by accident, Ambassador Grew was so placed that his bad ear was toward us, while his better ear had to listen to the continuous talk of the Emperor's brother.

The seating arrangement of the guests aroused my suspicion and, I bet it did Ambassador Grew's, too. But the Ambassador was helpless. If there was going to be a conspiracy against the United States between the Emperor of Japan and the President of the Philippines, the American Ambassador, whose duty was to protect American interests, would have been an innocent witness of the proceedings.

The conspiracy, however, did not take place. It was not even attempted, at least so it seemed to me. Emperor Hirohito thanked me for my good treatment of his subjects; told me that he had heard of the beauty of my country; asked me how many times I had visited Japan, and whether I had enjoyed my visits. I gave the appropriate answer to each question, and as we walked backwards bowing three times, we finally stepped out from the presence of the Son of Heaven.

Upon my arrival in America, I learned that my visit to Japan had been widely and diversely commented upon in the newspapers. I was misrepresented as having entered into negotiations with the Japanese Government, with the suggestion between the lines that the negotiations were more or less of a treacherous character.

It was incorrectly stated that on the occasion of my visit to Japan, there had been a great demonstration of armed force at a ceremony in my honor and that as a result of my conviction that Japan was unbeatable from the West, I returned to my country convinced that my people would have to make some special terms with the Japanese in order to avoid being attacked or dominated. The fact is that there never was any such demonstration of armed might in my honor or while I was there, and while I was in general aware of the Japanese military strength, I never thought that she was unbeatable from the West.

While I was in Japan, I stated in public addresses that it was our desire to be on good and friendly terms with Japan and with all the countries of the world, but that our special aim would be to maintain very close association with the United States even after the termination of any political ties between the two countries.

General MacArthur was present on one of these occasions and congratulated me on my address. When war broke out in Europe in 1939, I assured President Roosevelt that if the United States should become involved in the conflict the Filipino people would fight by her side to the bitter end.

CHAPTER XI

The Japanese Attack

ON MONDAY, the 8th of December (in the Far East), between five and six o'clock in the morning, my valet woke me up in my home in Baguio and said that Secretary to the President Vargas (Jorge B. Vargas) was calling from Manila over the long-distance telephone and insisted that he had to talk to me on a most grave and urgent matter. I felt in my bones that war between the United States and Japan had broken out. Nothing of less importance would have made Secretary Vargas feel justified in disturbing my sleep, for he knew I was in Baguio to recover from illness.

I took the telephone by the side of my bed and said: "George, what is on?"

"Mr. President," came the answer, "Pearl Harbor has been bombed by the Japanese and war has been declared."

"George, you are crazy," I retorted. "War may have been declared but the Japanese would never dare attack Hawaii! You are joking; Pearl Harbor is the best defended naval station in the world. Where did you get that nonsense?"

"Both the United and Associated Press have telephoned me, and General MacArthur has confirmed the report," he said.

"Do you know what has happened?" I asked.

"Nothing definite, but it seems that the surprise attack has had disastrous effects."

"Tell General MacArthur that I am coming down to Manila to-day and tell Colonel Nieto [my senior aide-de-camp] to rush up to Baguio immediately. Keep me constantly informed of everything."

"Yes, sir," answered Secretary Vargas and I hung up.

Baguio was the summer capital of the Philippines. Located there is what is called "The Mansion House," a modern building built and rebuilt by American Governors-General. It is on the top of a hill and the views from the Mansion are wonderful. A park with pine trees, flower gardens, ample lawns, a few fountains, an artificial lake, a tennis court and bridle paths form the beautiful grounds, in the center of which stands the summer Executive Mansion. I seldom stayed in this official residence. Mrs. Quezon in 1930 had built a house in Baguio, and year by year she gradually made of it a comfortable and attractive home. It is located on one of the nicest sites overlooking the city and the Burnham Park. The greatest attraction to Mrs. Quezon about our house was the modest imi-

Pier Seven on the modern water-front at Manila

Scene at the mouth of the Pasig River, Manila

Residents of Cavite evacuating the town after Japanese bombing raid of December 10, 1941

Reception hall of Malacañan Palace

Head of main stairway

President and Mrs. Quezon and their children on the porch at Malacañar

tation of the Grotto of Lourdes built inside the grounds. It took me a full month to convince Mrs. Quezon that she should leave our home in Pasay, outside Manila, for the historic Palace of Malacañan in Manila; but I never succeeded in making her go and live at the Mansion House in Baguio.

So when Vargas telephoned me I was with my younger daughter, Zeneida, spending a few days at our private house.

After the telephone conversation, I couldn't go back to sleep. For several months, I had been almost certain that war with Japan was inevitable in view of the positive stand taken by the United States vis-à-vis the so-called "China Incident" and the announced Greater East Asia policy of Japan. Indeed, I feared that war was an early probability when, upon the departure of Ambassador Nomura, Foreign Minister Matsuoka made a speech before the Japan-American Policy Association which could only be interpreted to mean that if America did not recede from her stand on the pending question, Japan would resort to war between the two governments. Matsuoka spoke no longer of merely the Greater East Asia policy; he spoke also of the *co-prosperity sphere* which, ambiguous as it may read to the uninformed, was plain enough to those who watched with open eyes Japan's expansionist moves. It was a positive assertion on the part of Japan that she would not tolerate Dutch restrictions of the amount of oil she might want to purchase from the East Indies—nor, for that matter, would Japan recognize anybody's right to deprive her of a pound of tin or rubber which she might desire. As it seemed to me, the co-prosperity sphere—after the Japanese incursions into, and seizure of, much Chinese territory—and the reference to the Southern Pacific, meant this much: that the Tanaka plan for the military expansion of Japan by land was being carried out and was about to be supplemented with the navy plan covering the conquest of the innumerable islands, large and small, in the Southwestern Pacific.

Whether Japan would have gone to war with the United States on all and every one of the above-mentioned issues, it is not important to discuss now. All I want to say is that in the appointment of Ambassador Nomura, I saw the last peaceful gesture of Japan in her diplomatic negotiations with the United States. In fact Matsuoka's speech said as much when it was stripped of its verbiage.

There was, however, a question in my mind that I could not satisfactorily answer. How could Japan fight America, potentially the strongest nation on earth? Japan, already poor in material resources, had been weakened by her war on China, according to the generally accepted view. Of one thing, though, I was certain. If Japan decided to go to war she would attack the United States without previous declaration of war. Such had been her policy when fighting any first-class power. Hence my insistence on preparing the Philippines for every eventuality as soon as I saw signs of what might come. But while I expected the surprise attack, it never occurred to me that Pearl Harbor would be the chosen target.

Therefore, the news from Vargas simply dumbfounded me. I saw at once that Japan was fully prepared for war to a degree that not even the experts had suspected. The gravest situation was confronting the Philippines.

Even so, it was not until I learned of the report of Secretary Knox, after his visit to Pearl Harbor, that I began to fear that no help could come to us in the Philippines from the United States. Secretary Knox's report, as given out, contained only very general information, but it was sufficient to make me reach this conclusion.

Before seven o'clock, my valet came again to my bedroom. A woman reporter from the Philippine *Herald* wanted a statement from me. I took a pen and a piece of paper and wrote these words:

"The zero hour has arrived. I expect every Filipino—man and woman—to do his duty. We have pledged our honor to stand to the last by the United States and we shall not fail her, happen what may."

Then I called over the long-distance telephone to my wife who, as usual, was at our rice farm in Arayat, busy making of it a sort of model farm and, at the same time, a profitable investment. With my wife were my two other children—Maria (Baby), my elder daughter, and Manuel, Jr. (Nonong), my only boy.

I gave my wife the bad news and advised her not to worry about it for everything would come out well in the end. I told her also that I was driving down that night to take her and the children to Manila with me.

After this conversation, I went down to have my breakfast. Major Speth, a retired American officer whom I had appointed Vice Mayor of the City of Baguio, and Mr. Sylvester, the American engineer who succeeded Mr. A. D. Williams in the Civilian Relief Administration, were in the living-room waiting for me. I had sent for Mr. Sylvester the day before to come up from Manila to study the safety of the air-raid shelters that were being built in Baguio. At the breakfast table was my daughter Zeneida. I greeted her with the news that Pearl Harbor had been attacked by the Japanese. "Daddy, how dare those Japs...!" she exclaimed.

The drone of airplanes was heard overhead. I asked Mr. Sylvester to go out to the porch and see whether those planes were ours, or of the enemy. He came back with the heartening news that they were American bombers. "Let us see them," my daughter suggested, and we followed her to the porch.

Ten thousand feet high in the air were flying seventeen planes in V formation. Before we could express our joy, we heard the explosion of bombs.

"Sylvester, how could you have mistaken those for American bombers?" I shouted. My chauffeur entered the porch carrying in his hand two bomb parts that dropped in front of my house when the bombers passed over it. Fifteen minutes later, Major Speth's chauffeur, stained with blood, reported to us that he had taken some people from Camp John Hay to the hospital. War had reached the Philippines!

I had Secretary Vargas called immediately to the telephone and I told him to inform General Mac-Arthur that Camp John Hay had been bombed.

"Summon a meeting of the Council of State* for to-morrow at 9:00 A.M.," I ordered.

After talking to Vargas, the Mayor of the City of Baguio, Mr. Valderosa, a Filipino, came to receive instructions if I had any to give.

"Just tell the people to be calm and follow the instructions previously given in case of air raids," I said.

Hardly was I through conversing with the Mayor when more bomb explosions shook my house. This time bombs had fallen outside Camp John Hay, not half a mile from my place. The house of a Filipino was wrecked and the owner's head blown off.

Major Speth then approached me and suggested

---

* The Council of State is the highest advisory council of the Chief Executive of the Philippines. It had been created by Governor-General Harrison. It came to an end during the administration of Governor-General Wood. It was revived by Governor-General Stimson, and I gave it more importance after my assumption of the presidency.

that we go out of the house to a less exposed place. We went to the other side of the road where there was a pine forest and sat down under its cover. Once again, we saw at a distance the Japanese bombers flying over Baguio as unmolested as if they were flying over Japan. At last I decided to take my car and go through the town to see how the people were behaving. Filipino Christians and Igorrots alike, they did not seem to be unduly alarmed although they had never before been in a real bombing. They walked in the streets and attended to their business as soon as the sirens blew the all-clear signal.

While I was on my way to the main street of the city, Colonel Segundo of the Philippine Army, Commandant of the Military Academy in Baguio, reported to me the damage done at Camp John Hay. "How are your cadets?" I asked him. "They are all right, sir," he answered. Since there were no air-raid shelters either at Camp John Hay or at the Academy, Colonel Segundo had ordered the cadets to disperse under the pine trees with their rifles and ammunition belts whenever the air-raid signal was given.

After the ride through the city, we went to the house of Major Speth which could not be seen well from the air and spent the rest of the day there. Once in this house, I sent for the Major of the Constabulary who had been charged with the duty of rounding up the Japanese nationals as soon as war broke out. He reported having performed his duty.

By noon, I was again called to the phone by Secretary Vargas.

"The Japanese," he said, "have bombarded Clark Field and the whole place is now afire."

"What are the American planes doing?" I inquired. Vargas did not know nor did I direct him to find out the answer. Up to this day, I never addressed that question again to anybody, for reasons that I shall state in the proper place.

My aide-de-camp, Colonel Nieto, arrived in Baguio late in the afternoon and gave as the reason for his delay that the road between San Fernando and Angeles was clogged with traffic due to the bombardment of Clark Field. He said further that the whole camp was ablaze.

As the sun was coming down behind the high mountains of the Benguet road, my automobile ran down the zigzag way to Manila. How could I foresee that it would take a long time before I could go back to Baguio again?

The eagerness of the Filipinos to fight, as well as the utter ignorance of our recruits and policemen at the beginning of the war as to how futile it is to try to kill, with rifles and shotguns, the Japanese flyers, is revealed by the following instances: In my house in Mariquina there were some soldiers of the presidential guard. Whenever they saw airplanes passing, flying low over my place, they would fire at the planes with their guns which, of course, made them targets for the

Japanese machine guns from the air. At last it became necessary for my aide, Colonel Nieto, to stay among the soldiers to prevent them from committing this kind of near-suicide. The same thing was done by Filipino soldiers stationed at Camp Murphy, located about one kilometer from my house. The worst case, however, was that of a policeman in Quezon City who, on seeing a plane passing only a few hundred feet over his head, drew his revolver and fired a shot at the plane. He was instantly killed by the aviator.

On my way to my farm in Arayat, which is about two hours by car from Manila, General Francisco, the Chief of the Constabulary, accompanied by the Constabulary Commander of Central Luzon, Major Rafael Jalandoni, met me on the road as I had previously directed them to do. I asked them to follow me to my house on the farm where I intended to discuss with them the general situation.

As I reached the balcony of the house where my wife was anxiously awaiting my arrival, I saw in the west a big fire and asked Major Jalandoni: "What is that?"

"The effect of the bombing of Clark Field," he answered. "Some hangars and some of the fuel stores have been hit, but most of the planes escaped; since those that were destroyed were only dummies, according to my information." Such also was the information obtained by General Francisco.

I greeted my wife who told me that the children

were already fast asleep. Then in a corner of the balcony I listened to the report of General Francisco. He had ordered that all the Japanese nationals in the Islands be taken to concentration camps, but be treated well. Our own people, he said, were loyal, although he was keeping watch on the Sakdalistas (members of an organization headed by Benigno Ramos, a well-known pro-Japanese) lest they might turn fifth columnists. I reminded General Francisco that in agreement with the American military authorities, the Philippine Constabulary, under my direction, would continue to be responsible for the maintenance of public order and would assist the Civilian Emergency Administration in carrying out the measures which had been promulgated for the protection of the non-combatant population. General Francisco assured me that as far as the Constabulary assignments were concerned, I could be certain that the men under his command would prove equal to their duty. After instructing General Francisco to take necessary precautions so that at any time day and night I might be able to get in touch with him, I gave him leave to return to Manila.

To Major Jalandoni, I said: "Jalandoni, you know that much as I regretted dispensing with your services as my aide, I decided to have you appointed to your present post because most of the disturbing elements of Luzon are to be found in Pampanga and Nueva Ecija. I rely upon you to see to it that peaceful citizens are protected against robbers." The little fellow, only about five feet, four inches high but decorated for extraordinary valor in action, stood up at attention and said with evident determination: "I shall not disappoint you, sir."

I left the balcony to call Secretary Vargas on the telephone. "Any more news, George?" I asked.

"Nothing more, Mr. President," he answered.

"Well, I am spending the night here at my farm and will continue the trip to-morrow morning. I want to have a meeting of the Council of State at eleven o'clock. Make sure that Secretary Sison is present so that I may be fully informed of the measures that are being taken by the Civilian Emergency Administration. I also want former Secretary Manuel Roxas * to attend the meeting." My telephone conversation with Secretary Vargas ended my official conferences on that long and distressing day.

---

* Manuel Roxas had been my Secretary of Finance, but had presented his resignation to be a candidate for senator. He had been elected by one of the largest majorities that any senator had received. He was, and if he is still alive, must certainly now be, one of the most outstanding Filipino leaders. He had been governor of his province when still a very young man and was elected Speaker of the National Assembly at the expiration of his first term as governor and was one of my strongest supporters until we broke our political association in 1934, on the occasion of our disagreement over the acceptance or rejection of the Hare-Hawes-Cutting Law by the Filipino people. Upon the inauguration of the Commonwealth Government and after the Nationalist Party had again reunited under my leadership, I trusted him with some of the most difficult and complicated problems that confronted the Commonwealth, with most satisfactory results.

I went to bed after chatting with the family. With my wife there were at the farm her two sisters, my niece Mary, and, at this moment, all our children. Around four o'clock in the morning, I was awakened by the noise of airplanes passing not very far away. I did not make a move for I assumed that those were our own planes reconnoitering. After an early breakfast, we moved on to Manila, the family forming quite a caravan. I went directly to my house in Mariquina to which I had moved from Malacañan Palace in December, 1940, when I had fallen ill. It is a country home situated on the cliffs overlooking the Mariquina river, with mango, papaya, banana and orange trees, and a poultry yard. It was one of the fine results of Mrs. Quezon's industry. Adjoining this plot, I had another lot of about fourteen acres which I turned over to the refugees from Germany, for their use free of charge, except for the payment of the land tax, for a period of ten years. I had informed the State Department that I would receive several thousands of these refugees in the Philippines and I started to demonstrate my faith in the policy I had adopted by making my own personal contribution to their care.

The first thing I learned on my arrival at my house in Mariquina was about the bombing early that morning of Nichols Field. The flames and smoke could be seen from the tower of the house. So I concluded that the airplanes that had awakened me at 4 A.M. were

Japanese planes flying towards Nichols Field outside Manila.

Before noon of December 12, 1941, I received a telephone call from General MacArthur to inform me that he was sending his aide-de-camp, Lieutenant Colonel Huff, to see me on a very important and urgent matter. I told the General I would see his aide immediately. I was in my house situated on the cliffs overlooking the Mariquina River. When Colonel Huff arrived, he told me that General MacArthur wanted me to be ready on four hours' notice to go with him to Corregidor. I was shocked. I never imagined that I would ever have to take refuge on Corregidor. I had known for years that the fortress of Corregidor had been built as the last stronghold of the American forces in the Philippines and as a safe refuge for American Governors-General in case of grave danger. But it had never crossed my mind, even after the war had started, and Japanese control of the air had been definitely demonstrated, that there would ever come a time when *I had* to go to Corregidor. I was no *American* Governor-General, but the *Filipino* President of the Commonwealth. It is true that while Major General Grunert was still in command of the Philippine Department, United States High Commissioner Sayre, in one of the conferences that I held with him and General Grunert, brought up the question of the evacuation from Manila, in case of necessity, of both the High Commissioner and the President of the Commonwealth. It was Mr. Sayre's opinion that we should be in the same locality. But I made it clear to both Commissioner Sayre and General Grunert that I felt it my duty to remain in the midst of my people, at whatever risk, because my presence would help to keep up their morale. General Grunert understood my feeling and thought it was right. Moreover, nothing was said in that conference to indicate that a Japanese invasion of the Philippines was a possibility as long as the American flag was still in the Islands.

After the appointment of General MacArthur as the Commanding General of the United States Army Forces in the Far East on July 26, 1941, Commissioner Sayre again and again brought up with me the question of our evacuation. He proposed that he and I should hold a conference with General MacArthur about this matter; but I always refused to take the initiative for this conference, and the High Commissioner failed to bring it about.

I was, therefore, wholly unprepared for the startling message from General MacArthur. I asked Colonel Huff to inform General MacArthur that I would see him that night at the Manila Hotel; that I would arrive at the rear entrance, so that we might meet without being seen by any one. After eight o'clock that night, I went through the unlighted streets of Manila to the darkened "Winter Garden" of the Manila Hotel—an air-conditioned hall where, before the war, people used to dance during hot tropical nights. Colonel Huff was there waiting for me, and, upon my arrival, immediately went for his chief.

General MacArthur gave no signs of being worried. He was perfectly calm and composed. I asked him the meaning of his message, and he explained that he was only preparing me for the worst in case the Japanese should land in great force at different places, in which case, it would be unwise to keep our small army scattered all over Luzon. It was General MacArthur's plan—as I understood him—if such a situation should develop, to concentrate his army in the Bataan Peninsula and on Corregidor where he was determined to fight until the end.

"But, General," I demurred, "why would I have to go to Corregidor in that case? The military defense of the Philippines is primarily America's responsibility and not mine. I have already placed every Filipino soldier under your command. My own first duty is to take care of the civilian population and to maintain public order while you are fighting the enemy."

I further said: "Were I to go to Corregidor, my people would think I had abandoned them to seek safety under your protection. This I shall never do. I shall stay among my people and suffer the same fate that may befall them."

General MacArthur was not in the least ruffled by my answer. He simply said: "Mr. President, I expected that answer from such a gallant man as I know you to be."

He tried to convince me that it was not a question of running away from my countrymen. He reminded me of our agreement to declare Manila an open city, to avoid its destruction by enemy bombs and also to save the civilian population from the cruel effects of modern warfare. He pointed out to me that so far the Japanese had only been bombing military objectives and that if they should continue to follow that practice, as under international law they were bound to do, when we left Manila there would be nothing there to require my presence.

Then I asked: "Do you mean, General, that tomorrow you will declare Manila an open city and that some time during the day we shall have to go to Corregidor?"

He gave me a most emphatic *no* answer. He did not even seem to be certain that we would have to leave the city at all. He informed me that the force under the command of the Filipino General Capinpin had succeeded in preventing the landing of the Japanese in Lingayen Gulf, about one hundred miles to the north of Manila. Evidently he was only preparing me in advance to leave the city on four hours' notice. Noting, I suppose, that I still hesitated, he reminded me of the fact that the safety of my person was not a mere personal matter, but of great import to the Government of the Philippines of which I was the head. He asserted that it was his duty to prevent my falling into the enemy's hands. He was also of the opinion that as long as I was free, the occupation of Manila, or even of the Philippines, by the Japanese Army would not have the same significance under international law as if the Government had been captured or had surrendered.

My parting words that night were: "General, I shall convene to-morrow the Council of State and hear their views; then I will let you know my decision."

In the course of the conversation, I had asked General MacArthur whom I could take with me in case I should decide to go to Corregidor with him. He told me frankly that conditions in the fortress did not permit the evacuation of many civilians to that spot. Therefore, I could only take such officials as I considered absolutely necessary, and also my doctors in view of the bad condition of my health. However, he advised me strongly to bring my family along.

Two other persons only were present while the conference was taking place—my inseparable aide-de-camp, Colonel Nieto, a strong chap who had many times taken me in his arms like a child whenever I was too sick to go up a staircase, but not sick enough to obey my doctor's order to stay in bed; the other man was Lieutenant Colonel Huff, aide-de-camp to

*Arch erected by the tenants to Mrs. Quezon on her birthday,
February 19, 1940*

School teachers and pupils on the President's farm at Mount Arayat

Mount Arayat Hospital, inaugurated February 16, 1941. The ambulance was presented by President Quezon

Mrs. Quezon with the manager of the farm, the doctor, and aides-de-camp of the President

Port Area between Pier Seven and Manila Port Terminal Building, bombed by the Japanese on
December 24, 1941

Coast Artillery Unit of the Philippine Army leaving Manila

General MacArthur. Neither of them heard what was said between the General and me.

When I got home, I called my wife aside and repeated to her everything that General MacArthur had told me. I wanted her advice. She felt that it would be very painful to leave and be away from our people. "But this is war," she said, "total war—and the Military Commander should know better what should be done to win it.

"The winning of the war," Mrs. Quezon added, "is the only question before us. Nothing else matters."

I agreed. She had put her finger on the right spot.

"How about you and the children—will you come with me?" I inquired. Instead of answering my question she asked me another: "What do you want us to do?"

"I want you to remain here. The Japanese will respect you and treat you with every consideration. I have always dealt with their nationals in the Philippines with courtesy and justice. And you have done the same."

Mrs. Quezon answered: "I shall do as you wish, but my preference is to be with you. Remember the sacred words, 'For better or for worse, in sickness or in health till death doth us part.'...

"However," she counseled, "let us think the matter over to-night and to-morrow we should hear what our children have to say. They are grown up enough to be heard."

On the following day and before the meeting of the Council of State which I had called for eleven o'clock, the family council took place. Every member of the family was willing to do as I wished; but, like their mother, who had said nothing to them of our conversation the night before, they preferred to go with me wherever I went.

Despite this unanimous sentiment on the part of my family, I was still determined not to subject them to the horrible life that I knew would await us on Corregidor once we were beleaguered there.

At eleven o'clock that morning, I held my first meeting with the Council of State after the Japanese attack on the Philippines. Almost every day I held those meetings until my departure for Corregidor.

It is simply unbelievable how the average Filipino reacts in the presence of peril. All the members of the Council came on time to attend the session, not one showing the slightest sign of either fear or worry. I felt ashamed of myself, for I knew I was both afraid and worried.

Those present at the meeting were: Vice-President Sergio Osmeña, Speaker Jose Yulo, Chief Justice Jose Abad Santos, Majority Floor Leader Quintin Paredes, Secretary of Finance Serafin Marabut, Secretary of Justice Jose P. Laurel, Secretary of Agriculture and Natural Resources Rafael Alunan, Secretary of Commerce and Communications Sotero Baluyot, Secretary of Public Instruction Jorge Bocobo, Secretary of Labor Leon Guinto, Secretary of Health Jose Fabella, and Secretary to the President Jorge B. Vargas, who was also Acting Secretary of National Defense. The former Secretary of Justice, Teofilo Sison, who was then at the head of the most important war organization of the Commonwealth, the Civilian Emergency Administration, was of course present, as well as the Chief of Staff of the Philippine Army, General Basilio Valdes, and the Chief of the Philippine Constabulary, General Guillermo Francisco. Senator Roxas also came in the uniform of a Major of the Philippine Army, inducted into the service of the United States. This Filipino official, one of our most able, upon the creation of the Philippine Army in the first year of my administration, with other members of the National Assembly entered the Military School for Officers in Baguio and he with the others had been commissioned as reserve officers of the Philippine Army. On learning of the declaration of war between the United States and Japan, Senator Roxas asked to be called into active service and was appointed by General MacArthur his liaison officer with the Government of the Commonwealth.

At the meeting of the Council of State, I addressed myself first to General Valdes to find out if the whole Philippine Army had already been inducted into the service of the United States, what their total strength was, where they were distributed, etc. I also wanted to know from him the strength of the United States

Army then stationed in the Philippines. General Valdes reported that on September 1, 1941, ten divisions of the Philippine Army were inducted into the United States Army; that of these, seven divisions were in Luzon, two divisions in Visayas, and one division in Mindanao, a total of eighty thousand men; that the United States Army consisted of ten thousand Americans and ten thousand Philippine Scouts. Then I asked General Francisco to report the actual number of the Constabulary Force, the steps he had taken in accordance with previous instructions, and such other information as he might have. General Francisco informed us that he had about six thousand men distributed in the provinces of Luzon, Visayas, and Mindanao; that he had given orders to round up all the Japanese and to take them to internment camps. He also mentioned the splendid service that was being rendered by the volunteer guards which had been organized by the Civilian Emergency Administration in every city, town, and barrio in the Philippines, and placed under the supervision and control of the Constabulary. These men, according to General Francisco, were working day and night without compensation, guarding the roads and bridges against possible sabotage, and were also helping in the evacuation of the civilian population from dangerous zones that had been so designated by the Military Command.

After hearing the reports of the two Filipino general officers about their respective assignments, I requested former Secretary Sison to inform the Council of the activities of the Civilian Emergency Administration. He confirmed what General Francisco said about the magnificent work that the volunteer guards were doing, pointing out the fact that they were receiving no compensation. He also reported that in the air raids of the day before against Clark Field in Pampanga and that morning against Nichols Field in Pasay, no heavy casualties had been suffered by the civilian population for the Japanese had bombed only military objectives, and those with surprising accuracy. I asked Secretary Sison the situation as to food supply, and he said that Dr. Victor Buencamino, the Food Administrator, had ample supplies in store, and that he had no fear the people might be starved even if the Japanese blockaded the Islands for several months.

At this point, the Secretary of Agriculture, Mr. Alunan, intervened and reminded us of what we already knew about the results of the policy which a few months before we had adopted, namely to make the people plant short-time crops. Secretary Alunan was optimistic as far as this aspect of the war situation was concerned. Secretary Guinto of Labor expressed gratification over the wholehearted coöperation that the labor elements were extending to the war efforts of the Government. Then I turned to Speaker Yulo, the chief member of the Council of State after the Vice-President, and asked him if the National Assembly would convene according to law to certify the results of the general elections which had just been held.* The Speaker answered that the majority of the members of the Assembly were already in Manila. I informed Speaker Yulo that I would call the National Assembly into special session to consider war measures. I adjourned the meeting of the Council of State to convene again the following day at the same hour unless sooner called by the President. Air raid or no air raid, the Council met every day until my departure for Corregidor.

I issued the call for the special session and I am proud and thankful to say that the members of the National Assembly attended to their duties despite the daily visits of Japanese planes over Manila. When it became evident that we were completely helpless against air attack and that it was most unlikely the Philippine Legislature would hold its next regular session which was to open on January 1, 1942, the National Assembly passed into history approving a resolution which reaffirmed the abiding faith of the Filipino people in, and their loyalty to, the United States. The Assembly also enacted a law granting the President of the Philippines all the powers that under the Philippine Constitution may be delegated to him

---

* In the general elections, the President, Vice-President, Senators, and Representatives for the ensuing administration had just been chosen, and the National Assembly, under existing law, was to convene in December to certify the election returns.

in time of war. This act would become invalid unless
reënacted after a certain period had elapsed.

During luncheon, Maria, my elder daughter, asked
my permission to organize her girl friends for the
purpose of soliciting public contributions to buy
Christmas gifts for the "boys at the front." In the
Philippines, public contributions may not be solicited
except with the permission of the Government, to
avoid racketeering. I applauded the idea and gave my
consent.

Maria and her friends, Helen Benitez, Lulu Reyes,
my other daughter, Zeneida, my nieces Mary and
Charing, and a large number of girls from the Philippine Women's University, the Centro Escolar University and Catholic colleges, worked every day, first
to solicit contributions and later to make up packages
in the Social Hall of Malacañan. How I admired those
young girls wrapping up their packages even while
the air raids were going on. God bless them! The
Philippines *Herald* and the *Tribune* helped the girls
with their publicity campaign. The last thing that
my daughter Maria did before leaving Manila was to
give instructions for sending these gifts to the boys at
the front. Indeed, due to this fact, we departed from
Malacañan and not from our house on the Mariquina on our hazardous voyage to the south, which
finally ended in Washington, D. C.

In the first week of the war, although I continued
to have fever every night and was being either carried

in somebody's arms or pushed about in a wheel-chair, I visited the Philippine General Hospital when I heard that many men, women, and children had been wounded in a very severe air raid on Camp Nichols. With me came my aide-de-camp, Colonel Nieto, my daughter Maria and my son Manuel, Zeneida having remained home with her mother. As we passed through the streets of Manila and its suburbs, with the presidential flag flying on my car, the people shouted, "*Mabuhay*—long live America, the Philippines, and President Quezon!"

In front of the headquarters of the Philippine Army there was a long line of young men waiting for their turn to enlist. It seems that the very defenselessness of Manila made these young men the more eager to fight the invaders. I stopped my car, made a sign to silence their cheering, and said, "My boys, I am proud of you," and went on. Later I learned that even after Manila's fall and after our forces in Luzon had retreated to Bataan, the Filipinos in the other Islands were seeking to enlist in the Philippine Army. If we had only had the necessary number of rifles, there would have been no lack of Filipinos to use them.

At the Philippine General Hospital, Dr. Antonio G. Sison, the Dean of the College of Medicine of the State University as well as the director of the hospital, met me in his physician's gown, stained with blood. He looked very serious and said: "Mr. President, there are already here many wounded and many more are arriving." No more competent physician or executive have I ever known in my life than Dr. Sison. Besides all this, he has both the physical and moral courage that make heroes of men. He was also my family physician. Placing me in a wheel-chair, he led me through the corridors to see the suffering victims. Doctors and nurses were all at work. Fortunately, since the inauguration of the Commonwealth Government, I had given special attention to hospital facilities. All over the Islands new hospitals had been built and the Philippines General Hospital in Manila had been practically doubled in capacity, equipment, and personnel. So this institution was ready to meet the unexpected demands upon it.

After leaving the hospital, I continued my drive and visited other sections of the city until nightfall. Seeing the effect that my presence had upon the people, I did the same thing on different days after the air raids, until I was compelled by circumstances beyond my control to leave Manila.

CHAPTER XII

Corregidor and Bataan

A̲T NINE o'clock in the morning of December 24, 1941, Colonel Huff, aide-de-camp to General MacArthur, came to inform me that, in accordance with a previous understanding, I was to leave for Corregidor at two o'clock in the afternoon. The last meeting of the Cabinet was held at ten o'clock the same morning, and we decided finally which of the government officials were to accompany me to Corregidor. To them all I revealed the agreement with General MacArthur that in order to avoid the destruction of the city and save the civilian population from the horrors of indiscriminate bombardment from Japanese planes and siege-guns, Manila was to be declared an open city.

My last instructions to my colleagues who were left behind were that they should do everything in their power to minimize the sufferings of the civilian population. "Keep your faith in America, no matter what happens. She will never let you down."

Every one of them wanted to accompany me, even though obliged to leave their families behind in Manila, but for lack of space and other obvious reasons, I could take only Vice-President Osmeña, Chief Justice José Abad Santos, Major General Basilio J. Valdes, Colonel Manuel Nieto, my aide-de-camp, and Serapio D. Canceran, my private secretary. I advised them to be ready at the Presidential Landing at two o'clock in the afternoon. It was a heart-breaking separation from men who, through thick and thin, for so many years had been my friends and my loyal supporters. But I was consoled by the fact that I was leaving behind a people on whom I could depend to do their duty by their country, regardless of the consequences to their lives and their fortunes.

In my heart of hearts, I was almost certain then that it would be a long time before we could meet again. I embraced everybody good-by and we parted. Immediately thereafter my family and my senior aide-de-camp, Colonel Nieto, accompanied me to the Palace of Malacañan. We found in the Social Hall here about fifty young girls with Mrs. Sofia de Veyra, the secretary to Mrs. Quezon, wrapping up the Christmas gifts for the soldiers, gifts which had been collected by public subscription upon the initiative of my eldest daughter Maria, with the help of her sister Zeneida, their cousins Mary Angara and Rosario Carrasco, and their friends Helen Benitez, Lulu Reyes and the Fabella girls. My two daughters immediately joined the girls and worked with them. By noon—at the usual time—Japanese bombers were flying over the city and began bombarding the Port Area in the immediate vicinity of the Presidential Landing, where, at two o'clock, we were supposed to embark. My last hours in the Palace of Malacañan could not have been more dramatic and inspiring. In that historic palace, the official residence of Spanish and American Governors-General, and then of the President of the Commonwealth, were those young girls completely unperturbed by the air raid and the bursting bombs, and attending to their self-assigned tasks. I thanked God that I was permitted to witness the patriotism, the courage, and the self-possession of the Filipino women who, throughout the history of their country, have never failed to share the sacrifices of the Filipino men. This breathtaking scene steeled my heart for the grim struggle ahead. Such a country, with such women, even though only in their teens, could never accept defeat! No Japanese planes, no Japanese Army, no Japanese Navy, not the whole combined forces of the Axis powers could ever permanently conquer the Filipino people!

By two o'clock in the afternoon, the Japanese bombers were still pouring bombs on the Port Area and on the bay. Hence, our departure was delayed. At three o'clock, although the all-clear signal had not been sounded, General MacArthur's aide, Colonel Huff, and Major Manuel Roxas, his liaison officer, came to Malacañan to inform me that the hour of departure had arrived. It was heart-rending to part from my wife's sister, Emilia, who had been my lifelong pal, and her daughter Mary, my dear niece. While my wife and children were embracing and kissing Emilia and Mary, I turned to Secretary Vargas, my faithful, hard-working, able, honest, and public-spirited secretary, to give him my final instructions. "God bless you, George, and lead you in the right path. You have my absolute confidence, and I am sure you will not fail me. Good-by." Vargas merely said, with suppressed feelings: "Mr. President, no matter what happens, you can count upon me, whether here in Malacañan, if the Japanese allow me to remain, or in my house in Kawilihan." No other word was said. That was enough for two men who had worked together in good and evil days for so many years.

From the Presidential Landing, in two launches, the party headed for the S.S. *Mayon*, nearly a mile away. Then I realized the air raid was not over, for there were still a few planes dropping bombs in the bay. They were trying to sink every ship in their view. Fortunately no member of my family noticed the danger to which we were exposed. They would have been gravely anxious, but for me, rather than for their own lives.

At last we boarded the S.S. *Mayon*, but the ship was not ready to move. The chief engineer and his first assistant had gone ashore to take some clothes and were not expected until the evening. The captain was there. For nothing in the world would he leave his ship, since the Japanese had become masters of the air over the bay. His name, now immortal, was Captain Aguirre. When, two months later, the *Mayon* was finally discovered by the Japanese bombers to be transporting supplies by order of General Mac-Arthur, this heroic man went to the bottom of the sea with his ship. I ordered the captain to sail, chief engineer or no. The ship-owner, Mr. Madrigal, my lifelong friend, was there to see me off. Under his direction, the third engineer was able to start the engines after one hour and a half of hard work, during which time the bombing of the bay did not cease. If the Japanese pilots had only known that U. S. High Commissioner Sayre, together with his wife and son, members of his staff and the President of the Commonwealth, were aboard the *Mayon*, they would never have let our ship get away. They would have been decorated by His Imperial Majesty Hirohito for having murdered two men whom His Majesty had deigned to receive into his august presence not long before. But evidently no fifth columnists were either in the vicinity of the High Commissioner's residence or in mine.

All the while, and until the last Japanese bomber disappeared from the sky, everybody on board, including Commissioner Sayre and I, had our life-belts on. No, there were two who did not wear them: my aide-de-camp, Colonel Nieto, and my daughter Maria, who put on her life-belt only when her mother commanded her to do it; but, at the first chance, she regularly took it off again, until caught without it by either her mother or by me. At six-thirty I was hungry, and asked that dinner be served. Our whole party took their seats at the tables, but the Commissioner and his family and party did not seem to have any appetite. I insisted that they join us, for it might be our last meal. The argument carried the point, and we all enjoyed the banquet. There were cocktails, wine, soup, fish, meat, a variety of fruits, dessert and coffee. It was perfect, but it proved to be for us all the last example for many a week, not only of a feast, but even of a simple, well-balanced and sufficient diet.

At dusk, we arrived at the pier of Corregidor, at the very spot where, with Major General Kilbourne, I had landed in 1935, to be received with a gun salute and a regimental guard of honor. This time only the commander of the Fortress, General Moore, and his aide-de-camp, were there to receive me. After taking me into his car, General Moore said: "You came just late enough to escape the bombing of Mariveles Bay. A French ship anchored in that bay was sunk half an hour before your arrival." Good luck seemed to be with us. We escaped two bombings, one at the start, and another at the end, of our trip across Manila Bay.

General Moore showed me to my quarters in the tunnel. I was to stay with the male members of my staff in the same lateral to which High Commissioner Sayre and his staff were assigned, and my wife and daughters were to share another lateral with Mrs. Sayre and the American ladies. Each lateral had but one shower, one toilet, and one wash basin for its occupants. There were also two small houses not too far from the tunnel, one for Commissioner Sayre and the other for me, which we could use when there were no air raids. General Moore apologized for thus piling us in a single, long, but narrow corridor, dark and without fresh air. As proof that this apparent disregard for our comfort and health was not due either to lack of courtesy or desire on his part properly to accommodate us, he informed me that the Supreme Commander of the USAFFE, General MacArthur, his Chief of Staff, General Sutherland, his aide-de-camp, Colonel Huff, the Quartermaster General, General Drake, the Adjutant General, Colonel Seals, the Chief Health Officer, Colonel Smith, and Major Roxas, the liaison officer, were also to share with us the same lateral. All told, there would be twenty-eight of us in that place.

I thanked General Moore and begged him not to worry about me. In a light vein I reminded him of the fact that I had been an insurrecto, well trained by actual experience to stand the hardships of war. "This is a first-class hotel," I remarked, "compared with those habitations during my days as a *guerrillero* against your army." General Moore appreciated the

Mrs. Quezon, Mrs. MacArthur, President Quezon, young MacArthur,
Miss Maria Aurora Quezon, in the bomb defense tunnel on Corregidor

Wounded Filipino soldiers awaiting medical attention at an advanced dressing station on Bataan Peninsula

joke. He thought, perhaps, that I would miss the splendor and comfort of Malacañan Palace. As a matter of fact, I did not. I was even grateful that in some insignificant way I could thus share the ordeal that our own soldiers at the front were going through at that very moment.

Before midnight of the same day, General Mac-Arthur, with his wife and son, his Chief of Staff, Major General Sutherland, Colonel Willoughby, chief of the Intelligence Service, Colonel Seals, Adjutant General, Colonel Huff, his aide-de-camp, and many other officers arrived at Corregidor aboard the steamer *Don Esteban.*

The following morning General MacArthur and I had our first meeting in Corregidor, a practice which thereafter we followed every day, and sometimes more than once a day until my departure from the Fortress.

It was Christmas Eve, which Catholics celebrate with a midnight mass. At 12 o'clock that night, my family and party and I heard mass inside the tunnel with an improvised altar. When the priest read *"Gloria in excelsis Deo et in terra pax hominibus bonae voluntatis,"* the heavenly song sung by the angels almost two thousand years before sounded in my ears with an almost ironical tone. Glory to God on high and on earth peace to men of good will. Peace! Where were the men of good will when in all parts of the globe men were butchering one another at that solemn hour? Did the Divine Child who descended upon the earth to preach brotherly love die in vain? ...

After the midnight mass it is customary among Catholics to wish everybody Merry Christmas. Who could give expression to that wish when all of us were sunk in the depths of grief? I kissed my wife and children. "Good-night, sweetheart; good-night, Dad"; and each went to bed.

It was an awful night, for I coughed all the time. From the beginning of the war my malady had gone from bad to worse. The lack of fresh air and humidity of the tunnel had an immediate effect upon my bronchials. But although awake, I refused to think. I closed my mind tightly and allowed no thought to come in. The decision had been made and I was determined to face its dire consequences. To ruminate over the past—the peaceful, happy, and steady progress of my people—or to remember the dear ones whom I had left behind would be a self-inflicted torture hard to endure. To look to the future was of no use. Victory, of course. Of this I was certain. But when? God only knew. In the meantime, for those who were in Corregidor or Bataan, including my family, there were only two alternatives—death, which was perhaps the less dreadful of the two, or long capivity in the hands of a ruthless enemy. All of that was in my subconscious mind, but I would not let it come up into my consciousness.

The following day was Christmas. I was dumb and stupid, but managed to appear unconcerned.

At eleven A.M. General MacArthur came to make a call. He and his family, with some members of his staff, had arrived in Corregidor several hours after us, quite late that night. He was going to occupy General Moore's house at the top of the hill and locate his office in another house near-by. He had left all the necessary orders for the declaration of Manila as an open city and had sent for the Japanese Consul General (then in detention) in order that the Consul might communicate this fact to the General in command of the invasion army.

Meanwhile, the American and Filipino troops were retreating to Bataan, fighting a delaying action so as to reach the Peninsula with their full strength. The orders were being carried out magnificently and to the letter. The Philippine Army was writing history. The General was certain that he and I would be proud of our handiwork. That was all for the present. He would see me every day at the same time and at any other time that there was some important news.

At noon there was a Christmas dinner, turkey for everybody, including the soldiers. Our lateral was in the hospital located in the tunnel, and we ate our meals in the dining-room for the doctors and nurses. We were served after them. The sight of the turkey gave me almost a thrill. Not that I cared for the meat of this bird, for I do not, but because it momentarily changed my mood. After all, the prospect did not look so bad. The U.S.A., I thought, must be well provided to stand a long siege. I was in high spirits during the dinner, and with the wine I had brought from Manila toasted our triumphal return to that city in time to celebrate in Malacañan the birthday of my wife, February 19th.

After dinner we went out of the tunnel for a breath of fresh air. The view of the deep blue sea and the green Mariveles mountain on that glorious, sunny December day was extremely exhilarating. Before I realized it, my mind was dwelling upon memories of a long and distant past—my days spent as an insurrecto on the tip of this very Peninsula, and my surrender in Mariveles. Would the Army, fast concentrating in Bataan, meet the same fate and surrender to the enemy as I had done forty years earlier? This thought brought me back to the realities of the situation which we were confronting. I went to my lateral to shut, not only my eyes, but my mind, again. I took a siesta and then played bridge until suppertime.

Another bad night with much coughing, and the 26th of December arrived.

After breakfast, Dr. Trepp and General Valdes, the Chief of Staff of the Philippine Army (and at this time acting Secretary of National Defense), who were staying in my lateral, and had heard me coughing on the two previous nights, suggested that I send some one to Manila to get all the medicines that I might need. Dr. Trepp is a native Swiss who had acquired Philippine citizenship. He is a lung specialist whom I took to Corregidor because of the recurrence in December of the year before of my tuberculosis. General Valdes, like the late General Wood, is a professional physician who had served in the first World War in France as Army doctor, and who later became an officer of the Constabulary, next Chief of that organization, and upon formation of the Philippine Army, succeeded General Paulino Santos as Chief of Staff.

On December 27th I sent my aide, Colonel Nieto, to Manila to get the required medicines.

My long association with Colonel Nieto first began at the time of his graduation from my alma mater, the College of San Juan de Letran. He had been a fine track athlete and perhaps the best fooball player of his day in the Philippines.

It is traditional in San Juan de Letran for the Dominican friars who conduct that college to tell the undergraduates of the student lives of those who have preceded them and later distinguished themselves in their careers. After my election as Resident Commissioner to the United States, and particularly upon my return to the Philippines in 1916 after the passage of the Jones Act, the professors of San Juan de Letran had spoken proudly of me. The whole student body went out to join in the public welcome which on that occasion was tendered me, and they formed a guard of honor in front of the college building when the Quezon Gate was opened in the old city wall facing the college. There I met young Nieto.

After the completion of his studies, Nieto offered his services to me. He was not interested in the salary, for his father, an old Spaniard who owned landed estates in the tobacco provinces of northern Luzon, had enough with which to support him. Of course, Nieto received a salary when I appointed him secretary of the Senate, of which I had become the President. From the time that he entered the public service he had always been by my side when he thought there might be any risk to my life. After my election as President of the Philippines, he was sent to the Officers' Training Camp in Baguio, where he graduated with distinction and was commissioned as Captain of the Philippine Army in the Reserve Corps. Later I called him to active duty as aide-de-camp. Nieto knows no fear. During the whole time that we were on Corregidor he never ran for the tunnel when bombs were bursting around us, and his loyalty has been such that I always felt that he would give his life to save mine. Some people, jealous of his prowess, have called him, disparagingly, my bodyguard. As a matter of fact, I never did have a bodyguard. Even as President of the Philippines I was accustomed to walk around in public without a policeman or a secret service man, or Nieto, or any one, by my side. On one occasion, my friend Roy Howard of the Scripps-Howard newspapers, who saw me alone in the midst of a large group of all kinds of people, advised me against it. I may say that it is not lack of fear, of which I have plenty, as I have discovered to my discomfiture on many instances, which caused me to be seemingly careless about my personal safety. Rather, it is my conviction that if a public man is marked to be eliminated, no amount of police, bodyguards or anything of the sort can save him, as history has shown again and again. Furthermore, I know the psychology of my people. They would have resented, as evidence of lack of confidence in them, their chosen President's always being surrounded by armed men. On the other hand, the Filipino returns lavishly, with a loyalty that knows no bounds, the affection and confidence of those whom he has elevated to high office. Of course, when there was real need for haste, motorcycle policemen preceded my car to open the traffic. On formal occasions either a cavalry or motorized artillery escort accompanied my car.

Reverting to my story: I sent Colonel Nieto to Manila aboard the presidential launch *Baler* and he came back the following day, the 27th. He had been to Malacañan Palace, had had a long conference with Secretary Vargas, then the Mayor of Greater Manila, and had seen Mr. Andres Soriano, who offered the one remaining plane he had for my family and me to use in order to go to Australia. Mr. Soriano's air service was a Philippine corporation which had been operating for some time before the attack on Pearl Harbor. Under the franchise granted by the Commonwealth Government, in case of emergency the Government had the right to take over and operate the airplanes owned by the company. Upon the beginning of hostilities Mr. Soriano had offered all his planes to General MacArthur, who, of course, accepted the offer, but allowed the company to continue the service until the Army actually needed them. It was one of these planes that was offered to me. With many thanks I declined it. Colonel Nieto also brought a copy of the newspaper containing General MacArthur's proclamation declaring Manila an open city. Here it is:

> In order to spare the metropolitan area from possible ravages of attack either by air or ground, Manila is hereby declared an open city, without the characteristics of a military objective. In order that no excuse may be given for a possible mistake, the American High Commissioner, the Commonwealth Government, and all combatant military installations will be withdrawn from its environs as rapidly as possible.
>
> The municipal government will continue to function with its police powers reinforced by constabulary troops, so that the normal protec-

tion of life and property may be preserved. Citizens are requested to maintain obedience to constituted authorities and continue the normal processes of business.

Later in the day General MacArthur stated that the declaration of Manila as an open city had been announced; that he was getting out of the city as fast as possible the few remaining armed forces there; that a delaying action was being fought by our men to cover the retreat of the Army to Bataan. After the conference with General MacArthur, I called my War Cabinet together to transmit to them the information just received. At this time the War Cabinet consisted of the Vice-President as Secretary of Public Instruction, Chief Justice Jose Abad Santos, Secretary of Finance and Agriculture, and General Basilio J. Valdes, Secretary of National Defense and Public Works and Communications. Also present was Major Manuel Roxas, who, though no longer a member of the Cabinet, was always invited to attend whenever a really important matter was to be considered.

On the 27th, General MacArthur reported that the Treasury Building and the old church of Santo Domingo had been bombed despite the declaration of Manila as an open city. It may be imagined with what indignation and pain we received this cruel news. Of course, no damage was done to the government gold and silver for, with the exception of small amounts that were kept in the Treasury in Manila for use as required, the rest had always been kept in a vault in Corregidor. The bulk of the paper currency, however, was kept in the Treasury for the ordinary use of the government and the people. In order to find out how much damage had been done to the Treasury, I sent Colonel Nieto again to Manila with instructions to Secretary Vargas to send as much paper currency as possible. This duly reached us on Corregidor.

On this same day General MacArthur reported another bit of information which distressed me personally even more than the bad news of the day before. The college of San Juan de Letran and the buildings of the Philippines *Herald* had been razed to the ground by Japanese bombs. The college of San Juan de Letran, as repeatedly stated in this story, was my alma mater. The Philippines *Herald* was a newspaper that had been published, on my initiative, by Filipino capital, in the English language, to express the Filipino point of view on public questions.

A Tokyo broadcast in English, Spanish, and Tagalog, addressed to President Quezon, offered the following conditions as prerequisite for the acceptance by Japan of the status of Manila as an open city: (1) that all military camps and establishments be withdrawn from Manila and the approaches to the city, and (2) that Filipino armies coöperate with the Japanese forces and cease all resistance.

Before noon on December 29th, Corregidor had its first taste of bombardment from the air. With my wife and children and a group of officers, including doctors and nurses, I was outside the tunnel when the sound of bursting bombs and anti-aircraft guns informed us that it was time to seek cover in the tunnel. Everybody moved in, but my daughter Maria was not in any hurry. Colonel Nieto had to push her in for my wife would not enter the tunnel before making sure that all the children were safe. Soon, through the main entrance to the hospital, the wounded began to arrive at the hospital. I asked my wife to go into her lateral and take the girls with her so as to relieve them of the distress of seeing our casualties. While the bombing was going on, my anxiety for General MacArthur and his family was indescribable. I knew that both his house and his office were at top-side, in the vicinity of the main hospital. The latter evidently had suffered a direct hit, for some of the wounded brought into the tunnel had been hit near the hospital. There was no one who could say what had happened to the General. One of General Moore's staff officers did report one fact which afforded some relief to my anxiety. According to this officer, there was an air-raid shelter near the house and the office.

On December 30th, the Japanese planes made their second visit to Corregidor, evidently with as much gusto as on the day before. But neither in casualties nor in property damage was their bombing so severe as the preceding one, and yet in our tunnel the effect of this second bombardment was bad. On the day before, the Japanese had directed their bombs only against top-side and while they practically demolished everything in sight up there, no bombs had fallen on "bottom-side." So the tunnel had not been in the least affected. The bombing of the 29th damaged the lighting system and broke the water pipes serving the tunnel. We were left in darkness. Casualties that were brought into the hospital had to be attended with flashlights. For some days we had to drink and cook in salty water.

The all-clear signal had hardly been sounded and some lights restored, when a long radiogram was delivered to me containing a proclamation of the President of the United States addressed to the people of the Philippines. On reading the message I was instantly electrified and thrilled. The dungeon where my sick body was lying lost its depressing gloom. I asked to be taken out to the open space, for the world was too small to contain the emotions that almost burst my heart. Indeed, I was so invigorated that I gave my wife a jolt when she saw me walking fast through the long corridor of the tunnel out into the setting sun. The receipt of the President's proclamation fortunately took place the day preceding my inauguration, and so it was a most welcome and timely addition to the address I had prepared. Indeed, I was almost tempted to dispense with my entire manuscript and limit myself to the reading of the President's message.

President Roosevelt's proclamation had at last broken wide open the doors of my conscious mind. After the receipt of the message, I held a Cabinet meeting and read it to them. Giving vent to my feelings, I told my colleagues that the sacrifices our country was making were not in vain. There was a future so brilliant and full of promise—no, not promise, but certainty. The Philippines would not only be independent and free, but its independence and freedom were to be protected and safeguarded by the "entire resources in men and materials of the United States."

The 30th of December, 1941, was the date set by law for the end of my first and the beginning of my second administration. At about 4 o'clock in the afternoon, the ceremonies of my second installation as President of the Commonwealth were held. A platform had been improvised in the leveled clearing outside the tunnel used as the officers' mess. Upon this platform the United States High Commissioner was seated on my right, the Supreme Commander of the United States Army Forces in the Far East, General MacArthur, on my left, Vice-President Sergio Osmeña to the right of the High Commissioner, and Chief Justice Jose Abad Santos, of the Supreme Court, to the left of General MacArthur. In front of the platform in the first row were my War Cabinet, the Commander of the Fort of Corregidor, General Moore, the Commander of Artillery, General King, the Quartermaster General, General Drake, and my family; behind there were the high ranking officers of the United States and Philippine Armies, my staff, doctors and nurses, a few American ladies, and the Filipino laborers of Corregidor led by Civil Engineer Castro.

The ceremonies were solemn; indeed, to me more solemn than those of my first inauguration, despite the fact that at that historic event of November 15, 1935, a brilliant and distinguished audience had assembled in full force.

On this my second inauguration, there was no adornment but the American and Filipino flags flying on either side of my chair, and before me only a limited audience. Yet, once again I say, it was more solemn than my first inauguration—nay, it was dramatic.

The Government to be inaugurated faced a life and death struggle. In 1935, my inaugural address was concerned with policies and plans for the future, to be carried out under the reign of peace; emphasis was laid upon the gratitude of the Filipino people for the boon they had received from the hands of the United States in the establishment of the Commonwealth and in the assurance that by 1946 that government would be succeeded by an independent Philippine Republic. Those expressions of gratitude were now being put to the crucial test. And we had stood true and kept the faith. The Government, our Army, our people all over the Philippines, even to the farthest corner, were now giving testimony of the reality of those expressions by their sufferings, their losses, and with their lives.

Chief Justice Jose Abad Santos administered the oath of office and I felt the burden of my new responsibility to be incomparably heavier than when confronted only with economic, social, and to a certain extent, political, problems. These, although enough to test the capacity of men better qualified than I was, now seemed to have passed into insignificance as compared with the one single problem lying ahead—war and war only, to face which required fortitude, determination and courage far beyond what I had been given by my Creator while in the womb of my mother.

After taking the oath, I delivered the following address:

> "On November 15, 1935, I took my oath of office as first President of the Philippines under the most favorable auspices. The Philippines was at peace and the Filipino people were happy and contented. At the inaugural ceremonies held in the city of Manila, there were present high dignitaries of the Government of the United States, and a vast multitude of Filipinos deeply grateful to America and thrilled with the vision of a bright future.

"Today I am assuming for the second time the duties of the Presidency under entirely different conditions. We are in the grip of war, and the seat of the government has been temporarily transferred from the city of Manila to a place in close proximity to the headquarters of our armed forces, where I am in constant touch with General Douglas MacArthur. All around us enemy bombs are dropping and anti-aircraft guns are roaring. In defenseless cities and towns air raids are killing women and children and destroying century-old churches, monasteries, and schools.

"Six years ago, there was every reason to believe that the Filipino people would be able to prepare themselves for independence in peace and without hindrance. In my first inaugural address, I outlined a program intended to lay the foundations for a government that will, in the language of our Constitution, promote the general welfare and secure to the Filipino people and their posterity 'the blessings of independence under a régime of justice, liberty, and democracy.'

"Our task of nation-building was in progress when suddenly, on December 8, 1941, the Philippines became the victim of wanton aggression. We are resisting this aggression with everything that we have. Our soldiers, American and Filipino, under the leadership of General Douglas MacArthur, one of the greatest soldiers of our times, are fighting on all fronts with gallantry and heroism that will go down in history. In the face of frequent air raids which are causing so much death, suffering, and destruction, our civilian population are maintaining their morale. Despite the enemy's temporary superiority in the air and on land and sea, we have been able to check the rapid advance of the invading armies. America and the Philippines may well be proud of the heroic struggle that our forces are putting up against the invader.

"At the present time we have but one task— to fight with America for America and the Philippines. To this task we shall devote all our resources in men and materials. Ours is a great cause. We are fighting for human liberty and justice, for those principles of individual freedom which we all cherish and without which life would not be worth living. Indeed, we are fighting for our own independence. It is to maintain this independence, these liberties and these freedoms, to banish fear and want among all peoples, and to establish a reign of justice for all the world, that we are sacrificing our lives and all that we possess. The war may be long-drawn and hard-fought, but with the determination of freedom-loving peoples everywhere to stamp out the rule of violence and terrorism from the face of the earth, I am absolutely convinced that final and complete victory will be ours.

"Soon after the outbreak of the war, I received a message from President Roosevelt expressing admiration for the gallantry of our soldiers and the courageous stand of our civilian population. Yesterday, the President of the United States issued a proclamation which, I am sure, will hearten our fighting men and thrill the soul of every American and Filipino in this land. This is the proclamation:

" 'News of your gallant struggle against the Japanese aggressors has elicited the profound admiration of every American. As President of the United States, I know that I speak for all our people on this solemn occasion. The resources of the United States, of the British Empire, of the Netherlands East Indies, and the Chinese Republic have been dedicated by their people to the utter and complete defeat of the Japanese War Lords. In this great struggle of the Pacific the loyal Americans of the Philippine Islands are called upon to play a crucial rôle. They have played, and they are playing tonight, their part with the greatest gallantry. As President I wish to express to them my feeling of sincere admiration for the fight they are now making. The people of the United States will never forget what the people of the Philippine Islands are doing these days and will do in the days to come. I give to the people of the Philippines my solemn pledge that their freedom will be redeemed and their independence established and protected. The entire resources in men and materials of the United States stands behind that pledge. It is not for me or for the people of this country to tell you where your duty lies. We are engaged in a great and common cause. I count on every Philippine man, woman, and child to do his duty. We will do ours. I give you this message from the Navy: The Navy Department tonight announces the Japanese Government is circulating rumors for the obvious purpose of persuading the United States to disclose the location and intentions of the American Pacific Fleets. It is obvious that these rumors are intended for, and directed at, the Philippine Islands. The Philippines may rest assured that while the United States Navy will not be tricked into disclosing vital information, the fleet is not idle. The United States Navy is following an intensive and well-planned campaign against Japanese forces which will result in positive assistance to the defense of the Philippine Islands.'

"My heart, and I know the hearts of all Americans and Filipinos in this country, are filled with gratitude for the reassuring words of the President of the United States. My answer, our answer, to him is that every man, woman, and child in the Philippines will do his duty. No matter what sufferings and sacrifices this war may impose upon us we shall stand by America with undaunted spirit, for we know that upon the outcome of this war depend the happiness, liberty, and security not only of this generation but of the generations yet unborn.

"Mr. High Commissioner, may I ask you to convey to the President of the United States our profound gratitude for the noble sentiments expressed in his proclamation. The Filipino people are particularly grateful for his abiding interest in our welfare and for his pledge to assure and protect our freedom and independence.

"General MacArthur, there are no words in any language that can express to you the deep gratitude of the Filipino people and my own for your devotion to our cause, the defense of our country, and the safety of our population. I trust that the time will come when we may express this sentiment to you in a more appropriate manner.

"To all Americans in the Philippines, soldiers and civilians alike, I want to say that our common ordeal has fused our hearts in a single purpose and an everlasting affection.

"My fellow-countrymen, this is the most momentous period of our history. As we face the grim realities of war, let us rededicate ourselves to the great principles of freedom and democracy for which our forefathers fought and died. The present war is being fought for these same principles. It demands from us courage, determination, and unity of action. In taking my oath of office, I make the pledge for myself, my government, and my people, to stand by America and fight with her until victory is won. I am resolved, whatever the consequences to myself, faithfully to fulfil this pledge. I humbly invoke the help of Almighty God that I may have the wisdom and fortitude to carry out this solemn obligation."

Then the United States High Commissioner read a congratulatory message from President Roosevelt which had been sent some time before the attack on Pearl Harbor.

After this, General MacArthur made a few remarks which were deeply felt by all present.

After the inauguration there was shaking of hands —strong, expressive, significant, hand-clasps. But none dared utter the word "congratulations." I hope not one of those present pitied me at that moment. I could not have borne it. Instead, the shaking of hands and the expression of their faces evinced confidence which was encouraging and inspiring. God knows I needed it.

On December 31st General MacArthur reported that his troops had fallen back to a line reaching within thirty miles from Manila. On the north our forces had readjusted and shortened their lines.

On this same day the National Treasurer, Mr. Apolinario S. de Leon, came with more paper currency and reported that Pio Pedrosa, one of the most trusted, efficient, and loyal servants of the Government, had been seriously wounded on the occasion of the bombing of the Treasury. With Treasurer de Leon came Mr. Franco, the Chief Electrician of the Bureau of Public Works, with a recording apparatus to make a record of the inaugural address which was to be broadcast from Manila, for Corregidor did not as yet have a broadcasting station.

By 8 o'clock in the evening of January 1st, the aide of General MacArthur came on behalf of the General to request that I join him at 9 o'clock that same evening at the house he was occupying not very far from the tunnel. At the appointed time I found there the General, his Chief of Staff, Major General Sutherland, the Chief of the Intelligence Service, Colonel Willoughby, and the United States High Commissioner, Mr. Sayre. At once it was evident that something serious was in the offing. General MacArthur read aloud to those present a telegram which he had received from Washington to the effect that if my evacuation could possibly be accomplished, I should be taken to Washington and function there as the head of the Commonwealth Government in exile and as the symbol of the redemption of the Philippines. The telegram further stated that if I was willing to be evacuated and in the opinion of General

MacArthur this was feasible, the General should effect it with the best means available to him or with the assistance of the Navy. Then General MacArthur read his proposed answer in which he stated that my evacuation was too hazardous to be attempted; that my departure would undoubtedly be followed by the collapse of the will to fight on the part of the Filipinos; that exclusive of the Air Corps which had no planes, there were only about 7,000 American combat troops, the rest being Filipinos. The telegram ended with a statement that both Mr. Sayre and I, having been informed of the contents of General MacArthur's answer, had expressed our concurrence.

There was a profound silence after the reading of the telegrams, the one received and the one to be sent. After a pause, I told General MacArthur that before giving assent to his proposed answer, I would have to lay the matter before my War Cabinet, discuss it with them and then make my own decision. At once there assembled in conference Vice-President Osmeña, Chief Justice and Acting Secretary of Finance Jose Abad Santos, Acting Secretary of National Defense and Public Works and Communications General Basilio Valdes, and my unofficial adviser, Major Manuel Roxas. I informed them fully of the contents of the telegram received from Washington, but said nothing of the answer proposed by General MacArthur.

The unanimous opinion of the Cabinet was that the

invitation to evacuate to the United States should be accepted if it could be done without serious risk to my life, for they thought that the Filipino people would want me to be saved from falling into the hands of the enemy or from being killed. Then, and without referring to the statements made by General MacArthur in his proposed telegram, I asked them if they did not think that my departure at that time would dishearten the Philippine Army and weaken their determination to fight. The Cabinet thought just the contrary, that is, if the Filipino generals were informed of the reason for my departure and especially if they could be assured that my trip to America would mean the timely arrival of help from the United States, then the effect of my trip upon the morale of the Philippine Army would be good. In any event, the Cabinet opined that the important thing to determine was the feasibility of my evacuation, that if this could be done in relative safety, the Filipino generals and their commands would feel strongly in favor of it. My colleagues were sure that the Army shared the people's desire to have the head of their government and their leader where he would be free from the encircling grip of the enemy. Major Roxas offered to go to Bataan and explain the whole thing to the Philippine Army. Then they asked me the opinion of General MacArthur as to the hazards of the trip. I told what General MacArthur stated in his proposed answer to Washington regarding this matter. Whereupon the Cabinet decided that I should refuse to make the trip for they were very hopeful that before Bataan and Corregidor were forced to surrender, sufficient help would come for the American and Filipino forces to take the offensive and drive the enemy out of the land. It should be borne in mind that the general belief among the Filipinos, both civilians and soldiers, was that Bataan and Corregidor had sufficient supplies of food and ammunition to resist six months' siege, and few doubted that within that time America would be in command of the seas and, therefore, able to send all the help necessary to beat back the invading army. For my part, I knew that at that time my evacuation to America could be made in comparative safety. Full control by the Japanese of the sea-lanes between Manila and Australia had not yet been established. I could have left on a surface ship from Corregidor to Mindanao, traveling at night. From Mindanao I could have flown to Australia, making the regular stops, for the airports in Celebes, Borneo, and the Dutch East Indies had not as yet been taken over by the enemy. As an alternative plan I could then have gone in a submarine to Panay and from Panay to Mindanao on a surface boat and from Mindanao to Australia in one continuous flight on a bomber as I did two months later. But neither to my War Cabinet nor to General MacArthur did I express this thought. I kept it to myself.

Moreover, I was doubtful if help could come in

time even with my presence in America. To me it was clear that if I accepted the invitation to evacuate there would only be one certain result—my safety and that of my family. Bearing in mind the proposed answer of General MacArthur, I saw that the Supreme Commander of the USAFFE was convinced of the need of my presence in Corregidor at that time, and I felt strongly that it was my duty to defer to his judgment. There was thus but one course for me to take. In the presence of the Cabinet I dictated the following letter to General MacArthur:

> I have carefully considered the telegram of General Marshall.... I have come to the conclusion that in so far as the suggested trip to the United States is concerned, I have no preference. I am willing to do what the Government of the United States may think will be more helpful for the successful prosecution of the war. My immediate concern is to secure prompt and adequate help from the United States, because our soldiers at the front and the Filipino people in general have placed their trust in this indispensable help....

It will be seen from the above letter that I did not directly decline the offer to evacuate. I left the decision on this matter in the hands of the Government in Washington, but I did emphatically state that my only concern was to win the war and I was ready to do anything that Washington might consider necessary to achieve this end. I did stress, however, the need for immediate relief.

My letter to General MacArthur was transmitted verbatim to the War Department. With this addition, he sent his telegram exactly as he had read it to me.

On January 2nd, General MacArthur informed me that the withdrawal of our forces to Bataan would be successfully completed in a day or two and that he thought that I should address a proclamation to the Filipino soldiers. I agreed that that was a magnificent idea and we discussed the question of making use of the proclamation of the President of the United States to the people of the Philippines. By this time, I had noticed that President Roosevelt had used the words "your independence will be *redeemed*" (italics mine), and I asked General MacArthur if he thought that the word "redeemed" had been used advisedly to indicate that the President had already come to the conclusion that the Philippines was lost as no possible help could reach us on time to save our situation. The General, while not expressing a positive opinion, suggested the possibility that the transmission of the presidential message might have been garbled. I decided that being in doubt as to the exact intent of the presidential language, I should not quote the President literally. So I used the word "preserved" instead of "redeemed," which, while not necessarily implying a promise of timely succor, could not be construed as meaning that all hope for help must be abandoned. Such a construction might weaken the fighting spirit of the men in the front.

On the 3rd of January, I issued the following proclamation:

> The people of America and your own countrymen have been thrilled by the gallantry with which you have been defending our country. I am grateful and proud for the resistance you have offered against such tremendous odds. You have performed deeds of heroism and valor which will live in the history of these stirring days. The service that you are rendering to your people and your country, to say the least, is the equal of that rendered by our fathers who fought and died in the battles for our liberty.
>
> The President of the United States, speaking for the Government and people of America, in a recent proclamation addressed to the people of the Philippines, solemnly pledged that the freedom of our country will be preserved and our independence protected. He asserted that behind that pledge stood all the resources of America in men and materials. You are, therefore, fighting with America because America is fighting for our freedom. Our salvation will depend upon the victory of American and Filipino arms.

America will not abandon us. Her help will not be delayed. The enemy's temporary superiority in the air, on land and on sea cannot last much longer. We must resist further advance of the enemy until assistance arrives and I trust it will be soon. The outcome of the battle of the Philippines will depend in very large measure on your firm and unyielding resistance.

I am aware of your sufferings, your privations, your sacrifices, and the dangers to which you are exposed. All these weigh heavily upon my mind, but I am consoled by the fact that I am sharing with you your trials and tribulations. Indeed, right now bombs are falling near me just as they must fall around you. But we cannot allow them either to daunt our spirit or weaken our determination to continue fighting to the bitter end. We must stand by our plighted word, by the loyalty that we have pledged to America, and by our devotion to freedom, democracy, and our liberty. We are fighting that the Filipino people may be the masters of their own destiny and that every Filipino not only of this generation but of the generations to come may be able to live in peace and tranquillity in the full enjoyment of liberty and freedom. Your duty—our duty—is to fight and resist until the invader is driven from our land. You must not give up a foot of ground when the battle joins. You must hold in place—and hold—and hold.

On January 6th, at the usual time of our conference, General MacArthur told me that the withdrawal of our forces to Bataan had been successfully completed without any serious loss either of life or material. Later in my conversation with Americans and Filipinos in command of our retreating forces, I formed the opinion that in this retreat General MacArthur out-manœuvered and outwitted the Japanese generalship. In that retreat, too, the men in command in the front lines proved their mettle and their ability to carry out the orders of the Supreme Commander. In this conference, General MacArthur also informed me that he was going to Bataan with the idea of staying there as long as it might be necessary. With great diffidence and as much diplomacy as I was capable of, I voiced the general feeling among Americans and Filipinos in Corregidor that General MacArthur should not take chances and risk his life, for if he were lost the consequences to the morale of the fighting men would be incalculable. For the first time, I repeated to General MacArthur the story told me by his orderly how he, the General, had almost lost his life in the first Japanese bombardment of Corregidor's top-side. In a rather light vein General MacArthur answered: "The Japs have not as yet fabricated the bomb with my name in it," and then more seriously, he said, "Of course, I understand what you mean and I also know that I have no right to gamble with my life, but it is absolutely necessary that at the right time the Supreme Commander should take these chances because of the effect all down the line, for when they see the man at the top risking his life, the man at the bottom says, 'I guess if the old man can take it, I can take it, too.'"

I asked General MacArthur to take with him Major Roxas so that Roxas might talk to the Filipino generals.

"Not this time," the General answered, "for I do not know as yet exactly the situation at the front, and since Roxas is not a trained and veteran soldier, the trip might be too much for him. When the situation is stabilized, it might be the occasion for sending Roxas."

The following day, General MacArthur, with his staff visited the front, and when we met again he told me that there was no reason for immediate worry; that he felt confident that he could hold Bataan and Corregidor for several months without outside help; that the morale of our forces was high; that those Filipino reservists who had only had five and a half months' training, had become veterans in less than one month actual fighting against a determined and superior force. Although this report could not be more encouraging, it plainly implied that we could not stem the flood of Japanese assault indefinitely. More and more I realized what would be the inevitable result unless help from America was forthcoming. I could no longer take the same fatalistic mental attitude that I was able to assume in the first days of my stay in Corregidor. I began to worry about the soldiers at the front. In the Philippine Army there were the best of the youth of my country, the sons of the rich and influential Filipino families, partaking equally with the sons of the lowliest, in the hardships and the casualties of the war. As days passed by, with bombs dropping on Corregidor or not, this thought weighed more heavily upon my mind—and my conscience. After all, although the Tydings-McDuffie Act or Independence Law, provided that during the transition period of the Government of the Commonwealth, the President of the United States could muster into the service of the Federal Government all the organized forces of the Commonwealth, the Philippine Army had been of my own creation. Neither President Roosevelt nor any department of his government had made the slightest suggestion to me that I create an army to fight with America for America and the Philippines while the American flag was flying over the Islands. Had I not created the Philippine Army, only the Philippine Scouts, a part of the United States Army and the Philippine Constabulary under my command, with a limited number of officers and men, would have been subject to call by the President of the United States when war broke out. Therefore it was evidently my responsibility to God and my people that thousands of my countrymen would die and the survivors perhaps be taken as

Unit of Philippine Scouts moving into Pozzorubio on December 20, 1941

In Washington, President Quezon greets Lieutenant John D. Bulkeley, U.S.N., who piloted the Navy torpedo boat which conveyed the President and his family and party to the point of departure in the southern Philippines for Australia

prisoners of war, if, because of some unsurmountable obstacle, the aid from America could not arrive on time. Not only this but it was also upon my initiative that the whole Filipino people had rallied to the standard of America and offered everything they had in manpower and resources in defense of the American flag. Of course, I knew that this was our duty—a duty imposed by our gratitude to America and our sworn loyalty to her. And I also knew that the Filipino people felt this double obligation as strongly as I did. But, withal, I was staggered by the immensity of the sacrifice. To find out how the men at the front felt, I determined to send on January 10th, the Chief of Staff of the Philippine Army and Acting Secretary of National Defense, General Valdes, accompanied by my aide, Colonel Nieto, to visit our forces in Bataan and report to me the situation. They came back on the night of the 11th and spoke in enthusiastic terms of the prevailing spirit among our forces. They had seen all the command posts of the Filipino generals, the headquarters of the Philippine Army and also conferred with some subordinate officers. They failed to see General Wainwright at his headquarters because he was inspecting the front lines. From high and low among the Filipinos in Bataan, General Valdes received assurances of their determination to fight on and of their confidence in beating the Japanese if they could only have protection from the air.

When General MacArthur came to see me on the morning of the 12th, I communicated to him the report given to me by General Valdes and Colonel Nieto, emphasizing the evident expectation of our people at the front that help especially in airplanes would come from America.

Purely on my own responsibility I telegraphed President Roosevelt on January 13th, expressing my belief and desire that the whole force of America should be directed first against Japan in the Far East. I sensed that even among the American officers who were in Corregidor this was the general opinion and wish, although no one would express his opinion.

On January 15th, the Japanese bombed Corregidor's middle-side for more than one hour starting at 1:30 P.M.

After the visit made by General Valdes to the front, my eldest daughter, Maria, began asking my permission to go to the front and visit "our boys." She wanted to know whether the Christmas gifts which she and her friends had sent them from Manila had safely reached their destination; and furthermore, she wanted to visit them in my name since due to my ill health and physical weakness I was unable to make the trip. She had already found something to do in the tunnel. She and her sister had offered their services to the chief nurse and were making the beds for the patients and also folding gauze for the operating room. But she was not satisfied with this. She insisted that she should visit the front. I would not answer "no" for I did not wish to weaken her will to serve the cause, nor would I say "yes" for I knew that her mother, already worried about my health, would spend the most painful hours of supreme anxiety while she was at the front. So I told her that the matter had to be submitted to General MacArthur whose permission was necessary for her to go to Bataan. When General MacArthur came to see me, I told him the whole story and he, of course, said that under no circumstances would he allow my daughter to go to Bataan. We agreed, however, that I should not disappoint her by telling her plainly what the General said; so I informed Maria that General MacArthur felt that she had to wait until the situation became more normal at the front and then there might come a time when he would allow her to go. Day after day, my daughter would ask me if General MacArthur had decided definitely one way or another about her trip. I procrastinated.

Meantime, General Francisco and General De Jesus had been in Corregidor to see me at my request. They told me that the amount of rice given to the Filipino troops was insufficient and that if they had to be fed with only that amount of rations they would not be able to endure the fatigue of day and night engagements. They called my attention to the fact that every officer and man not seriously sick or wounded was continuously in the line without even temporary relief, for we had no reserves. They also told me of the increasingly grim determination on the part of our men to fight as they learned of the abuses and atrocities committed by the Japanese soldiers, especially the raping of Filipino women. "If we only had airplanes, we would lick these Japs in short order, Mr. President," they said. I told General De Jesus, our Chief of the Intelligence Division, to find the Governor and Assemblyman from Bataan and send them to me so that I might instruct them to coöperate with the military authorities in organizing the fishermen of the province to provide fish for the soldiers. The large number of civilians from Pampanga and Bataan who came inside the lines greatly increased the difficulties of the food supply.

At this conference General Francisco delivered to me the following telegram from the Constabulary Commander in Negros Oriental:

> Civilian military situation Negros Oriental excellent. About fifty thousand civilians of military age ready for induction into the Army. Civil activities being carried on as usual. Morale of people very high. Entire population very happy to receive the news that the President is well and safe.

After my conference with the above cited Filipino generals, I called in the Cabinet to discuss with them the food situation in Bataan and see if we could do something about it to help the Army. Vice-President Osmeña told me that there was plenty of food in Cebu, and Major Roxas, on his part, said that there was plenty of food in Capiz and Iloilo, but the question was how to bring these supplies to Bataan. I suggested that there was one Coast Guard vessel in Mariveles, the *Banahaw*, which we might send to Capiz, which was nearer to Corregidor than Cebu. I sent right away for the captain of the *Banahaw*, but he reported that the ship was not ready to sail and that it would take at least two days to prepare for sea. Then Major Roxas informed me that the S.S. *Legaspi*, a merchant marine ship which was engaged in inter-island traffic before the war, was available, and he suggested that I send for the captain and ask him to go to Capiz and get supplies. I discussed the matter with General MacArthur. To him I repeated what General Francisco and General De Jesus had said to me about the rice situation and asked him whether he had any objection to my discussing this matter with the captain of the S.S. *Legaspi*. General Mac-Arthur was so happy to think that we might be able to bring food from the Visayan Islands that he authorized me to tell the captain of the *Legaspi* that if he made the trip, he would compensate him and all the sailors generously, and moreover, would decorate them on their return.

I sent for the captain and another Filipino officer who was in charge of a small boat, also in Mariveles, but which was in no shape to make a voyage. They came to see me for the first time on January 20th. The name of the captain was Lino Conejero. I told them that it was in their hands to save our soldiers in Bataan, and although I knew that the trip from Corregidor to Capiz and back was most hazardous, I did not hesitate to appeal to their patriotism in the confident expectation that they would not hesitate to render this service. Captain Conejero, in the most casual manner, answered me without hesitation:

"Mr. President, all you have to do is to give the order and I will leave as soon as I can." Then I told him of what General MacArthur had promised to do for them. And on my part, I also offered to reward them from the funds of the Government of the Commonwealth with a full month's salary to each officer and sailor of the ship. Then I took them myself to the headquarters of General MacArthur to inform the General of the result of my conference with them. General MacArthur, with undisguised emotion, shook hands with the captain and the first officer, and in his usual appealing style said a few words which almost brought tears to the eyes of these men of the sea. On the morning of the 21st, I again saw Captain Conejero and gave him my final instructions to the Governor of Capiz. We proceeded at once to telegraph the governors of Iloilo and Capiz to turn to and help the Army to get all possible rice and other food supplies which could be assembled by the time the S. S. *Legaspi* arrived in Capiz. General MacArthur, on his part, telegraphed General Chynoweth giving him full instructions as to what should be done. I felt very much encouraged the whole day, and my spirits were so high that in the afternoon I was strong enough to visit the coast artillery batteries of Corregidor. I invited my daughter to accompany me and we saw some of the batteries manned by Philippine Scouts and Philippine Army soldiers. We made the trip in one of the Army cars accompanied by an American officer designated by General Moore, and by a Filipino captain who was in the artillery. With me were General Valdes, my daughter, and Colonel Nieto. The dust on the road was so thick that not even by closing the windows of the car could we be free from it. Some of the bombs had done so much damage to the road that attempts at repair had not improved it much. The sight of these soldiers practically unprotected from air attack almost broke my heart, and I could only say a few words to them: "Boys, I am proud of you. Our people will forever be grateful for your gallant defense. God bless and keep you." On my return to the tunnel, I coughed more than ever before, and on the following day I had a severe attack of asthma with spasmodic coughing which left me breathless and almost suffocated. By midnight, they had to give me a dose of morphine. I also had a very high fever. On January 23rd, I had another severe attack which required another injection of morphine. In the afternoon they took me out of the hospital in an ambulance to a cottage near the one where General MacArthur slept at night with his wife and son. The following day I was taken back to the tunnel where I had another attack in the afternoon, following which I was again carried to the house. In order that in the daytime I might have a place to lie in bed near the tunnel, a tent was constructed for me at the rear end of the hospital outside the tunnel, so that from January 26th until I left Corregidor this tent became my living and sleeping quarters.

CHAPTER XIII

Communications with Washington

O N January 28th a radio broadcast from Tokyo gleefully announced that a new government had been established in the Philippines, and that it had pledged its adherence to Japan's Greater East Asia Co-prosperity Sphere Policy. The broadcast also gave the names of the Filipinos who were supposed to constitute this new government. The effect of this broadcast among Americans on Corregidor, including the United States High Commissioner, members of his staff, and some officers of the United States Army, was very bad. Filipino officers who came to see me from Bataan later in the day were eager to find out what I thought of the announcement made by Tokyo. Having known for many years the men who were alleged to constitute this new government and having tested during that time on many occasions their loyalty to the United States as well as their personal loyalty to me, I felt certain that whether the creation of this new government was a fact or not, if the men who constituted it were those mentioned in the radio broadcast, they could be depended upon under any and all circumstances to commit no act of disloyalty, either to America, to the Philippines, or to me, the head of their government. So I told the young Filipino officers from Bataan that there was nothing to fear from those whom we had left in Manila, and I asked them to return at once and communicate this information to their commanders. General MacArthur, in our conference that day, was also reassured by me, although I did not find him as skeptical as High Commissioner Sayre who had come to ask me if I would not give out a statement repudiating the action of those Filipinos and reminding them that the day of reckoning was not far away. I told High Commissioner Sayre that I would not make any such statement, first, because I was sure of my men, second, because it seemed to me ridiculous that in my powerless situation, I should adopt a threatening rôle. Moreover, knowing the psychology of my people, I felt that if those men had been hesitating in the face of a situation that would try men's souls, any evidence of my faith in their loyalty would in itself serve to fortify their determination not to betray me; whereas, any indication that I considered them lost to the cause and practically traitors, would perhaps force them to go over to the Japanese. I therefore emphatically refused to adopt the suggestion of High Commissioner Sayre, and I told him that I considered the matter closed. However, fearing the effect in the outside world of Tokyo's broadcast, I proceeded at once to write a letter to General MacArthur, asking him that some parts of it be given the widest possible publicity. This is what I wanted publicized:

> I have been mortified by the radio broadcast from Tokyo asserting that a new government has been established in the Philippines, which government has pledged its conformity with Japan's New East Asia Policy.
>
> I know what the real sentiments of my people are and I am certain that their stand is not changed despite the military reverses of our forces. I am likewise convinced of the loyalty of the men who have accepted positions in the so-called new government.
>
> I want you, therefore, to give publicity to the following statement: "The determination of the Filipino people to continue fighting side by side with the United States until victory is won has in no way been weakened by the temporary reverses suffered by our arms. We are convinced that our sacrifices will be crowned with victory in the end and in that conviction we shall continue to resist the enemy with all our might."
>
> Japanese military forces are occupying sections of the Philippines comprising only one third of our territory. In the remaining areas constitutional government is still in operation under my authority.
>
> I have no direct information concerning the veracity of the news broadcast from Tokyo

that a Commission composed of some well-known Filipinos has been recently organized in Manila to take charge of certain functions of civil government. The organization of such a commission, if true, can have no political significance not only because it is charged merely with purely administrative functions but also because the acquiescence by its members to serve on the Commission was evidently for the purpose of safeguarding the welfare of the civilian population and can, in no way, reflect the sentiments of the Filipinos towards the enemy. Such sentiments are still those I have repeatedly expressed in the past: loyalty to America and resolute resistance against the invasion of our territory and liberties.

The foregoing statement was publicized in the Philippines both by printed leaflets and radio broadcasts, and it had an immediate reassuring effect so far as the Filipinos were concerned, both in the occupied and in the unoccupied territory.

In my letter to General MacArthur I also made certain statements which were intended not so much for General MacArthur as for the President of the United States.

I said in part:

At the same time I am going to open my mind and my heart to you without attempting to hide anything.

We are before the bar of history and God only knows if this is the last time that my voice will be heard before going to my grave.

My loyalty and the loyalty of the Filipino people to America has been proven beyond question. Now we are fighting by her side under your command despite overwhelming odds. But, it seems to me questionable whether any government has the right to demand loyalty from its citizens beyond its willingness or ability to render actual protection.

This war is not of our making. . . .

Despite all this, we never hesitated for a moment in our stand.

We decided to fight by your side and we have done the best we could and we are still doing as much as could be expected from us under the circumstances. But how long are we going to be left alone? Has it already been decided in Washington that the Philippine front is of no importance as far as the final result of the war is concerned and that, therefore, no help can be expected here in the immediate future, or at least before the power of resistance is exhausted? If so, I want to know, because I have my own responsibility to my countrymen whom, as President of the Commonwealth, I have led into a complete war effort. I am greatly concerned as well regarding the soldiers I have called to the colors and who are now manning the firing line. I want to decide in my own mind whether there is justification for allowing all these men to be killed when for the final outcome of the war the shedding of their blood may be wholly unnecessary. It seems that Washington does not fully realize our situation nor the feelings which the apparent neglect of our safety and welfare have engendered in the hearts of the people here....

In reference to the men who have accepted positions in the commission established by the Japanese, every one of them wanted to come to Corregidor, but you told me that there was no room for them here. They are not "quislings." The "quislings" are the men who betray their country to the enemy. These men did what they have been asked to do, while they were free, under the protection of their government. Today they are virtually prisoners of the enemy. I am sure they are only doing what they think is their duty. They are not traitors. They are the victims of the adverse fortunes of war and I am sure they have no choice. Besides, it is most probable that they accepted their positions in order to safeguard the welfare of the civilian population in the occupied areas. I think, under the circumstances, America should look upon their situation sympathetically and understandingly.

I am confident that you will understand my anxiety about the long-awaited reinforcements and trust you will again urge Washington to insure their early arrival.

Without delay, President Roosevelt answered my letter to General MacArthur in a radiogram addressed directly to me as follows:

> I have perused your message to General Mac-Arthur and I appreciate completely your position. I am fully sensible of the profundity and honesty of your feelings with reference to your unavoidable obligations to your fellow-country-men and I solemnly state that I would never ask of you and them any sacrifice that I believe without hope in order to further our attainment of the goal towards which we are all pressing. I desire, nevertheless, to emphasize as strongly as possible that the superb defense of our soldiers in Bataan is a definite contribution in bringing about an eventual and complete overwhelming of the enemy in the Far East. The deficiency which now exists in our offensive weapons are the natural results of the policies of peaceful nations such as the Philippines and the United States who without warning are attacked by despotic nations which have spent years in preparing for such action. Early reverses, hardships and pain are the price that democracy must pay under such conditions. However, I have dedicated to the accomplishment of final victory every man, every dollar and every material

sinew of this nation; and this determination to attain victory necessarily includes as an' objective the restoring of tranquillity· and peace to the Philippines and its return to such government as its people may themselves choose. Although I cannot at this time state the day that help will arrive in the Philippines, I can assure you that every vessel available is bearing to the Southwest Pacific the strength that will eventually crush the enemy and liberate your native land. Vessels in that vicinity have been filled with cargo of necessary supplies and have been dispatched to Manila. Our arms, together with those of our allies, have dealt heavy blows to enemy transports and naval vessels and are most certainly retarding his movement to the south. By the trans-African route and lately by the Pacific route our heavy bombers are each day joining General Wavell's command. A continuous stream of fighter and pursuit planes is traversing the Pacific; already ten squadrons of the foregoing types are ready for combat in the South Pacific area. Extensive arrival of troops are being guarded by adequate protective elements of our Navy. The heroes of Bataan are effectively assisting by gaining invaluable time, and time is the vital factor in reënforcing our military strength in this theater of war.

Words are inadequate to convey to you my esteem and appreciation for the totally magnificent showing of faithfulness, heroism and

President Roosevelt greets President Quezon of the Philippine Commonwealth, and his family, at the Union Station in Washington on May 13, 1942: Mrs. Quezon, Manuel Quezon, Jr. President Quezon, President Roosevelt, Captain John McCrea, Miss Maria Aurora Quezon, Miss Zeneida Quezon

President Roosevelt signs the United Nations Agreement, as the Philippine Commonwealth and Mexico become new members during Flag Day ceremonies at the White House, in the presence of representatives of the twenty-six original United Nations

President Roosevelt has a word with President Quezon of the Philippine Commonwealth, after the signing of the United Nations Agreement

First Philippine War Cabinet Meeting held in Washington at the Commonwealth's office building, 1617 Massachusetts Avenue: Vice-President Sergio Osmeña; Lieutenant Colonel Andres Soriano, Secretary of Finance; Resident Commissioner Joaquin Elizalde; President Quezon; Major General

spirit of sacrifice that the Philippine people, under your superb guidance, have shown. They are maintaining the most glorious standard of all free people.

Those parts of your message to General Mac-Arthur which you request be brought to the attention of the world at large are being broadcast from Washington. Your speech and your actions will encourage not only your fellow-countrymen but all those throughout the world who are partners in the battle for democratic ideals and liberty in the right of self-government.

The message of President Roosevelt was not only admirable in its form and substance but was evidently all that could be expected under the circumstances described by him. The human sympathy and understanding of this great man in the face of an almost intrusive radiogram from me, especially if contrasted with the attitude of other heads of governments in dealing with people under their sway, could not be overestimated. Yet I must confess that my grave concern for the welfare and security of my people and the incalculable loss of life on the part of our soldiers was not put at rest. If I could only be sure that the Dutch East Indies and Singapore would hold out long enough to keep the sea-lanes open during the period which I felt certain the American and Filipinos in Bataan and on Corregidor would hold, then I felt that bombers, fighters and pursuit planes, and the troops to which the President's radiogram referred, would reach the Philippines in time for the Army of MacArthur to take the offensive and drive out the Japanese. But would Singapore and Java fight as long and as well as we were fighting? The destruction of the *Prince of Wales* and the *Repulse* right at the beginning of the war was a sinister revelation of the basic weakness of the defense of Singapore—lack of adequate air power. The easy gains which the Japanese were making through the supposedly impassable jungles of the Malay Peninsula (as was daily broadcast to us) raised increasing doubts of the impregnability of Singapore, contrary to what we in the Far East had assumed to be the completeness of English fortifications. And it was clear to me that, if Singapore fell, the Dutch East Indies would be an easy prey to Japanese land, sea and air forces, despite the fact that the whole American Asiatic Fleet had joined the Dutch East Indies fleet.

With Singapore and the Dutch East Indies in the hands of the enemy, Bataan and Corregidor were doomed. That was the dreadful and horrible thought which haunted me day and night after receiving the foregoing message of the President of the United States. I did not conceal my serious misgivings from General MacArthur. But he would always retort: "I will bring you in triumph on the points of my bayonets to Manila."

In the meantime my health was not improving. [I

was ill and confined with tuberculosis when I went to the tunnels of Corregidor.] I was being carried in a wheel-chair in and out of the tunnel during the frequent air raids and bombardments. Rumors about the doubtful attitude of the Filipinos in the occupied territory, especially in Manila, were being circulated and these increased beyond expression my anxiety. One day when information regarding the situation in the Malay Peninsula and Singapore convinced me that the surrender of this English fortress was only a question of weeks at most, I told General MacArthur that I was not certain that my stay in Corregidor was of any practical value to either the defense of Bataan and Corregidor or to the maintenance of the morale of the civilian population. This, together with my rapidly declining health, caused me to feel that perhaps I would render better service to America and the Philippines if I went to Manila and allowed myself to be made a prisoner of war by the Japanese. [I wanted them to know I was not afraid and not even if it cost me life itself.]

On February 6th, General Aguinaldo, in a radio broadcast addressed to General MacArthur, urged him to surrender in view of the futility of continuing to fight against superior enemy forces. Although I would not condemn in my own mind this attitude of Aguinaldo, despite the fact that he was my enemy, as an act of treason and for this reason refused to enter into a public controversy with him as was suggested to me by Commissioner Sayre, his actions at this time reminded me of his conduct under similar circumstances when he was the President of the Philippine Republic and Commander-in-Chief of its forces. It will be remembered that when General Aguinaldo was convinced of the superiority of the American forces, many years before, he had been willing to enter into negotiations with the American authorities in Manila on a basis other than independence. Recalling this incident, I also remembered that great Filipino character, Apolinario Mabini, and what he had done even after he had been captured and was a prisoner of war in the hands of the American army. Mabini, a paralytic, refused to take the oath of allegiance even after he had been deported to Guam, and only took the oath when the whole people of the Philippines had accepted the sovereignty of the United States and expressed their willingness to coöperate in carrying out the policy of ultimate freedom propounded by the United States Government.

I told General MacArthur my fear of the effect on our people, especially the less educated classes, of the promise of independence made by Premier Tojo in his speech before the Japanese Diet, wherein he said that Japan was ready to give the Filipinos "independence with honor." This promise which was used by Aguinaldo as further reason for urging the surrender of our forces might well have had the effect of weakening the Filipino leaders if they found the people in general to be won over to Tojo and Aguinaldo; so I informed General MacArthur that I was seriously considering placing myself in the hands of the Japanese and defying them, in the belief that such action on my part would solidify the opposition of the Filipinos to any Japanese influence. General MacArthur told me that, in his opinion, that would be a mistake, that he thought the Japanese were too smart to make me a martyr, knowing as they did that in so doing they would forever win the enmity and hatred of the Filipino people. He believed that the Japanese would allow me to go to Malacañan and would advertise this fact, but would allow no Filipino to get near me; and that without my knowledge or consent they would give out statements, as coming from me, telling the Filipinos that they should coöperate with Japan and advising the Filipino soldiers at the front to surrender and abandon the American forces. Moreover, General MacArthur said that he feared that my action might be misinterpreted abroad. To this last consideration I retorted at once that I was not interested in the judgment of outsiders so long as I was satisfied that I was acting in accordance with my duty as in conscience I saw it. The struggle on the part of the American and Filipino armies was heroic, but in a sense it was a futile one. It might even be questioned that the entire American army at that date if present could have defended the Islands against the vast numbers of men, machines, matériel of the Japanese forces. However, his remarks as to what the Japanese might do did impress me. Knowing something of the Japanese, the views of General MacArthur seemed perfectly reasonable, so I told the General I would think more about the matter.

After further consideration, I came to the conclusion that it might be an unwise thing for me to attempt to imitate Mabini. The Americans in those years long ago had dealt with the Filipino revolutionaries entirely above board. When they captured Mabini they did not conceal from the Filipino people the courageous stand of this patriot. Nor did they pretend that they were treating him as other than a prisoner of war. So Mabini died as the noble and great man that he was in the eyes of his countrymen and of the world. Whereas, in my case my sacrifice would not only have been in vain but might have carried with it my eternal dishonor, for it might not have been possible for any one but me and my Japanese jailer to have known or to furnish proofs of what I had done or been trying to do.

There remained, however, what, in my opinion, was a larger question—the possibly useless sacrifice of the Philippine Army, and why shall I not say of the American Army as well, for my heart had gone out to those heroic men and women, officers, soldiers and nurses who, after all, were fighting in defense of my country at the same time that they were fighting to maintain the honor of their flag. At last, I thought I found the key to the problem. I would ask the President of the United States to authorize me to issue a public manifesto asking the Government of the United States to grant immediate, complete and absolute independence to the Philippines; that the neutralization of the Philippines be agreed at once by the United States and the Imperial Japanese government; that within a reasonable period of time, both armies, American and Japanese, be withdrawn; that neither nation should occupy bases in the Philippines; that the Philippine Army be demobilized, the only organized force remaining in the Islands to be the Philippine Constabulary for the maintenance of law and order; that Japanese and American noncombatants who so wished be evacuated with their own army under reciprocal and fitting stipulations. It was a great anxiety of mine to achieve independence for my people under the Americans. I wanted it done before the Japanese who played no part in this development could claim credit for it.

When I submitted this question to my Cabinet, Lieutenant Colonel Roxas expressed serious doubts as to the effect such a proposal would have on President Roosevelt, and Vice-President Osmeña was inclined to agree with Roxas. They frankly expressed to me their fear that the President might think that we were weakening in our stand, or might misunderstand our motive. I told them that I was gravely concerned as to the reaction of the people, as well as of the Filipino leaders, to the offer of independence made by Premier Tojo, and I expressed the conviction that if Japan were to actually establish an independent government in the Philippines, the masses of the people who knew very little of the history of Japan in Manchukuo would fall into the trap and our leaders would be powerless in the face of such a situation. On the other hand, if the Japanese government should refuse to accept my proposal, the Filipino people and our forces would discover at once the perfidy of Tojo's promise of independence, and our spirit of resistance to Japan would naturally be strengthened.

Again I explained to them my misgivings as to the ability of our forces to prolong their resistance with so little food and so much dysentery and malaria—a resistance which might be further weakened by their knowledge that the civilian population had accepted "independence" at the hands of Japan. After hearing my views, the Cabinet unanimously approved the sending of the message to the President of the United States. On the next day, President Roosevelt sent me the following answer:

> I have just received your message sent through General MacArthur. From my message to you of January 30, you must realize that I am not lacking in understanding of or sympathy with the situation of yourself and the Commonwealth Government today. The immediate crisis cer-

tainly seems desperate but such crises and their treatment must be judged by a more accurate measure than the anxieties and sufferings of the present, however acute. For over forty years the American Government has been carrying out to the people of the Philippines a pledge to help them successfully, however long it might take, in their aspirations to become a self-governing and independent people, with the individual freedom and economic strength which that lofty aim makes requisite. You yourself have participated in and are familiar with the many carefully planned steps by which that pledge of self-government has been carried out and also the steps by which the economic independence of your Islands is to be made effective. May I remind you now that in the loftiness of its aim and the fidelity with which it has been executed, this program of the United States towards another people has been unique in the history of the family of nations. In the Tydings-McDuffie Act of 1934, to which you refer, the Congress of the United States finally fixed the year 1946 as the date in which the Commonwealth of the Philippine Islands established by that Act should finally reach the goal of its hopes for political and economic independence.

By a malign conspiracy of a few depraved but powerful governments, this hope is now being frustrated and delayed. An organized attack upon individual freedom and governmental independence throughout the entire world, beginning in Europe, has now spread and been carried to the Southwestern Pacific by Japan. The basic principles which have guided the United States in its conduct towards the Philippines have been violated in the rape of Czechoslovakia, Poland, Holland, Belgium, Luxembourg, Denmark, Norway, Albania, Greece, Yugoslavia, Manchukuo, China, Thailand, and finally the Philippines. Could the people of any of these nations honestly look forward to a true restoration of their independent sovereignty under the dominance of Germany, Italy or Japan?

You refer in your telegram to the announcement by the Japanese Prime Minister of Japan's willingness to grant to the Philippines her independence. I only have to refer you to the present condition of Korea, Manchukuo, North China, Indo-China, and all other countries which have fallen under the brutal sway of the Japanese Government, to point out the hollow duplicity of such an announcement. The present sufferings of the Filipino people, cruel as they may be, are infinitely less than the sufferings and permanent enslavement which will inevitably follow acceptance of Japanese promises. In any event is it longer possible for any reasonable person to rely upon Japanese offer or promise?

The United States today is engaged with all its resources and in company with the governments of 26 other nations in an effort to defeat the aggression of Japan and its Axis partners. This effort will never be abandoned until the complete and thorough overthrow of the entire Axis system and the governments which maintain it. We are engaged now in laying the foundations in the Southwest Pacific of a development in air, naval and military power which shall become sufficient to meet and overthrow the widely extended and arrogant attempts of the Japanese. Military and naval operations call for recognition of realities. What we are doing there constitutes the best and surest help that we can render to the Philippines at this time.

By the terms of our pledge to the Philippines implicit is our forty years of conduct towards your people and expressly recognized in the terms of the Tydings-McDuffie Act, we have undertaken to protect you to the uttermost of our power until the time of your ultimate independence had arrived. Our soldiers in the Philippines are now engaged in fulfilling that purpose. The honor of the United States is pledged to its fulfillment. We propose that it be carried out regardless of its cost. Those Americans who are fighting now will continue to fight until the bitter end. Filipino soldiers have been rendering voluntary and gallant service in defense of their own homeland.

So long as the flag of the United States flies on Filipino soil as a pledge of our duty to your people, it will be defended by our own men to the death. Whatever happens to the present American garrison we shall not relax our efforts until the forces which we are now marshaling outside the Philippine Islands return to the Philippines and drive the last remnant of the invaders from your soil.

The effect of the foregoing telegram on me was overwhelming. I thought I could read between the lines more than what the President had actually said. I suspected that he had gone so far as to tell General MacArthur that if the Filipinos desired to quit, which they did not, no obstacle should be placed on our way; that the President of the Philippines with his whole Government and his (Philippine) army could surrender if they wanted to, as long as they did not compromise any of the rights of sovereignty of the United States over the Philippines; but that the American forces should fight for their flag and in defense of the Philippines to the last man. The Filipinos wanted to fight to the bitter end because of their gratitude to the United States and because they resented the ruthless invasion of their homeland.

I first knew President Roosevelt when he was Under-Secretary of the Navy. I had close and almost personal relations with him after he had become President of the United States. From the first time that I had met him, his irresistibly winning smile had attracted me to him. I gave him from the beginning my personal affection. From my official dealings with him, I had come to the conclusion that he was a great statesman—with broad human sympathies and a world-wide knowledge of affairs; a leader of men, with physical and moral courage rarely seen in a human being. I had become convinced of his extreme regard for the welfare of the Filipino people and his abiding faith in liberty and freedom for the human race. But I did not know, nor did I suspect that this man was so great as to be able to renounce the power, which was given him by the Philippine Independence Act, to compel the Filipino forces and people to stand by America in the defense not of America but of the Philippines during the period before complete independence. When I realized that he was big enough to assume and place the burden of the defense of my country upon the sacrifice and heroism of his own people alone, I swore to myself and to the God of my ancestors that as long as I lived I would stand by America regardless of the consequences to my people and to myself. We could not in decency be less generous or less determined than President Roosevelt. Without further discussion with anybody, I called my Cabinet and read them my answer to President Roosevelt, as follows: "I wish to thank you for your prompt answer to the proposal which I submitted to you with the unanimous approval of my Cabinet. We fully appreciate the reasons upon which your decision is based and we abide by it."

That was the end of my worries. The course of the ship was definitely charted and at the helm I was ready to break through every rough sea, every torment and every hurricane. Nothing in the world would steer me away from my course. I pondered over the general situation and came to the conclusion that if the fight was to be carried on, Corregidor was not my place. I had to leave that beleaguered fortress at whatever risk and be with my people in the unoccupied territory so as to arouse to the point of supreme heroism the patriotism and loyalty to America of every man, woman, and child. It was also necessary to marshal the resources of the country to provide supplies and cash for the Army in the Visayas and Mindanao and to send food to Bataan and Corregidor by every possible means at our disposal. After discussing the plan with my War Cabinet, I submitted the program or plan to General MacArthur who instantly approved it. Then I sent it. Colonel Roxas went to the front to prepare the Filipino generals for the news of my departure when the time came for making it known to them. On his return to Corregidor, Colonel Roxas reassured me that the Philippine Army would understand and fully approve of my departure. Then I asked General MacArthur to inform Washington of my plans. I also authorized him to destroy the silver currency we had in Corregidor if such action became necessary because of impending seizure by the Japanese. My order to this effect must have convinced

President Roosevelt that I meant what I said when I informed him that I abode by his decision, for on February 15 I received the following telegram from him:

> A radiogram just received from General MacArthur informed me that you have ordered that the silver currency, property of the Commonwealth Government, be destroyed, if such action becomes necessary because of impending seizure by the Japanese. It is extremely gratifying to have this added evidence of the absolute fidelity of your government and yourself to the United States and of your willingness to sacrifice in behalf of the ideals for which we are all striving. I am sorry that the necessity for secrecy prohibits my making public your splendid action for such indication of absolute singlemindedness of purpose of the United Powers inspires all our peoples to an accelerated exertion toward ultimate triumph.

The next day General MacArthur informed Washington that it was my wish, concurred in by my War Cabinet, that the seat of the Philippine Government should be transferred to the free territory of the Islands, at first in the Visayas. We had expressed the feeling that we members of the Government would be of greater service to the cause if we could have direct contact with our countrymen, which was not possible from Corregidor.

The message further outlined our plan to maintain the unity and heighten the morale of the Filipino people in the free portion of the Islands, in order to oppose more successfully the enemy.

General MacArthur concurred heartily with our plans and requested the authority to use submarines to get us out of Corregidor, which was approved by Washington.

President Quezon addressing the House of Representatives on June 2, 1942. He said that death, ruin and destruction had not daunted the spirit of the Filipinos

The Pacific War Council meets on the occasion of Mr. Churchill's visit to the United States in June, 1942

CHAPTER XIV

Through the Blockade from Corregidor

(Note: The following chapter has been prepared by former Governor-General Francis Burton Harrison, who was adviser to the late President Quezon. At President Quezon's request Governor Harrison kept careful notes of the former's expressed views on the subjects involved in this chapter. Governor Harrison was greatly assisted by data furnished to him by Colonel Manuel Nieto, President Quezon's principal military aide, who accompanied him in all his journeys after leaving Corregidor.)

ON DECEMBER 30TH, shortly after our arrival in the fortress, I had been asked by President Roosevelt to come directly to Washington, but I declined the invitation, for I was anxious to remain in the theater of war, where I felt that my presence would be of service at that time.

Finally, after nearly two months of siege and bombardment and upon the advice of General MacArthur and of my doctors, we decided to leave Corregidor for the, as yet, unoccupied zones of the Philippines. We felt that we might thus be able to encourage continued resistance in the free portions of our islands, and, above all, get some much needed food for our armies.

The supplies hastily gathered in the narrow

confines of Bataan and Corregidor had become greatly depleted and the food ration was already reduced to half.

It was understood as we left, that, on account of differences in plans and of immediate destinations, High Commissioner Sayre was to await the return of our submarine for the departure of himself and his party.

The departure took place, of course, after eleven o'clock at night when the moon had set. As the enemy was firing upon us from Cavite, no chances could be taken.

The moment was tense and dramatic; each clasp of the hands seemed to convey a question as to what fate had in store for us and for them.

General MacArthur and all the High Command of the fortress were at the dock to bid us good-bye, and with them came General Manuel Roxas, then a colonel, and the only representative of my Government to be left on Corregidor. On him I conferred full powers as Executive Secretary of the President in the following order:

OFFICE OF THE PRESIDENT
OF THE PHILIPPINES

Corregidor
February 18, 1942

DEAR SECRETARY ROXAS:

I have today designated you to act as Secretary to the President. In this capacity you are authorized, when in your judgment the circumstances so require, to act in my name on all matters not involving any change of policy. You are familiar with the policies of my administration, and I expect you to be guided by those policies in all matters of government requiring action or intervention on your part.

With respect to the assets of the Government now deposited in the Treasury Vaults, as you know, I have authorized General MacArthur to destroy the silver currency when in his judgment the military situation requires such action. As to the paper currency, you are authorized to withdraw from the vaults such amounts as may be necessary for official purposes, but always upon proper requisitions or vouchers. When in the opinion of General MacArthur it becomes necessary or convenient to take such action, you are also authorized to destroy the said currency. For this purpose you should designate or cause to be designated a group of officials to act as a Destruction Committee. This committee should certify the destruction, and counterpart certificates should be prepared in your files and sent to the proper officials in Washington for purposes of record and future references.

You are authorized to appoint a paymaster and such other officials as may be necessary to assist you in the performance of your duties.

Sincerely yours,

MANUEL L. QUEZON

Hon. Manuel Roxas
Corregidor

With me there went, of course, my family, Vice-President Osmeña, Chief Justice Jose Abad Santos, Major General Basilio Valdes, Father Ortiz, S.J., our Chaplain, and my senior aide, Colonel Manuel Nieto. The rest of my own party, including Lieutenant Colonel Velasquez, who had been serving as Chief of Staff of a division on Bataan, now my junior aide, Lieutenant Colonel Andres Soriano, now Secretary of Finance of my government, who had been serving at the front as intelligence officer on the staff of General Alfred Jones, my private secretary Serapio Canceran and my doctors had left the night before us on the fine inter-island steamer the *Don Esteban*. They could only travel by night, of course, stopping en route at three carefully selected hide-outs during the daytime.

On our departure from Corregidor I discarded the wheel-chair which had been necessary during the crisis of my illness while there.

As we boarded the submarine *Swordfish* I shook hands with Commander Chester C. Smith of Boise, Idaho; he looked so young and innocent! Yet, on his way up to meet us he had met a Japanese transport and had promptly launched a torpedo and sunk it.

After threading the complicated mine-field which guarded the entrance to the bay, we rose to the surface and traveled the rest of the night through quite a rough sea.

Poor Mrs. Quezon was sea-sick as were my two daughters who lay together in a tiny bunk, the feet of each to the other's head. As for my son Manuel, aged fifteen, he took all of his adventures like a little man. For him, the really important feature of the submarine was the wonderful food. He ate two dinners, one after the other, thus wiping out the memories of two months of short rations on Corregidor. He still talks of that food.

The next day, at the break of dawn, we submerged through all the long hours of daylight above. This was an experience I found very hard to endure. Most men, I suppose, who have once been prisoners, as I had been for six months after the Philippine insurrection, suffer in after life from claustrophobia! At all events, something seemed to have gone wrong with the air-conditioning of that submarine, and it was for me almost intolerably hot and stuffy. The following day, Sunday, February 22nd, at 2:40 A.M., we arrived at San Jose de Buenavista, in Antique province, which was our point of rendezvous with the S.S. *Don Esteban* which arrived an hour later.

The Visayan Islands had not yet been occupied at any point by the enemy. To the southward they had seized the ports of Davao and Zamboanga on the great island of Mindanao and had occupied the Sulu Archipelago. The narrow seas about us were constantly patrolled by war vessels of the enemy.

In the Visayas, there were no considerable quotas of our Army, and those in the service consisted for the most part of raw· recruits or draftees. When their turn eventually came, they put up a gallant resistance.

Bombing was already going on in Iloilo, but this, as yet, had achieved no very material damage. One incident brought us almost comic relief from the deadly serious nature of the situation.

As soon as this grim war fell upon our peaceful and prosperous land, I had proclaimed daylight-saving for reasons recognized by all the peoples engaged in this conflict. But in the Visayas, at least, this measure had brought to us benefits quite unexpected. The Japanese, as is well known, operate on an exact schedule adopted long before hostilities begin. Everything with them is like a railroad time-table. Their rule, it seems, is invariably to bomb airfields at lunch-time—twelve o'clock noon. But after my proclamation of daylight-saving time, twelve o'clock Japanese time was one o'clock Philippine time, and at that hour people had not always returned to their work from luncheon. In Iloilo the members of the Lopez family, who owned an important airfield near that city, thanked me profusely for the lives I had saved by my proclamation. When the Japanese bombed their airfield near Iloilo, there was nobody there—they were all still at lunch.

General Quimbo and Colonel Powell were sent in a launch by General Chynoweth, chief of the armed forces in Panay, to receive us. I decided to continue the trip to Iloilo by car accompanied only by my military assistants. Vice-President Osmeña and Secretary of Justice Santos boarded the *Don Esteban* which took them to Iloilo, at which capital they arrived at 10 P.M. of the same day.

We reached Iloilo at 7:30 in the morning and put up temporarily on the property of the Lopez family in a little nipa house on the beach. My object was, if possible, to keep my movements secret—an effort which was unsuccessful because word got around among the people, and it was necessary for the police to be called to prevent the house being over-run.

The people begged me to explain what they were not able to understand—the reason for the bombardments and the war. They did not comprehend that in an armed conflict between the United States and Japan, our land necessarily became part of the field of battle. In each look I found intense anxiety to know when these horrors would come to an end. I answered as best I could and exhorted them to continue their struggle for the cause of democracy in the certainty that sooner or later the United States would come to our relief.

At midday I proceeded to Ajui, site of the

sugar factory of the Elizaldes, a place appropriate for my headquarters in the Visayan Islands. The people in charge of the factory prepared for us a meal which seemed to us most lavish. This constant reference to the prosaic subject of eating might appear out of place to one who has been enjoying a good table. This is not the case, however, with those who, like us, had lived for more than two months on half rations, the half ration consisting of tinned goods without such indispensable items as coffee, milk, butter, etc.

At three in the afternoon, I received the military and civil authorities of the three provinces of Panay. There were present, with General Chynoweth, the governors, provincial treasurers, auditors and attorneys and the manager of the branch of the Philippine National Bank. Panay was, through its proximity, supplies and facilities for shipment, the point from which one could most easily provide food supplies for the troops on Bataan and Corregidor. After giving instructions concerning the vital necessity of sowing rice and corn, I increased the price to be paid by the Government for these supplies and pointed out the patriotic duty of everyone to aid in their shipment to Corregidor and Bataan. Here I must say that those provinces reacted with the liberality and hospitality legendary among the Filipino people and I desire to make particular mention of Governor

Hernandez of Capiz Province, who was in charge of the affair. From the well-to-do people down to the poorest, everyone brought what he could of fish and dried meat, rice, corn, fruit and eggs, which latter were particularly needed in the hospitals of Bataan and Corregidor. Thanks to this assistance which lasted until the only two vessels at our disposal were sunk by the Japanese, it was possible for our forces to continue fighting a month or so longer without starving.

That same night, I decided to go to Negros and after dinner in Iloilo I went aboard the *Don Esteban*.

The fixed lights of the strait which separates Iloilo from Negros were extinguished and the captain did not dare to make the crossing. Since it was not prudent, on the other hand, to voyage by day, because the enemy air force was constantly raiding the few vessels which could take provisions to Corregidor, I disembarked in Guimaras, a little island at the mouth of the Iloilo River, where I passed the day, while Colonel Nieto returned to Iloilo to arrange with the Quartermaster Department the assignment of the S.S. *Princess of Negros* for my use during an inspection of the Visayan Islands.

This permitted me to send immediately the *Don Esteban* to Corregidor with food supplies. She made a successful trip, but on her return she was bombed and sunk by the enemy. For the heroic crew of this vessel and of the S.S. *Legaspi*, which were unprovided with any means of defense, navigating in waters patrolled by enemy submarines and destroyers and under skies filled with airplanes, all words of praise sound feeble. Only men endowed with extreme patriotism and courage could have carried out these tasks.

In the *Princess of Negros* I proceeded to Bacolod, capital of the Province of Western Negros. This is the principal sugar growing territory of the Philippines, and here are found the largest sugar factories. Here, also, the extreme tension between factory owners, planters and workmen, brought about by the war, naturally had become greater than in any other part of the country. These difficulties were so severe that the only course open to me was to direct the suspension of grinding and to authorize certain loans by the Government bank to enable wage payments to be made.

Except for this, the Island of Negros had not yet been seriously affected by the war although news had been received of the bombardments, pillage, sacking and other calamities in Manila. Knowing so little of the war, they displayed that peculiarity of human beings who feel that they are remote from all danger and, with the utmost good faith, think of life in terms of enjoyment, entertainment, music and good times generally. To those of my party, however, who had seen so closely the horrors of war, this attitude seemed a shocking desecration.

Two days later I decided to go to Eastern Negros, where we arrived on the 27th of February, and from here to save time I decided to send in advance Vice President Osmeña and Secretary of Justice Santos to Cebu, and I directed the Insular Treasurer, Andres Soriano, to go to Mindanao.

In this period and while I was traversing that province rapidly, not remaining more than two days in any town, since I assumed that the Japanese would learn of my stopping places, I will tell of only one, among many, of the frustrations which the Japanese encountered. We took with us to the Visayan Islands the remainder of the paper money of the Filipino Treasury which had not been destroyed on Corregidor, foreseeing that it might be necessary to use it in the payment of the troops in the southern islands. For this story, the actual amount of the funds in question is not important; it is enough to say that there was a good fistful of millions, exposed always to the dangers of our journey.

On the 16th of March at midnight a flash announced to me the presence of Japanese destroyers in the Tanon Strait between the islands of Negros and Cebu, exactly where our *Princess of Negros* was at anchor with these funds on board destined for the city of Cebu. At once I sent my aide, Colonel Nieto, to the steamer to

take charge of the funds—a thing which he succeeded in doing before dawn. Twelve hours
later, the *Princess of Negros* was captured by a
Japanese destroyer. My hair still stands on end
when I think how nearly that money fell into
Japanese hands.

The Governor of Iloilo, Tomas Confesor,
who later on, in the jungles at the head of the
guerrillas of Panay, was to distinguish himself
as one of the most extraordinary figures of the
resistance against the invaders, had just arrived
at Negros from Manila, whence he had escaped
on board a small boat. He brought me the first
direct impressions of events there, since the capture of that capital by the Japanese.

With General Homma, Supreme Chief of
the Japanese Occupational Forces, there entered
into Manila Hideico Kihara, who for many
years had been Japanese Vice-Consul in Manila
and until November, 1941, had been Consul
General in Davao. Kihara was a good mixer
and had built up a number of friendly relation-
ships among the Filipinos for which reason he
was being utilized as advisor to the Japanese
Army.

Homma, advised by Kihara, convoked the
entire official staff of the Filipino Government
who had remained in Manila, at the head of
whom were Jorge Vargas, my executive secretary, and Jose Yulo, the speaker of the Philippine Assembly. Homma produced a plan of or-

ganizing a commission which should have in its charge the administration of civil affairs and should serve as a liaison between the military forces of occupation and the people.

But notwithstanding the advice which I left for them before my departure to the effect that if they should be given an opportunity to coöperate in the administration of civil government, they should accept it in order that the interests of the people and public order and respect for property should be safeguarded, their answer was no!

They were then told, as Governor Confesor related to us, that in view of their attitude, the Japanese found themselves obliged to place this duty in the hands of Filipinos who were more sensible and coöperative, that is to say, pro-Japanese or more pliable Filipinos.

The officials then asked for twenty-four hours to make a decision, during which time it was their intention to send a courier to Corregidor to find out my opinion, but communication was already broken.

There remained, therefore, no alternative but to accept or permit the placing of the interests of the Filipino people in the hands of individuals who might be mercenary, irresponsible and unscrupulous, which would have spread alarm and demoralization throughout the country. Finally, their sense of responsibility came to the fore and they accepted the Japanese proposal, but not without laying down the condition that they should not be asked to renounce their loyalty already given to the United States.

In their zeal, these Filipino officials went even further. Although, logically speaking, the head of the new commission should have been Yulo because he was speaker of the Assembly, elected by popular vote, they decided that it should be Vargas, who held only an appointive position, in order that none of their acts might be interpreted as bearing popular sanction or the endorsement of the public.

In an earlier chapter on the battle of Bataan, some account has already been given of atrocities practiced by the Japanese. In the provinces around Manila there had been wanton and unnecessary bombings of several towns, working great destruction upon innocent people in places where there were absolutely no military objectives. But by far the most shocking story of atrocity perpetrated by brutal Japanese soldiery, evidently grown completely out of hand, was the number of cases of rape upon Filipinas in the provinces. Many of the girls died from this brutal treatment and nothing could have been more certain to leave a permanent scar of deep hatred among the Filipinos against the conquerors than these awful crimes.

Adopting the technique of the Germans in France, the Japanese had made earnest efforts in Manila more than anywhere else to capture the hearts of the Filipinos, hoping, no doubt, to reconcile them to Japanese rule and to wean them away from their loyalty to the United States. In this they made a dismal failure. On the surface our people were calm in the presence of the enemy who had invaded their country and occupied their cities. But to those who knew them well, as I do, it was hardly a matter of surprise to learn how deep was their hatred of the invader and how strong remained their devotion to the United States.

While the Japanese High Command and military officialdom lavished smiles and respectful gestures on the Filipinos in social affairs, with the enlisted men it was quite the other way. The ruthless and fanatical Japanese soldier indulged in his cruel sport of slapping the first Filipino youth or old person who dared to pass in front of him with an air of indifference or smoking a cigarette, which for them constituted lèse-majesté. No woman who struck their fancy was safe from outrage.

A complete revision of Philippine schoolbooks had been begun by the Japanese within six weeks of their triumphant entry into our capital. General Masaharu Homma, the Commander in Luzon, proposed the gradual elimination of English from our schools to be replaced by a wider use of Tagalog. We, ourselves, had already adopted Tagalog as our national language, in order still further to consolidate our people, and to reduce the use of other Malay dialects found in the different provinces. Nevertheless, English will probably always rank with Spanish in the Philippines as a requisite for all higher education. But General Homma's proposal had a far different and more revolutionary purpose. He wished, as he declared, to "eliminate the blind dependence upon Anglo-American culture and civilization," and to promote among the Filipinos the "consciousness that they are Orientals."

A recent Japanese broadcast by Domei stated that the Filipinos had lost the Oriental virtues owing to their association with Spain and the United States, and added, as proof of that assertion that they "thought only of clothes and how they looked."

I am not aware that Vanity Fair is an exclusive monopoly of the Western world, but all of us must acknowledge that there are many virtues in Oriental philosophy and discipline. We Filipinos should be in a position to profit by the rich cultures of both the West and East. But the Japanese will never be able to accomplish by such appeals the absorption of the Filipino race into their body politic. The differences between us are too profound and too long established.

The Filipino is, psychologically speaking, a Westerner. His concept of honor is, by heredity, Spanish: gallant, although generally

For my old friend President Quezon on
his arrival from Corregidor and in token of his
triumphant return to the Philippines

Franklin D. Roosevelt

To President Quezon

With the admiration and affection
of an old comrade-in-arms of
"the fox holes of Bataan and the
batteries of Corregidor"

Douglas MacArthur

humble and not presumptuous, he reacts violently against the least act of contempt.

Of all the excesses committed by the Japanese, those which insulted the dignity and honor of the Filipinos are without doubt the ones which will leave the deepest and most irreconcilable wounds and make forever impossible any cultural union of any kind between the two races. General MacArthur has always held that the Philippines is a Latin-American nation and should be so treated. There were four hundred years of Spanish colonial empire in the Philippines which, even though imperialistic and inquisitorial in its operations, was in certain of its phases respectful of religious instruction, of culture, and of civilization.

The Philippines is the only Christian country in the Far East, a fact which alone inevitably identifies us with Western civilization.

Before the Japanese themselves had decided whether their own religion should be Shintoism or Buddhism, the Roman Catholic religion already existed in the Philippines, and there had been already founded the University of Santo Tomas, that spot which the Japanese have now converted into a concentration camp for Americans.

Fifty years of association with American ideals, as inspired and practised by the United States in the Philippines with altruism and generosity, have finally rounded out our apprenticeship and fixed our Western characteristics.

We were told that the Pope had consented to receive a Japanese Ambassador at the Vatican. As there are some fourteen million Roman Catholics in the Philippines, now under Japanese domination, we welcomed this decision of the Holy Father. He could thus do his best to care for his flock in the Philippines. We learned that the Archbishop of Manila, Monsignor O'Daugherty, had been requested by the Japanese authorities to direct all his parish priests to coöperate with the Army of Occupation. He had refused on the ground that he had had no opportunity to consult with his parish priests, and as they were all Filipinos and he was an American of Irish birth, he did not know how they would take it from him. Then the occupying authorities brought two Japanese Catholic priests down to Manila, and through them the coöperation of the Church was sought.

We learned further that all the Protestant missionary clergy had been well treated, and that there had been no looting of church property, nor destruction of church buildings, Catholic or Protestant, except for the unfortunate demolition of the old buildings of Santo Tomas University in Manila on the day when the shipping in the Pasig River was bombed. The new buildings of Santo Tomas, some distance outside Manila, were now being used as a concentration camp for American, English and Dutch civilians of military age. The women and children and old men who were citizens of those nations were, at the beginning, left in their own houses, and were allowed to be provisioned by their own Filipino servants, though some of them were sadly inconvenienced by want of money.

A good example of Japanese propaganda was the fabricated story of my death at the hands of the Americans, as was published in all the newspapers of Manila.

It had become a question of honor for the Japanese to end as soon as possible the campaign in the Philippines which was already taking too much time and constituted a cause of shame for their army, which had announced that our islands would be conquered within twenty-five days.

Singapore, Java, Sumatra, and Borneo, had already been conquered by the enemy and a part of the air and naval forces which had been concentrated in those regions could now be directed to hasten the conquest of Bataan, Corregidor and the Visayan Islands. So Tojo decided to send to the Philippines, General Yamashita, conqueror of Singapore, to replace General Homma who was at one time reported to have indulged in the traditional hara-kiri.

The change was soon noticed not only in the increased pressure of the land and air forces on

Bataan and Corregidor, but also in the naval activities which now commenced to draw a more rigid circle around the Visayan Islands and Mindanao.

Cebu, which is the second capital in importance of the Philippines, was bombarded almost every day by enemy naval forces, an unmistakable indication that they intended to make that city their immediate objective.

I felt that it was not prudent for the Vice-President to continue in Cebu and asked him to return. Things began to get difficult in that region and the long-cherished hopes of everyone for reinforcements from the United States began to wane. The symptoms were unmistakable; we were definitely in retreat.

My fears were soon justified. On March 17th, Colonel Soriano returned from Mindanao, whither I had sent him on a secret mission. He brought a letter from General MacArthur addressed to me, whose content speaks for itself:

HEADQUARTERS U. S. ARMY FORCES IN
THE FAR EAST

March 16, 1942

MY DEAR MR. PRESIDENT:

As I radioed you yesterday, an entirely new situation and prospect has developed. The United States is moving its forces into the southern Pacific area in what is destined to be a great offensive against Japan. The troops are being concentrated in Australia which will be used as the base for the offensive drive to the Philippines. President Roosevelt has designated me to command this offensive and has directed me to proceed to Australia for that purpose. He believes this is the best way to insure the success of the movement. I was naturally loath to leave Corregidor but the Washington authorities insisted, implying that if I did not personally assume the command the effort could not be made. As a matter of fact, I had no choice in the matter, being peremptorily ordered by President Roosevelt himself. I understand the forces are rapidly being accumulated and hope that the drive can be undertaken before the Bataan-Corregidor situation reaches a climax. I left there several days ago and by the time you receive this note, will have flown to Australia. I want you and your family to join me there. We have been completely identified together for many years, and you have been at my headquarters since the beginning of the war. It is the natural and proper thing for you to do to rejoin me at my headquarters in Australia in the great drive for victory in the Philippines. The Filipinos and the world at large would acclaim this in every way, and it would enthuse and inspire them. This is an entirely different proposition from the one we previously discussed which involved your leaving the country merely for the sake of security. The plan would be to have you fly from Del Monte in three of our big B-17 bombers. The trip would take only nine hours and be done at night, and it does not represent a serious hazard. You could do it with no jeopardy whatsoever to your health. Flying at night would be at no higher altitude than eight or nine thousand feet, and the flight surgeons assure me that you would have no physical difficulty. General Sharp, who is in command here, will aid and assist you in every way. You will find him entirely sympathetic and coöperative. Inform him when you are ready as it will take me a little time to set the plan up.

I am retaining full command here in the Philippines and have left part of my staff at Corregidor, pending my return there. Roxas remains there. All communications for me go there just as before. I am sending this note by Soriano, who has read its contents.

We all join in expressions of love and devotion.

Affectionately,
Douglas MacArthur

His Excellency,
The President of the Commonwealth of the
Philippines

My own reaction is contained in the following telegraphic answer:

Buenos Aires, Neg. Occidental
March 17, 1942

General MacArthur:

Your letter received and I accept your plan stop I need the three fast boats in Zamboanguita tomorrow night stop If they are not available send M/V *Dumaguete* which was at Iligan yesterday and the two fast boats referred to in your radiogram just received.

D o n

This decision naturally made a radical change in the state of affairs. I desired that the few remaining members of my Government accompany me. The Secretary of Justice, Jose Abad Santos, decided, however, to remain behind. A little later he was made prisoner by the Japanese in Cebu. They offered him his liberty on condition that he would agree to make a campaign of pro-Japanese propaganda throughout those provinces. He refused and they shot him. Jose Abad Santos was one of the great figures belonging to the nation. The Filipinos will never pardon the Japanese for that crime.

With my military staff, doctors and personnel, I again sought to fulfill the duty which in that crisis I considered sacred; namely, to leave to each one the decision whether to remain or to accompany me. They all agreed to come with me.

CHAPTER XV

To Australia and the United States

(Note: The following chapter has been compiled by Colonel Manuel Nieto, P.A., who was President Quezon's principal military aide. At the request of President Quezon's family, he has consented to serve as the late President's literary executor. Colonel Nieto was with President Quezon on Corregidor, left with him in the submarine for the Visayan Islands, and was with him daily on all his journeys and in the United States up to the time of the President's death on August 1, 1944. Colonel Nieto kept careful notes of his important conversations with President Quezon and from these, supplemented by other records, he has compiled this chapter of history.)

MARCH 18th was without doubt the most critical day of all our journeys, since leaving Corregidor. On this date, our lives, even though we did not suspect it, were in greater danger, and the bravery of some of our countrymen came more into evidence than at any other time. Our departure had been fixed for ten o'clock that night and the place of rendezvous with the P-T boats had been determined—the Zamboanguita Beach at the extreme southern end of the Island of Negros.

General Wainwright, left by General MacArthur in command of the land and naval forces in the Philippines (since the air forces

[302]

had become only a vague recollection) was given the charge of arranging immediately, within the resources at his command, for my evacuation from the Visayan Islands, and on him was laid the duty of guaranteeing my arrival at destination safe and sound. This was a rather large order, taking into account the activities of the enemy who seemed to have been well-informed of our movements and had taken steps to obstruct them.

Finally, flashes began to arrive concerning destroyers on raids south of Cebu, east and south of Negros, and north of Mindanao. Believing that there might be exaggeration and false alarms in these reports, I detailed my aide and Colonel Soriano not only to observe with their own eyes what was going on but to familiarize themselves with the terrain where, later on that night, we would have to go on board the P-T boats in the most complete blackout. As far as Zamboanguita Beach, they traversed the coast in a car, and Soriano took off in a small rickety airplane piloted by Major Fernando—an act which nearly cost them their lives. In his anxiety to make a complete survey of the entire course which we would cover, he and his pilot nearly reached Mindanao and were obliged to return, since night was coming on. They had to make a forced landing on the beach near Dumaguete with no gas, no beacons and no landing lights. A man proves himself in times of danger, and Soriano, whom I never before had seen in that situation, gave convincing proofs of his character. For this and other services, I conferred on him a degree of Military Merit.

There now was no doubt that the enemy destroyers were not simply around by chance but were following a deliberate plan of patrolling that part of the coast. In the meantime, our observers took for new destroyers all the vessels which were passing by, although in reality it was only the original ones returning. There was a time when they reported the presence of seven. Naturally, this news alarmed General Wainwright, who ordered immediately the postponement of our departure until the following day. Later on, we knew that three of the seven destroyers reported by our nervous observers, were the P-T boats which came to take me away.

Despite General Wainwright's order, I felt it necessary to push on. It was 10:30 at night. Something told me that since we were obliged to undertake this journey, the sooner we did it, the better. Nothing gives such courage as necessity.

We arrived at Zamboanguita about midnight after experiencing the difficulties natural to a journey in caravan in the most complete darkness. The road ran along the coast and any light could cause our destruction. The exodus was painful and was made more so by the people who, alarmed by the news, clogged up the road with vehicles and baggage, prepared to flee into the mountains from the Japanese invasion, which they felt was imminent.

At Zamboanguita, the P-T boats were not at the place agreed on. What should we do? Should we take this as a providential sign that the journey should be suspended, as General Wainwright had ordered? When I recall those moments in which everything was confusion and darkness, within and around me, aware of all the dangers which surrounded me, suffering on my own account and on account of what I felt those dear to me—wife, children, relatives and friends—were suffering in silence, I almost believe that I was brave without knowing it.

For a moment, my sense of responsibility found comforting relief through the intervention of an act of God. The P-T boats were not there. It was midnight. The thing definitely indicated was to retrace one's steps and I so ordered.

I gave up thinking, since thinking was only suffering, and even continued suffering can bore one. I gave myself up to the designs of Providence with the fatalistic renunciation of one who leaves everything to the will of God.

Silence reigned again, this time not even broken by the usual chatter of my daughters.

We had completed almost half of the return journey. Suddenly, the sound of a horn, distant at first but growing in volume. A few minutes later, the lights of an approaching car illuminated the road. I ordered the chauffeur to stop. Two men, one of them with beard and waterproof hat, made themselves known. The army officer was Colonel Soriano; the "old sea-dog" was Commander Bulkeley, in charge of the squadron of P-T boats. His ferocious aspect, far from repelling me, caused in me a feeling of security. They had just arrived at Dumaguete and told me that there was no time to lose. I argued that my departure had been postponed by order of General Wainwright until the following day.

A brief conversation took place between Bulkeley and me:

"Mr. President, we must not delay. One of the P-T boats of my squadron has already been lost. Tomorrow may be too late."

In reply, I asked him: "Do you guarantee to put me on Mindanao tomorrow?"

"On my word of honor," answered Bulkeley, stoutly.

Up to this time, all the decisions which involved risk of life for my wife or children had been taken after consultation with them, both when we left Manila for Corregidor and when we departed from there in the submarine. This time, however, I assumed sole responsibility.

We resumed the journey. When we arrived at the wharf in Dumaguete, it was three in the morning. We proceeded on board—a job by no means simple, considering the number of persons who composed my staff and the quantity of baggage to be loaded on the two small P-T boats. It was necessary, moreover, to leave room for the crew of the P-T boat which had been wrecked in a fish trap that afternoon. At the end I had to leave behind my Secretary, Serapio Canceran, who followed in a sailing-canoe.

We had no time to lose since it was necessary to reach Mindanao before daybreak. Suddenly a violent wave released the propeller of one of the torpedoes on deck. This immediately commenced to spin very rapidly and produced a terrible whistling sound like the escape of compressed air. At the same time, a great flame shot up many yards into the air.

This seemed to us to be our end. The alarm and confusion of the passengers on deck whose instinct of self-preservation made them hurl themselves toward the opposite side of the boat from the fire, can hardly be described.

We then heard the voices of Bulkeley and Soriano seeking to restore calm and order. I sought to explain to myself what was going on, and in my ignorance I could only think that a fire, however innocent its cause, was not the proper surrounding for an instrument as deadly as a torpedo. Shortly thereafter, order was restored. Later on, I was informed that thanks to the presence of mind of Bulkeley and of the two torpedo men, Houlihan and Light, the situation was promptly saved. These men rapidly unlashed the torpedoes and launched them into the sea.

This had been no minor accident. According to Bulkeley, if the flame had succeeded even in heating up the charge of explosives in the torpedoes nothing would have remained of the boat or ourselves. It is perhaps unnecessary to say that following this incident I conferred upon Bulkeley, Houlihan, and Light the Distinguished Conduct Star of the Philippines.

At 6:30 in the morning, we tied up to the dock at Oroquieta on the northern coast of Mindanao.

We went ashore and I sought to pass unrecognized through the crowd on the wharf but it was not possible. We went directly to the church, where we gave thanks to God in our gratitude. In the meantime, our transportation for Del Monte was being made ready. Here, as may be guessed, I took good care to arrange the journey by land. I stopped in Dansalan, where we conferred with the military and civil government authorities.

To the Moros who, in all the Philippine territory, inhabit only the islands of Mindanao and of Jolo, and whose independent and belligerent character I had found it necessary on more than one occasion to suppress with armed forces, I took the opportunity to say that the time had now arrived when we would be happy to see them display their prowess against the Japanese.

In Del Monte during the three days while we were awaiting the arrival of the planes, I lodged in a nipa house which an old friend built on a hill with the idea of remaining there for whatever time the war might last.

When I had been preparing to leave Corregidor, my first intention was to take along with me Colonel Manuel Roxas, but he felt—and rightly—that someone had to remain there to maintain the morale of the Filipino troops. When I left Corregidor I conferred on him the powers of Executive Secretary of the President.

While I was in Negros, when the infiltration of the Japanese forces began, and prudence counselled the selection of the person who would succeed to the presidency of the country in case something should happen to me and to Vice-President Osmeña, I selected, under the powers granted me by the Constitution, Colonel Roxas as our successor and issued the following Executive Order:

Whereas the danger of the President of the Philippines being either killed or captured by the enemy is always present; and

Whereas, public interest demands that the succession to the Presidency be provided for so that at no time may the country find itself without a lawful head of the Government of the Commonwealth,

That in case I or Vice-President Osmeña should be unable to perform these duties, the Secretary to the President should become the President.

Having notified President Roosevelt of this arrangement, I received a reply approving the action.

I had previously arranged for Roxas to visit me in Mindanao and had there discussed with him the matter of his joining me in my trip to Australia, basing my opinion on the argument that the loss of the battle of the Philippines, which it was necessary to admit dating from the order given to General MacArthur to leave, put an end to our mission in the southern islands. I furthermore stated that I needed his services and assistance. He replied that he would do whatever I ordered but that his own thought was that it was his duty to remain in the islands.

He seemed to feel that in his own particular case, as a soldier, to leave the country would be tantamount to desertion, and notwithstanding that he recognized as well as I did that we were lost in a military sense—because to continue hoping for reinforcements was vain and the days of Bataan and Corregidor were numbered—he insisted upon remaining. He knew,

Mrs. Quezon

murdered him X But oh, how proud I am of him!
I was right, absolutely right when
I almost envy him for he had occasion to do what
I wanted to do myself — to tell the Japanese that
we want nothing from them.

If Roxas has been murdered he is the
greatest loss that the Filipino people have
suffered in this war. He can't be replaced. And
I don't know how long the race will produce
another Manuel Roxas.

He saved his people from eternal
ignominy. Had he accepted the offer Japan might
have already established a Manchukuo or a
Nanking regime in Manila with him
as the President. And see how well informed
those Japanese are of as to who is who in
the Philippines they did not offer the Presidency
to Vargas, or Laurel, or Aquino, or Yulo or Paredes —
only to Roxas.

Let us hope for the best. Can we not make
him Major General or give him some decoration?

Facsimile of a portion of President Quezon's tribute
to General Manuel Roxas

of course, that his only choice of fate would be to become a prisoner of war if he returned to Corregidor, or if he remained at large, to perish of hunger and illness in the jungles.

That in Roxas there is a leader is clearly shown in his political career. He was born in the Province of Capriz, and after filling practically every public office, provincial and national, he became Governor of the Province and subsequently was elected a representative to the Philippine National Assembly, of which he was chosen Speaker. When, with Osmeña, by himself, he went to the United States on various missions, representing the interests of the Philippines, Roxas distinguished himself by his brilliant talent, his statesmanship and his remarkable ability in using English.

When General MacArthur organized the Filipino Army, Roxas was among the first to come forward, and when the Japanese attack began, he promptly placed himself at the disposition of General MacArthur.

The Filipino people could not afford to lose Roxas. It was my duty to save him and for this reason I was so insistent upon his accompanying me. But, on the other hand, I asked myself whether I was certain of being saved my own self. That doubt in my mind and his own insistence upon remaining, influenced my final decision.

When I reached Washington later on, and my illness continued to drain away my health, and when the responsibilities and problems of the government in exile increased, how many times did I regret not having forced him to come with me. This feeling was heightened by the news that he had been taken prisoner, because I feared that the Japanese, being aware of his ability, would offer him the presidency of the puppet government and, upon his rejecting it, as I was sure he would, they would shoot him, as they had Justice Santos.

In a letter to General MacArthur, which I wrote on January 6, 1943, from Washington, I said this:

Not long ago, I sent you a telegram through the War Department requesting that you try to get Roxas out of Mindanao. I reiterate that request. To me it is of the utmost importance to save Roxas and bring him to the United States. Of course, if he is alive I have no doubt that he is doing a fine work wherever he may be, but I cannot conceive that he can do anything nearly as important as what he could do in the United States at this time. When the time comes for our return, we would, of course, take him along.

Please, General, find Roxas. He is needed by the Filipino people in the years to come.

In another letter which I felt that I must write to General MacArthur, I gave expressions to my feelings in these words:

The news that Roxas fell into the hands of the Japanese has broken me almost completely, for I suspect that after his insistent refusal to be President of the Philippines the Japanese might murder him.

But oh, how proud I am of him! I almost envy him for he had occasion to do just what I wanted to do myself—to tell the Japanese that we want nothing from them.

If Roxas has been murdered he is the greatest loss that the Filipino people have suffered in this war. He can't be replaced and I don't know how long [before] the race will produce another Manuel Roxas.

He saved his people from eternal ignominy. Had he accepted the offer, Japan might have already established a Manchukuo or a Nanking regime in Manila, with him as the president and see how well informed those Japanese are as to who is who in the Philippines! They did not offer the presidency to Vargas or Laurel or Aquino or Yulo or Paredes —only to Roxas.

Let us hope for the best. Can we not make him a major general or give him some decoration?

In recording now the work of my Government during our stay in the Visayan Islands and Mindanao, it must be understood that my official authority was unaffected by the war, except in regions actually occupied by the Japanese. Martial law was not established in the islands by the American Government.

The military forces in Mindanao were under command of General Sharp who with Chynoweth in Panay and Hillsman in Negros, had really no substantial means of defense.

But how great is the ingenuity and tenacity of man! This military post had only one bull-dozer—that famous machine which can demolish living rock. They assigned it to the Del Monte airfield. Now these men under General Sharp with this bulldozer accomplished the miracle of excavating the mountains which surrounded the airfield and making a hangar large enough to hold fourteen P-40 planes.

To prove that they had not forgotten us, the Japanese planes came over us on various occasions during our stay in Del Monte.

At 10:30 in the evening of March the 26th, with military punctuality the three large bombers which General MacArthur had sent from Australia to pick us up made their landing.

In planning our departure for Australia it was arranged that Vice-President Osmeña was to travel in one plane and I in another so that both might not perish in one accident. Americans, who are so air-minded and so accustomed to travel by plane, cannot understand, I suppose, the apprehension with which I boarded an airplane for the first time.

With me and my family, in our plane, came General Valdes, my aide, and Dr. Trepp. With Vice-President Osmeña went the rest of the personnel. At 11:20 P.M. we took off from the Del Monte airfield. My feelings on thus leaving my native land I will not attempt to express.

We are already far on our journey. I was worried lest the great altitude should affect my heart because I recalled the difficulty which I had at only five thousand feet in Baguio, our summer capital; but, at the same time, I realized that to travel high was necessary to avoid enemy planes. Thus, consideration for the heart was sacrificed because it was the lesser of two evils.

If it came to the point, we could always take oxygen.

The trip lasted nine hours. In normal times, we would have landed at Port Darwin but at that date this port was being bombed every day by the Japanese from their bases in Timor. We landed on Bachelor Field, which is sixty miles away.

We were now in Australia but this was only a mile-post on our long journey. We had to keep on by plane. Outside of travel by water, flying was the only means of traversing those immense lands in the north of Australia where roads and railroads are unknown.

We departed for Alice Springs not in a bomber this time but in a Dutch transport plane of the type which covered the route from Java to Europe; the passage took five hours. Alice Springs, a name which seemed to suggest something of the type of summer resorts in America, turned out to be a little village of which the predominating feature was the flies found in such enormous numbers that the people there have to protect themselves with mosquito nets which hang from their hats down below their shoulders. We passed two days here because the plane in which Vice-President Osmeña was journeying had to make a forced landing through lack of fuel, and it took two days to locate it.

Certainly, I did not envy the Vice-President that experience since one of the worse features in it for him—a man with the most punctual appetite which I have ever encountered in my life—was not the flies which prevented him from getting out from the plane but the absolute absence of food. I have known few men with as good a disposition as Osmeña in the face of every kind of vicissitude and obstacle; he could encounter them with a contagious elegance provided, however, that at twelve noon the repast was ready.

We covered, finally, the last stage of our plane trip. Six more hours brought us to Adelaide. There we were received by Colonel Huff, one of General MacArthur's aides. That same day, we took the train for Melbourne, where we arrived the following morning. General Mac-Arthur, with his entire staff, were in the station to receive us.

The people of Australia greeted us with great

enthusiasm and were loud in their expression of gratitude for our long resistance on Bataan. They believed that this had given them time to prepare their own defense, and so had probably saved them. The Governor-General was most kind and appreciative. When I told him that my junior aide, Colonel Velasquez, had been in the front line at Bataan, he spent fully five minutes in talking with Velasquez. He thanked us all for our delaying battle which, he said, had preserved the future of the Australians.

Upon our arrival at Melbourne, I asked General MacArthur to send to the Philippines the following proclamation:

HEADQUARTERS U. S. ARMY FORCES IN THE FAR EAST

IN THE CLEAR PRIORITY

NR 50
WAINWRIGHT
FORT MILLS
Publicize the following proclamation of President Quezon:

"To the Filipino People and the Philippine Army: At the request of General MacArthur, I have left the Philippines and joined him at his headquarters in Australia. On previous occasions, suggestions have been made to me that I leave the Philippines, but I have refused to do it, determined to carry on with the affairs of Government in Philippine territory.

"Upon the appointment of General MacArthur

to command the Allied Forces in this part of the world, he invited me to join him upon the ground that we could continue to coöperate as we have done in the past better if we were together than if we were separated and with the difficulties in the means of communications. Having no other objective in mind than to free the Philippines, I did not hesitate to accept the suggestion of General MacArthur despite the hazards that the trip involved. And so I am here where I expect to be able to be of assistance in the reconquest of every foot of territory of my beloved country. It is my hope that the results of the appointment of General MacArthur to the High Command and my having followed his advice to join with him will soon be felt in the Philippines.

"I call upon every Filipino to keep his courage and fortitude, and to have faith in the ultimate victory of our cause.

"(Signed)   MANUEL L. QUEZON"
MACARTHUR

While at Melbourne, we received news of the tragic fall of Bataan. Here follows the press statement given by me upon that sad occasion, on April 11, 1942:

The fall of Bataan closes a chapter in the history of the Filipino people for freedom as heroic, if not the most heroic, that we have ever fought. Side by side with their American comrades, first under the personal leadership of General MacArthur and later of Lieutenant General Wainwright, our forces fought without air support against a foe that had, at all times, absolute command of the air and the seas, and an overwhelming superiority in number of land forces. This fight lasted as long as resistance was humanly possible, for our forces gave up only after they had become exhausted from lack of food and continuous battle. I am proud of the part that the Filipino forces have taken in this epic battle and I am profoundly grateful to the whole army which has thus vindicated the honor and right of the Filipino people to become an independent nation. Their country and their countrymen will consider every man who took part in this battle as a national hero and will feel undying gratitude for the service they have rendered.

The loss of Bataan has not ended the war in the Philippines. Corregidor, the Visayan Islands, and Mindanao are still fighting the enemy and I am certain that all these places will be defended as long as there are means with which to defend them.

The Filipino people will stand by and with America and our allies to the bitter end.

Melbourne
April 11, 1942

We spent several days looking for a suitable house and I had not yet been able to confer with General MacArthur with relation to the campaign to be undertaken from there to retake the Philippines—perhaps because I became aware immediately of the shattering of our hopes. The forces which General MacArthur had expected to find on arriving in Australia were not there; in fact, were not even on their way. Whatever forces could be gathered were desperately needed to defend Australia, which was at that time on the point of being invaded by the enemy. Only a few days previously, two Japanese submarines entered the harbor of Melbourne, itself, but luckily were discovered in time and sunk before they could do any damage to the number of transports gathered there.

It was evident that there was nothing I could do in Australia but "vegetate," and I am not made for that. But, on the other hand, would I be able to do anything in the United States? I did not know. Probably not. Certainly I could do nothing to hasten the sending of forces which, if they had not already reached Australia, had failed to do so because of a situation which my presence would do nothing to solve.

I consulted on this matter with the members of my Cabinet; Vice-President Osmeña was of the opinion that our proper place was in the United States, not only that we might cause to be recognized what the Filipino people had done for the United States but that we might contribute to the prompt dispatch to General MacArthur of the forces necessary for the prompt retaking of that country.

Osmeña honestly believed that Providence had guided our steps toward the accomplishment of a mission which did not end in Australia but in the United States, and he was so emphatic in his statements that he offered to go alone in case I should decide not to make the journey. In reality, if the matter had depended upon him alone, we would have gone to the United States in the same submarine in which we took passage from Corregidor. He actually proposed this to me but of course I was not in favor of this plan. In this same session of the Cabinet, the advisability of taking with us to Australia General Roxas and Colonel Romulo was discussed. The capture of the latter, who had often spoken on the radio from Corregidor against the Japanese in the broadcast entitled "The Voice of Freedom," would have meant his death; hence, it was considered very necessary to remove him to Australia.

I felt that the Vice-President was right on the question of our going to the United States, and followed his judgment. MacArthur agreed with this and prepared our passage aboard the *President Coolidge*.

On going aboard, I left a letter for General MacArthur which reads as follows:

Melbourne, Australia
April 19, 1942

MY DEAR GENERAL MACARTHUR:

On the eve of my departure I desire to write down a few thoughts that I earnestly hope will make some impression on you.

[321]

I am certain that, despite your new responsibilities and very high place in this great conflict, your heart is still with the Philippine Army which you have created, especially after the misfortune which has befallen it, not for lack of courage or will and ability to fight, but because of lack of means with which it could put up a winning battle. Remnants of the Philippine Army are still in Mindanao waiting for you to come and give them a chance to fight back victoriously. Until you are ready to return in force, there will be very little that can be done for them except to send them supplies. But there is a group there for whom something can and should be done at once. I am referring to the Philippine Air Corps men who are now in Mindanao. Won't you pick a few of those men and bring them here and constitute a squadron with them so that they might do their bit in the fight in the air that is going on? I am told that these boys can hold their own against the enemy.

The general feeling of depression and helplessness which the Filipinos both in the Philippines and abroad feel would in part be relieved with the knowledge that a unit of the Philippine Air Force, no matter how small, takes part in the reconquest. This would make us all feel proud and encouraged. I therefore appeal to you and fervently hope that you will do what you can to bring a few Filipino pilots from Mindanao, give them planes and create a unit with them.

I would also appreciate it if you could give the Silver Star to General Valdes, Colonel Nieto, Lieutenant Colonel Soriano and Lieutenant Colonel Velasquez. Every one of these men have dared death in Bataan and in the trips they have made with me. I know they have the courage which deserves that decoration.

There are many Filipinos who are here in Australia, all of them either officers and crews of ships that have been taken over by the USAFFE, or Filipino soldiers. I hope the United States Government will take care of them and pay their salaries until the war is over. Should there be cases that the American Army cannot properly care for, I give you full authority to order Lieutenant Colonel Jose McMicking, whom I am appointing as disbursing officer, to pay such sums of money as you may think equitable. I am leaving sufficient amounts in the Commonwealth Bank of Australia to cover this.

It is hardly necessary for me to reiterate my grateful appreciation for everything that you, General Sutherland, General Marshall, and the rest of the men under your command, including General Sharp of Mindanao and others, have done for me. I confidently expect that we are not parting company for good, but that we will continue the work which we have started of making the Philippines and the Filipino people prosperous, happy, free, and a strong nation.

With love to you, Mrs. MacArthur, and Arthur, I am, as ever,

Devotedly yours,
Manuel L. Quezon

At the farewell, General MacArthur was on board with his staff; General Sutherland, General Marshall, his deputy Chief of Staff, General Willoughby, and others. I embraced General MacArthur with that feeling of presentiment of coming misfortunes which always seems to me to exist during farewells.

Again I found myself aboard the sumptuous *President Coolidge*, in which I had more than once crossed that ocean which no longer could be correctly called Pacific. What a change! The floating palace had been converted into a troopship. Those salons for pleasure, for reading, for dances and concerts, were changed into a scaffolding of cots which reached up to the ceiling.

The crossing took eighteen days without untoward events but with the idea of danger constantly present through the daily drills with life-preservers on, and the eternal zigzagging of the steamer to avoid submarines. On the morning of May 8th we reached San Francisco.

At last we were again on American soil, ready to take up our life long struggle for independence with the aid of the Government and people of the United States. We were met at the dock by Assistant Secretary of the Interior Chapman, who represented Secretary Ickes, and by Lieutenant General De Witt, who represented General Marshall.

I found on our arrival in San Francisco that President Roosevelt had sent us a special railway train to bring us across the continent. When we reached the Union Station in Washington, there stood the President himself to welcome us. Back of him I saw a reception committee made up of members of the Cabinet and of all the living Governors-General and High Commissioners of the past twenty years.

We were conveyed to the White House as guests for overnight, and the dinner that evening was attended by the President and the members of his Cabinet. To them, in response to a gracious toast by the President, I gave the bare outline of some of our recent experiences, concluding with a quotation from my address made at Manila on Hero's Day, before the students of the University of the Philippines, just six days before the first Japanese attack upon us. I had told them:

I pray that our people may be spared the horrors of war, but if it comes to us, I shall welcome it for two reasons: first, that we may show the people of the United States that we are loyal to them; second, that you may learn to suffer, and, if needs be, to die. For many years now of the material prosperity which has come to our wealthy families under American sovereignty, you have become soft—you think only of dancing and cabarets. But only those who know how to suffer and to die in order to be free are worthy of that freedom.

On June 2nd I had the pleasure of addressing the House of Representatives in the historic hall where I had spent seven years of my young life as Resident Commissioner from the Philippines. I felt greatly honored by the invitation to address the House, as its guest, and recognized many friends among the members present.

I told them the story of Sergeant Jose Calugas of the Philippine Scouts, and had read into the record the citation for the award of the Medal of Honor to this, the only Filipino who has as yet received that high honor.

AWARD OF THE MEDAL OF HONOR

By direction of the President under the provisions of the act of Congress approved July 9, 1918, a Medal of Honor was awarded by the War Department in the name of Congress to Jose Calugas, sergeant, Battery B, Eighty-eighth Field Artillery, Philippine Scouts, United States Army, for conspicuous gallantry and intrepidity above and beyond the call of duty in action with the enemy at Culis, Bataan Province, P.I., January 16, 1942. When the battery gun position was shelled and bombed until one piece was put out of action and casualties caused the removal of the remaining cannoneers to shelter, Sergeant Calugas, mess sergeant of another battery, voluntarily, and of his own accord, proceeded one thousand yards across the shell-swept area to the gun position and joined the volunteer gun squad, which fired effectively on the enemy, although heavy bombing and shelling of the position continued.

Two days later, on June 4th, I spoke before the Senate of the United States. This was an occasion which impressed me very deeply. I must confess that while in the past I had always hoped to become one day President of my own country, it had never entered my head, in my wildest dreams, that I, the Baler boy, would one day be invited to address the Senate of the United States.

In giving an account of the Filipino participation in this war, it would be improper to omit the man most closely associated with that participation, General Douglas MacArthur. I do not desire to pen a eulogy for one whose military career, covering two wars, has already accomplished the task.

All Americans know this, as well as the intense zeal with which he carried out our plan for the organization of the Philippine Army. Equally well-known is the military genius with which he directed the American-Filipino forces which so heroically defended the freedom of the Filipino people, the integrity of their land, and the honor of the American flag.

Those of us who have seen him in the most anxious days when Japanese bombs were shattering to pieces everything around him, have learned that this man's courage was greater than his caution. He never sought a shelter or covered his head with a helmet in the midst of the worst air raids. On the Rock of Corregidor, Douglas MacArthur was a rock of strength and a source of inspiration for all who fought by his side.

General MacArthur knows better than anyone the complexities of warfare in the Pacific because he found himself surrounded by these problems from the very first day of the attack. He knows how to defeat the Japanese, and the values and factors of the strategic-psychological kind upon which peace must be established in the Pacific regions. Certain it is that in planning his return to the Philippines, which he considers his second fatherland, he is following his own wishes for the accomplishment of a legitimate revenge, but apart from the sentimental side, he sincerely believes that the Philippine Islands are the only strategically sound road to Japan.

INDEX

INDEX

[331]

INDEX

Malalos Congress, 43
Malay Peninsula, 265
Manchukuo, 270
Manila Bay, 33, 34, 63, 160, 213
Marabut, Serafin, 200
Marinduque, 89
Marin, Father Valentin, 28
Mariquina, 189, 199-200
Mariveles, 64, 75, 76, 77, 218, 251
Mariveles Bay, 213
Marshall, General George C., 240,
  277-278, 323, 324
Marshall, Thomas R., 128, 130
Martin, Congressman, 117
Martin, Lieutenant, 39
Mascardo, General, 48, 50, 52, 54,
  55, 56-57, 59, 61, 62, 63, 64, 65,
  67, 69, 75, 78
Mascardo, Major, 53-54, 58
Mason case, 94-99, 100
Masonic Order, 70
Matsuoka, Yosuke, 183, 184
Mayon, 211, 212
McCoy, General Frank R., 139
McDuffie, John, 152
McKinley, President, 40-41, 43,
  69, 88, 92, 123, 124, 130
McMicking, Lieutenant Colonel
  Jose, 323
Melbourne, 316, 317, 318, 320
Miciano, Dr., 83
Miles, General N.A.,
Miller, Lt. Lawrence, 76-77, 83
Mindanao, 168, 169, 170, 202, 239,
  276, 283, 289, 298, 303, 306, 307,
  308, 310, 318-319, 320
Mindoro, 89, 92, 93
Monrovia, 143
Monte, 66-67
Monte de Piedad, 84
Montojo, Admiral, 35
Moore, General George F., 213,
  214-215, 217, 225, 228, 253
Moro-maro, 3, 4
Morong, 61, 63, 64

Moros, 7, 168-169, 308-309
Murphy, Frank, Justice, 149-150,
  157, 161, 164

Nacionalista Party, 27-28, 111
Nationalist Party, 143, 158, 192
Nagasoki, 109
Nakamori, Lieutenant, 55
Natividad, General Benito, 44
National Assembly, 106-108, 110
Navotas, 67, 70, 73, 83
Negritos, 60
Negros, 250, 287, 288, 289-290, 303,
  309, 314
Negros, 169
New York, 109
Nichols Field, 194, 203
Nieto, Colonel Manuel, 182, 189,
  190, 198, 206, 209, 212, 219, 220-
  22, 223, 225, 247, 248, 252, 282,
  287, 289, 302, 319
Nomura, Ambassador, 183, 184
Nueva Ecija, 30, 38, 191

Ocampo, Pablo, 107, 111
O'Daugherty, Archbishop
  Michael, 296
Offley, Governor, 93
Orani, 60, 64
Orion, 64, 66, 77
Oroquieta, 308
Ortigas, Francisco, 85
Ortiz, Father, 282
Osmeña, Sergio, 26, 27-28, 107,
  108, 131, 139, 140, 143, 144, 145
  148, 149, 150, 158, 200, 209, 227,
  237, 251, 269, 282, 285, 289, 309,
  311, 316, 320, 321
Otis, General Elwell S., 37, 40

Paco, 6
Pact of Biaknabato, 31-32, 33, 42
Palanan, 9, 59, 74, 77
Pampanga, 35, 48, 52, 59, 64, 72,
  142, 191, 203, 250

[333]

INDEX

(1)